Editing: Ma Anand Urmila, Ma Kamaal
Design: Ma Christina, Ma Puja Abhar
Illustrations: Ma Prem Ganga
Typesetting: Ma Divyam Sonar
Production: Ma Deva Harito
Printed by   Thomson Press (India) Ltd.
Publisher: Rebel Publishing House Pvt. Ltd.,
                 50 Koregaon Park, Pune, 411001, India

Copyright © 2000 Osho International Foundation
Osho ® is a registered trademark of Osho International Foundation, used under license.
All rights reserved.
Originally published as *Bhaj Govindam*
ISBN 81 - 7261 - 161 - 7

THE
SONG
OF
ECSTASY

OSHO

Spontaneous talks given
to disciples and friends at
Osho Commune International,
Pune, India

OSHO

THE SONG OF ECSTASY

Talks on Adi Shankara's
Bhaj Govindam

CONTENTS

1. Always Sing the Song of the Divine — 1
2. Sowing the Seed — 39
3. The Search for Nirvana — 75
4. Every Step Is the Destination — 105
5. The Bondage of Hope — 135
6. The Great Transcendence — 163
7. A Song of Life — 191
8. This World Is a School — 219
9. The Essence in Life — 249
10. Just One Moment... — 277

INTRODUCTION

Osho, the enlightened master for the twenty-first century, has mentioned Adi Shankaracharya, an enlightened mystic of eighth-century India many times, but here for the first time we are given a series of talks on the mystic and his teachings. Here we are introduced to a different Adi Shankaracharya — one who can sing in his ecstasy, one who can create a song and dance of his joy in life with an enlightened perception.

Osho begins the series with "The first and the basic sutra to be understood, is that truth is attained in emptiness and is lost in words.... Language is created by man. Truth is not created by man, it is his discovery. It is neither to be created or proved, but only to be unveiled." Here Osho begins to unveil the secret, "Language is the veil. Thoughts are the only obstacle." Again we are directed inward into meditation, to bring out the mystery and mastery of our humanness.

Hearing Osho mention this master many times I had formed in my mind a character for Adi Shankaracharya – the great teacher, Shankara — as a dry debater of the scriptures. Adi Shankara went around the country, from one end to the other, arguing, debating and defeating all the renowned scholars, theologians and the so-called traditional religious leaders of that time who had turned the search for one's self into merely a mental exercise, an academic discussion. In these debates he continually insisted on bringing the search for one's self, of

INTRODUCTION

one's enlightenment, back to where it should be – the search within.

This popular song, which is in the Sanskrit language, is sung throughout India and is known as "Bhaj Govindam."

"Oh fool! Sing the song of the divine, sing the song of the divine." These words introduce the sutras of this song, leading us into Adi Shankara's perceptions that many will find will cut to the bone. One by one he cuts all delusions away from you, all supports and constructs that you might have used for the way of life you have chosen up to now, allowing a fresh opening, a new beginning. This song contains the truth, the beauty, the clarity and the power of this enlightened master's teaching.

At the same time Osho is continually exhorting us, from his own understanding, "Oh fool! Sing the song of the divine, sing the song of the divine."

Kamaal

ALWAYS SING THE SONG OF THE DIVINE

Oh fool!
Sing the song of the divine,
sing the song of the divine,
sing the song of the divine,
because at the time of death
the memorization of grammar will not save you.

Oh fool!
Drop the desire of accumulating wealth,
awaken right understanding,
make the mind desireless,
and be contented and happy
with whatsoever you gain through your own labor.

Do not be infatuated
by the beauty, the breasts, the navel
and the waistline of a woman.
These are nothing
but the contortions of flesh and fat
— contemplate this again and again.

Life is as transient and unstable
as a droplet on the lotus leaf.
Understand it well that the world
is suffering from the disease of ego
and is wounded by sorrow.

The family takes interest in you
only as long as you are capable of earning money.
As old age comes and the body becomes decrepit,
no one in the house even bothers about you.

Only as long as there is life in the body
do the people in the family care for you.
The life gone out, the body fallen lifeless,
even one's own wife is afraid of it.

A child is obsessed with playing games,
a young man is obsessed with young women,
the old are obsessed with worries.
Man never turns towards the divine.

THE SONG OF ECSTASY

The first and the basic sutra to be understood, is that truth is attained in emptiness and is lost in words. Truth is attained in silence and lost in speech. Truth has no language; all language is untruth.

Language is created by man. Truth is not created by man, it is his discovery. Truth is. It is neither to be created nor to be proved, but only to be unveiled, and this unveiling of the truth happens only when all the noise of language inside stops, because language is the veil. Thoughts are the only obstacle.

When a child is born he has no language. He doesn't come with any scripture, any religion, any caste or any nation, he arrives as an emptiness. The sacredness of emptiness is unique – emptiness is the only virginity, the rest is all perversion. The child arrives like a fresh flower, without even a scratch on his consciousness. He doesn't know anything. But the child's capacity to know is pure. He is like a mirror where nothing is yet reflected but the mirroring capacity is total and pure. Later on there will be many reflections; his knowledge will increase, but the capacity to know will go on decreasing – because the emptiness will become full of words, the emptiness will cease to exist. It is as if the reflections in the mirror go on sticking to it and don't disappear. Then the mirror's capacity to reflect will go on decreasing.

A child is born; he doesn't know anything, but his capacity to know is pure. That is why children learn quickly and old people only with difficulty. This is because the old person's capacity to learn has become less – he has had enough of everything. A lot has been written on his slate; now his paper is no longer blank. To write something new, the paper has to be made blank all over again. You can attain truth only if you can again become like the newborn child. So the arrival of the child into this world is the first birth, and the second birth is when sainthood is born in him. Whosoever goes through the second birth is *dwija*, twice born, and he is the real *brahmin*.

The scriptures say that all are born like *sudras*, untouchables. It is very rare that someone becomes a brahmin; most of the people are born like sudras and die like sudras. Who is a brahmin? Not the one who knows the Vedas, because anyone can know the Vedas. Not the one who has memorized the scriptures, because anyone can memorize scriptures. Memorizing the scriptures is just memory, not true knowledge. Only he is a brahmin who knows the *brahman*.

You have come here. You may not know that your coming here is actually the quest for being a brahmin – the quest to know the brahman.

Shankara wrote the first verse of this sweet song when he was passing through a village and saw an old man who was memorizing the rules of grammar. He felt pity for this old man who was on his deathbed – he had wasted his whole life and now he was wasting the last moment too. During his whole life he had never remembered the divine, and even now he was busy with grammar. What will he gain by memorizing the rules of grammar?

Swami Ramateertha went to America and the Americans were deeply impressed by him. He was a unique person, a living *vedantin*. For him the divine was not a borrowed idea it was an actual experience – he was luminous with his experience. The simple heart of America was greatly impressed by him. This heart of America is very simple; the reason is that America has no past, no history, no tradition. The country is only three hundred years old. Its heart is as simple as that of a child; it is not covered with many layers of words of knowledge and scriptures. So the people of that country loved Ramateertha. They listened to his words attentively, as if he had brought the message of nectar, of the deathless. They danced and sang with him.

Ramateertha returned to India. He thought that if a country like America – which has no tradition of religion, where people are absolutely materialistic – could be so impressed by his talks and by his personality, then what will happen in India? "I am coming back to my home country whose tradition is thousands of years old. Its history is so old that nobody knows when it started, it is hidden in darkness. The land where the Vedas, the Upanishads and the Gita were created, the land where people like Buddha, Mahavira and Shankara were born. With this background the people of India will listen to me eagerly, as if I am distributing diamonds." When such a miracle could happen in America where people are materialistic, where they cannot understand godliness, where their connections with the divine are broken, then what would happen in India? But what actually happened in India Ramateertha could never have imagined!

He thought that it would be better to enter India through Benares, the old city of Kashi, because this is the city which has witnessed the whole glorious past of India. Buddha delivered his first sermon there, Shankara declared his universal victory in scriptural debating there, Jaina *tirthankaras* were born there. There is no other city older than Kashi in the whole world. Even Jerusalem is new; Mecca and Medina are also new. Kashi is the oldest place of pilgrimage. It is the first city on earth to have become civilized.

So Ramateertha came to Benares and gave his first discourse, but just in the middle of the talk a *pundit* got up and said, "Stop! Do you know Sanskrit?" Ramateertha couldn't understand this interruption. He was a carefree man. He didn't know Sanskrit. He knew Urdu and Persian very well. He had never thought about what the knowledge of Sanskrit had to do with the Vedas, with brahman and with knowledge – the divine can be realized without knowing any language. In spite of being illiterate Kabir knew, the illiterate Mohammed knew; the flowers of that knowing blossomed in the life of the carpenter's son, Jesus. For this one doesn't have to be a scholar.

So Ramateertha was quite surprised by the question and he replied, "No, I don't know Sanskrit." The pundit started laughing.

The other people got up to leave and said, "When you don't know Sanskrit, then how can you know the Vedanta? First go and learn Sanskrit, then come to teach others."

After this Ramateertha went to the Himalayas, and the sad part of the story is that he gave up wearing the *sannyasin* clothes. When he died he was not in his ochre robes, because he thought: "Why be a part of a tradition whose religion has become stuck in mere words, whose *sannyas* has become only scholarliness and who thinks that the knowledge of Sanskrit is necessary to know Vedanta?" So when he died he was not in his ochre robes. He had given up sannyas.

Tradition has polluted even sannyas. America could understand him, but India could not. America is ignorant – that is why it could understand. India is very knowledgeable – a bit too knowledgeable. Without knowing, India has the illusion of knowing too much. Its mind has become scholarly, but not wise, it has become so full of words that there is no space left for the wordless, and religion has nothing to do with words. Therefore you should be more attentive to what I do *not* say than to what

I say to you. When I speak, don't pay too much attention to my words, be attentive to the empty space between the two words. It doesn't matter if you miss my words, but do not miss what is unspoken. One has to read the brahman between the lines. One has to search the brahman between the words. It happens only in the gaps. When I am quiet for a moment you wake up, you look at me attentively. That is when you give me the chance to come close to you so that I can caress your heart.

Religion is not in the rules of grammar, it is in singing the song of the divine. And it is not in *your* song of the divine; when even the song is lost, only you are left. When all words disappear, only an emptiness surrounds you. You don't even speak because there is no need to speak to existence; it knows without your speaking. Your speaking is not going to add anything more to this knowing, and anyway, what can you say? Whatever you say will be nothing but your crying, and if unhappiness is to be conveyed then it is better to convey it through crying, because only your tears will be able to express what your words cannot.

How can you express your gratitude in words? Words are too small and gratitude is too vast, it cannot be contained in words, it can be expressed only by dancing. If there is nothing to be said, then it is better to remain quiet so that the divine may speak and you may listen.

Bhajan, devotional singing, *kirtan*, divine songs and dance — these are the means of expressing the feelings. Shankara is hinting that without saying anything you yourself should become a song, a divine song. These verses are very simple, these sutras are direct, and they are written by a genius like Shankara. In the whole of Shankara's literature there is nothing more precious than Bhaj Govindam. Shankara is basically a philosopher. Whatever he has written is very complex; it is all words, scriptures, logic, analysis and thinking. But Shankara knows that godliness cannot be attained through logic, analysis and thinking; the way to attain is to dance and sing — through feeling and not through thinking.

The path of Shankara's realization is through the heart and not through the head. That is why, although Shankara has written commentaries on the Brahmasutra, the Upanishads and the Gita, you will find his innermost feelings expressed in these small verses; here he has opened his heart. Here Shankara doesn't speak like a scholar or a thinker, here he expresses himself like a devotee.

> Oh fool!
> Sing the song of the divine,
> sing the song of the divine,
> because at the time of death
> the memorization of grammar will not save you.

Oh fool! Sing the song of the divine. What is the foolishness? Shankara is not calling you names by addressing you as 'fool.' In fact it is a very loving expression. *Oh fool! Sing the song of the divine, sing the song of the divine, sing the song of the divine.*

What is the meaning of foolishness? Try to understand it. Foolishness doesn't mean ignorance. To be a fool means to think yourself to be knowledgeable when you are ignorant. It is the scholars who are the fools and not the ignorant ones. Why call the ignorant, fools? The ignorant is just ignorant; he doesn't know, that is all. It has happened many times that the ignorant one has come to know and the knowledgeable one has not reached anywhere, because the one who doesn't know has no ego, he is humble. Since he doesn't know, he doesn't make any claim to know. But the scholar who doesn't know, thinks that he knows. Because he has learned words and scriptures and he can repeat the rules of grammar, he gets lost in all these things.

There is a Sufi story.

To earn his living a Sufi *fakir* used to work as a ferryman on a river. One day a village pundit wanted to go across the river and the fakir offered to take him across free of charge. He used to charge one or two *paisa* for the journey. The pundit sat down in the boat and the fakir started rowing. They were the only people in the boat.

The pundit asked him, "Can you read and write?" What else can a pundit ask? He wants to teach others whatever he knows himself. We can give to others only what we have. Pundits are obsessed with their so-called knowledge. He could not see the radiance of the fakir, he took him to be an ordinary boatman, but the fakir was an extraordinary man. The pundit didn't know that the godliness about which he had been contemplating, hearing and discussing was present in this extraordinary man. It was peeping through him. If he'd had eyes to see he could have found in the fakir all that he had dreamed about and read about in the scriptures. Something was present there. But all that the pundit could ask was, "Do you know reading and writing?"

Well, even if a pundit meets God he is sure to ask, "Where is your certificate? What is your education?" A pundit has his own world, he lives in his own world of words and scriptures.

The fakir replied, "No, I don't know reading and writing. I am absolutely illiterate and rustic." If there was an iota of awareness in the pundit he would have seen the utter humility of the fakir. To accept one's own ignorance is the first step towards self-knowledge. If one accepts one's ignorance wholeheartedly then it can become the last step also. When you are acutely aware of not knowing anything then your ego is bound to disappear, its very foundation will give way. The building of the ego will fall down and you will slip into egolessness. That is the door from where one can be in contact with the divine.

The fakir said, "I know nothing. I am absolutely illiterate."

On hearing this the pundit remarked, "Then one-fourth of your life is wasted."

The boat sailed a little farther. The pundit asked again, "But you surely must know arithmetic at least? It is necessary for maintaining accounts."

The fakir said, "I don't possess anything, so there is no need to maintain any accounts. Whatever I earn during the day, I spend by the evening. I don't earn more than the need of my daily bread. By the night again I am a fakir. Then in the morning I start earning again. Existence has been providing enough for me until now, so why should I worry about tomorrow? If somebody gives me money, it is all right. If somebody doesn't give me anything, even then it is all right. I have lived up to now and will be able to live in the future also. Neither the giver gives anything which lasts forever nor the one who doesn't give takes away something which may be a loss forever – it is all just a play."

On hearing this the pundit said, "Well, half of your life is wasted." Just at that time a storm started, the boat began to toss in the waves and it seemed that it may sink any moment. The fakir laughed because the pundit became very frightened. Who will not, when death is imminent? The pundit used to talk of deathlessness, used to say that the soul is immortal, but these scholarly claims of the soul, of deathlessness, are of no use when faced by death.

The fakir asked him, "Do you know how to swim?"

The pundit answered, "No, not at all."

The fakir said, "Then the whole of your life is wasted! I am going to jump because this boat will sink."

> Oh fool!
> Sing the song of the divine,
> sing the song of the divine
> because at the time of death...

Perhaps Shankara knew the story which I have just told you...

> ...the memorization of grammar will not save you.

When you are about to be drowned, when death surrounds

you, you will be saved only if you know how to swim... swimming in death. If you don't know how to swim in death, then death will drown you. It has drowned you many times before too, but you have not woken up yet, you have not yet learned to swim. At the time of death your knowledge of languages – no matter how many languages you know – as well as your knowledge of grammar, will be absolutely useless.

Death is the criterion. Whatever is useful at the time of death is wisdom and whatever is useless at the time of death is scholarliness. Go on testing whatever you know on this criterion. Keep this touchstone always with you, just as a goldsmith goes on testing the gold on the touchstone. Whatever is useful, helpful at the time of death, is true knowledge, and whatever is useless and deceptive is nothing but scholarliness.

Can anything which is useless in death be useful in life? What is of no use even in death, how can it be useful in life? – because death is the ultimate, the culmination of life. It is the pinnacle of life. It is the festival of life. Whatever is useful in death is useful in life. Although it is easy to deceive in life it is impossible to deceive in death. Death exposes everything.

Whom is Shankara calling a fool? He is calling that person a fool who doesn't know the truth but who has memorized grammar, who knows the words and scriptures and can repeat them, explain them. Shankara is calling the pundit a fool. His very words: *Oh fool! Sing the song of the divine, sing the song of the divine, because at the time of death the memorization of grammar will not save you,* prove that he was using the word fool for the pundit; otherwise all of a sudden there was no need to mention about grammar. It is not the fool or the ignorant whom we consider as such, it is the pundit who is memorizing grammar, he is the fool.

The pundit is memorizing grammar, and this has become a big burden in India, so much so that almost every person has this false notion that he knows the divine just because he knows the word 'God.' Remember that the word 'God' is not godliness, just as the word 'water' is not water. When one is thirsty the word 'water' is of no use and actual water is needed to quench the thirst. At the time of death the principles and theories of immortality are of no use; the actual taste of immortality is needed.

Once I was traveling during the summer. It had not rained that year in the area. The train stopped at a station where a man was selling water – ten paisa per glass. He was calling out, "A glass of water for ten paisa." He went on selling the water and collecting the money.

A man sitting near me asked him, "Won't you sell it for eight paisa?"

Hearing this the water-seller didn't even stop and he said, "Then you are just not thirsty!"

Yes, he was right. When you are really thirsty, you don't worry about eight paisa or ten paisa. Only those who are not thirsty can think of bargaining. The water-seller's remark appealed to me. When you are thirsty you cannot think of saving two paisa, in fact you are ready to give everything at that time. The bargaining goes on only while you are not thirsty.

You say that you are a Hindu, a Mohammedan, a Christian; this only means that you are not yet thirsty. When one is thirsty one doesn't bother about being a Hindu, a Mohammedan or a Christian. When one is really thirsty you ask for the divine; temples, mosques or *gurudwaras* don't mean anything to you and these cannot quench your thirst. One doesn't bargain when one is thirsty.

The meaning of renunciation, the meaning of sannyas, is that you are thirsty and you are ready to stake everything.

People say, "Yes, we want to know God, but at present there are lots of other things to be done, there are lots of problems to be sorted out." So they go on postponing religion to the last. God is the last on the list of your necessities and the last of necessities is never fulfilled. He remains the last. One day you will be finished, you will never be able to attain him. When one necessity is fulfilled, ten others arise. When one ambition is fulfilled, thousands of others arise. Religion always remains the last. The divine doesn't come nearer even by an inch. Everything depends on whether religion is the first or the last on your list of life. A fool is one who keeps religion as last on his list, and certainly that person is not a fool who has it as first on his list, he has started waking up. He has understood properly that he may accumulate any amount of wealth, but eventually death will snatch it away from him, so there is no sense in wasting time in accumulating things which will be snatched away in the end.

Oh fool! Sing the song of the divine.

The meaning of bhajan should also be understood. You will see lots of people doing bhajan, singing the song of the divine, but they are not really doing bhajan, they are doing it very superficially. It may be a sort of recreation for them as they have not staked their life. It may be just an enjoyment for them, and this type of enjoyment they can get from any other song or from any other music.

Bhajan means that there is a deep agony in your inner being; a sound arises from your inner depth. Your whole life is at stake as if it is a question of life and death. If you want to sing the song of the divine then you have to lose yourself. If you want to save yourself and to be devotional to Govinda, God, then you are deceiving yourself.

Bhajan in itself is the climax. It is the ultimate. The disciples of Ramakrishna used to be very careful that when he is walking on the road nobody should say "Rama, Rama," or "Jai Rama," because even if a stranger saluted him by saying "Jairam-ji," he would stand there overwhelmed with emotion and ecstasy and he would start dancing right in the middle of the road. The disciples used to be embarrassed. The policeman would arrive and tell them to clear the chaos on the road. If he was invited to some wedding, then nobody would bother about the bride and the bridegroom and all of them would gather around him.

Once, one of his admirers had invited Ramakrishna to his daughter's wedding so that he could give his blessings. The wedding ceremony was about to start, when somebody called out "Govinda," one of the names of God. There was a big crowd and somebody was shouting, "Where is Govinda?" Ramakrishna heard the name of Govinda and started dancing, and the bhajan of Govinda started! That wedding place changed into a divine scene. The marriage party was no longer a marriage party. The wedding ceremony was no longer a wedding ceremony; it was altogether a different thing.

Bhajan means that there is a constant flow of the remembrance of the divine within you twenty-four hours a day. That constant flow was there within Ramakrishna. so when anyone uttered the name of Rama, Krishna or Govinda, the inner flow would erupt. The slightest outer stimulus would reveal the inner dance, the inner music, the inner sound. It is just like a well which is full of water – if somebody puts the bucket in the well it will come out full of water. In the same way, if someone uttered the name of Rama, the inner bhajan, the inner remembrance, would be expressed outwardly.

Bhajan is not something which you can do at your own convenience. Bhajan is a continuous remembrance. When it starts it never ends, it goes on and on – a continuous remembrance inside your being.

> Oh fool!
> Sing the song of the divine,
> because at the time of death
> the memorization of grammar will not save you.

Death is not going to ask you, "How much do you know

about the scriptures?" Death will reveal how much truth you have known. At the time of death, only what you have known yourself will remain with you, and what was known by others and what was borrowed by you from others will be lost. If scripture is borrowed then it is useless, but if the scripture is revealed to you then you have reached the same source where the *rishis* of the Upanishads had quenched their thirst. In that case, the Upanishads are not mere scriptures for you; then they are the expression of your own realization, of your own knowledge.

People ask me why I speak on Shankara, Buddha or Christ... I can also speak directly. I tell them that I am speaking directly, because in this song of Shankara's, he has said the same thing which I would like to say, and he has said it so beautifully that it just cannot be improved upon. He has said the last word, so there is no need to repeat it. I am not speaking on Shankara because it seems to me that he knows; the question of my having belief in Shankara does not arise. It is because I have also drunk water from the very source from where he drank and this song was born in him.

> Oh fool!
> Drop the desire of accumulating wealth,
> awaken right understanding,
> make the mind desireless,
> and be contented and happy with whatsoever
> you gain through your own labor.
> Oh fool, always sing the song of the divine.

Give up the desire of accumulating wealth. 'Wealth' doesn't mean the wealth you know as wealth. Here wealth means all that which you go on collecting or accumulating... all that is wealth which you accumulate according to your desire – even knowledge. When you are accumulating knowledge you are accumulating wealth.

One person goes on counting how much money he has put in

his locker, another one is counting how much knowledge he has accumulated, how much information he has gathered and how many scriptures he has read, but both of them are accumulating. The third person may be accumulating renunciations, counting how many fasts he has done. The fourth may be accumulating fame – he may be counting how many people have faith in him, how many worship him and how many follow him. Whatever you accumulate and whatever can be accumulated is wealth, and this wealth is very deceptive because outside you may go on accumulating, but you remain poor within.

Whatever is accumulated outside cannot be taken inside, and death will snatch away what you cannot take inside, because you alone can go through death and nothing else. Only your being will pass; flames will not be able to burn it, arrows will not be able to pierce it. Only *you* will be able to pass through the gate of death, you in your purity and nothing else.

If you have accumulated only the outside wealth you will remain poor while passing through the gate of death. If death proves you to be poor, then it means that the wealth accumulated during life was nothing but a deception. Wealth is only that which can go with us; otherwise the rest is nothing but trouble. What you are accumulating appears like wealth to you, but actually it is not so, it is only trouble. You also come to know after accumulating that the trouble has increased.

The real wealth will bring contentment, the real wealth will bring peace, will bring fearlessness. This real wealth will resonate in your life – that you have attained, that you have arrived, that you have come home. A fragrance of restfulness will begin to emanate from you. But there is no such thing in you. With the increase of so-called wealth your life stinks more, it becomes more unhappy and more fearful. The amassing of this wealth creates thousands of worries. This wealth doesn't bring peace, it only disturbs peace.

Oh fool! Drop the desire of accumulating wealth...

Yes, give up the desire to accumulate. Why are people so mad about accumulating?

Once I used to live in a house whose owner was mad about collecting things. He even used to collect such things which were absolutely useless. His house was like a junk-house, I used to wonder how he managed to live in it. One day I was standing out in the garden and, while he was talking to me, his younger son came out and threw away an old, used, broken broomstick. Immediately he became restless. He kept looking at the broomstick as he talked to me. I knew that my presence was disturbing him, so I told him that I shall be back in a few minutes and I went in.

When I came out I found the broomstick had disappeared. He had taken it in. I followed him in and caught him red-handed. He was standing there with that broomstick. I asked him, "Why have you brought it in?"

He said, "Well, it may be needed sometime."

I said, "But it is useless now."

He protested, saying, "No, no, it may be of use sometime. Why throw it away? Let it stay."

This is the mania of collecting things. What is the reason for this? Why does man want to accumulate? Really, there is a big emptiness inside which has to be filled, and it has to be filled up with anything, otherwise you feel very empty. If you possess nothing, then you feel very empty inside. Just think: if you have nothing to possess, you will be free and empty inside.

Friends come to me for meditation. When they have meditated for some time – say for a month or so – they start seeing that emptiness inside themselves. That emptiness was always there, but it was not noticed. Meditation makes you more aware – awareness increases and then one becomes aware of the emptiness. Then a very peculiar thing happens. Whosoever feels that inner emptiness starts eating a lot. One or two cases of this type come to me every day. They say, "What are we to do? We never used to eat so much food. The effect of the meditation is such that we want to eat all the time."

I explain to them that the reason for this is that meditation has shown you the inner emptiness and this emptiness hurts, so it has to be filled up. You therefore fill up this emptiness with money, position and fame. By accumulating things and sitting amongst them, one feels that one has something. Those who don't have anything have the desire of accumulating. But those who have something don't accumulate, they are sufficient unto themselves. Just 'being' is so fulfilling that there is no need to collect anything.

That is why we worshipped Buddha, we worshipped Mahavira, we worshipped Shankara, because we noticed that their wealth is within them; there is something in them and because of this the emptiness has disappeared. There is some light within them and because of this the inner emptiness has become a fulfillment, the inner emptiness has become truth. Meditation brings emptiness.

If you are in haste you will have the desire to fill up the emptiness. But if you are not in haste and if you accept the emptiness and you are ready to live with it, then you will find that gradually the emptiness gets filled up by itself. Nature doesn't tolerate emptiness. You create the emptiness, nature fills it up. God doesn't tolerate emptiness; if you create emptiness, God fills it up. Only emptiness is needed, fullness comes on its own. Just like when it rains, water from all sides will rush into a pit; in the same way, when you become empty, the divine rushes towards you from all sides.

If you make a pit, existence will fill it up. Half of the work is done by you, half by existence. But your doing is not so important, the real work is done by existence. All that you have to do is to be ready, to be empty. That is why all the enlightened people go on insisting, "Don't accumulate. Don't have the desire to collect things"... because if you fill yourself, then you

are not giving a chance to the divine to fill you.
I have heard a story:

Once, Krishna sat down for a meal. Rukmini was serving the food. Krishna had hardly taken the first morsel when all of a sudden he got up and ran out. But no sooner had he reached the door than he came back and sat down.

Rukmini couldn't understand this behavior. She asked him, "Why did you run? For what? Then why did you turn around at the door? You ran as if some house was on fire and you had to extinguish it before having your meal. But then you came back as if nothing had happened."

Krishna replied, "Yes, certainly something was on fire, but by the time I reached the door it was extinguished, so I came back. One of my devotees was walking on a street of the capital. People were throwing stones at him, his forehead was bleeding and he was calling, 'Govinda, Govinda!' He was neither reacting nor trying to save himself. He had trusted himself to me entirely. So to save him I had to run."

When one becomes helpless like that man, existence has to take care of him. When a person becomes so empty that in spite of being stoned he is doing nothing to save himself, he is not even running away and not even reacting, then the whole existence comes to save him. When there is a pit, water rushes in from all sides to fill it up. Rukmini asked, "Then why did you come back?"

Krishna replied, "By the time I reached the door he had changed his mind. He had picked up a stone in his hand. He himself was reacting so I was not needed anymore."

God is needed when you are helpless, and in that helpless condition when you call on God, then that is bhajan, devotion. There is no need to say the word 'God' aloud; the inner emotion is enough. When your eyes full of love look towards the sky, when your heart is opened towards the sky and you are making no effort to do anything from your side, that is the moment when the divine rushes towards you. If you become a pit, he is always ready to fill it up.

Mohammed used to say that if you take one step towards Allah, he takes a thousand steps towards you. But if you don't take even one step...and that one step is very necessary because until and unless you give him the invitation, how is he going to come? Even if he wants to come, how is he to come? In spite of your not inviting him, not asking him to come, if he comes to you, your doors will be closed. Even if he knocks you will think that it is the mind. Even if he calls you loudly you will not be able to hear him because of your inner turmoil.

> Oh fool! Drop the desire of accumulating wealth,
> awaken right understanding...

Intellect means your cunningness; right understanding means your wisdom. That is why as the world is becoming more and more clever, it is becoming more cunning too. It was expected that education would make people simple and innocent, but the surprising thing is that with the increase of education man is becoming more cunning, more dishonest and more of a hypocrite. He has become expert in exploiting others.

Cleverness means efficiency in this world, and good sense means efficiency in the inner world. The worldly people may think that the person of good sense is stupid. They are bound to say so because he will ask, "What are you doing?"

It was because good sense prevailed that Buddha gave up his home, his palace, his kingdom. The charioteer who had gone to see him off at the boundary of his kingdom was an ordinary servant, but even he said, "Please excuse my impertinence, but I can't help telling you that what you are doing is absolutely stupid. Have you gone mad? The whole world craves for such a palace and for such a kingdom. You are fortunate enough to have them, but you are giving up all these things. Where else will you get such a beautiful wife? Where else will you get this wealth, these comforts, these luxuries, this type of family and this respect? You had better come back."

Certainly the old charioteer is more worldly wise than Buddha, so he is giving this advice.

Buddha said, "I quite understand what you are saying. But where you see the palace I see only flames of fire; where you are seeing beauty I see death; what you see as wealth is only a deception of wealth for me. I am in search of real wealth, I am in search of a real home which cannot be snatched away one day. My search will continue until I get it. For the sake of this search I am ready to stake everything, because why not stake something which is eventually going to be taken away, it is only a matter of time? If I attain something which cannot be lost by staking something which is going to be lost, then this deal is not bad. It is just a matter of time. If I can stake what is to be snatched away tomorrow anyway, for something which can never be taken away, it is not costly."

Good sense has prevailed upon Buddha and the charioteer is indeed wise about the world.

Buddha became enlightened and returned home after twelve years. But his father was angry. He said, "Don't be stupid! Come back home. You have deceived me, deceived your wife and the newborn child. In spite of all these things I will forgive you, because I have the heart of a father. Come back, your begging on the road doesn't look right. And why do you beg? You can give alms to thousands of beggars every day."

Even now Buddha seemed stupid to his father. The religious intelligence always appears as stupidity to the worldly wisdom, and people generally think it to be utter madness. But to the person who has this religious intelligence, this worldly wisdom seems stupidity.

It is you who have to take the decision. Without this decision you cannot enter the world of religion. Until worldly wisdom seems stupidity to you, you cannot attain good sense. When you see worldly wisdom as foolishness, when you see worldly cleverness as deception, when you see the futility of worldly fame, of position and of reputation, then it means that the seed of right understanding has sprouted in you.

> ...awaken right understanding,
> make the mind desireless,
> and be contented and happy with whatsoever
> you gain through your own labor.

This is true regarding all types of wealth – about the outer wealth also, which one gets with one's own effort. Whosoever is satisfied with it, his life will be full of morality. And the same is true about the inner wealth also: when the inner wealth is obtained by one's own effort he will be religious within.

Memorizing the scriptures, means that you are committing theft. You are stealing the knowledge hidden in the scriptures; you didn't get it by your own effort or hard work. It is all borrowed and stale, you are just holding on to the other person's knowledge. Don't construct your building on it. Its foundation is on sand, so it will crumble down in the slightest gust of wind.

Just a few days ago I was telling a Zen story.

One evening a Zen monk knocked at the door of a Zen monastery. It is a tradition of the Zen monasteries, that if any traveling monk wants to rest there he has to give the right reply to at least one question. He has to earn the shelter to rest in by giving a correct reply to one question otherwise he cannot halt at the monastery, he has to continue his journey.

The head of the monastery opened the door and asked the guest a very old puzzle of the Zen monks. The puzzle is: Which is your original face, the basic face? the real one which was yours even before the birth of your father and mother? This question is regarding the soul. What you have received from your mother and father is the body; your face was also received from them. But what is your basic face, the original face? What is your nature?

And Zen monks say that the reply to this question cannot be given in words, its reply should be a living expression. As soon as this question was asked, the traveling guest monk took off his shoe and struck the face of the monk who had asked the question.

The host stepped aside, saluted and said, "You are welcome! Come in!"

After they had dinner together, they sat down by the fire at night and started talking.

The host told the guest, "Your answer was wonderful."

The guest asked, "Have you yourself experienced this answer?"

The host said, "No, I have not experienced it. But I have read many scriptures and have learned from them that the one who gives the correct reply doesn't hesitate. You replied without any hesitation and your reply said everything.

On the basis of the scriptures, I understood that you have come to know the reply, because through your reply you said, 'You fool! You are asking the question in words and you are wanting the reply without words; you are asking about the original face which you also have. Therefore by striking your face with the shoe I am saying that this face is not your original face – it deserves a shoe-hit.'"

The host said, "So I understood your reply. I have also read the scriptures and such replies are written in them."

The guest didn't say anything. He went on sipping his tea. Upon this the host became a little doubtful. He looked at the face of the guest carefully and what he saw was very dissatisfactory. He said, "Friend! I am asking you once again: Have you really experienced the answer or not?"

The guest answered, "I too have read many scriptures. I have read that this is an appropriate reply to the question you asked. But the fact is, I have not experienced the answer."

Scriptures can be very deceptive because the replies are also written there. But to repeat the answer from the scripture is just like using the answers written at the end of the arithmetic book. One reads the problem, then turns the book and sees the answers at the end. In this way you will give the right answer, but you will never know the method by which one reaches that answer. The answer will be correct, but you will remain wrong, because if you had passed through the method you would have evolved, you would have developed.

Another person's answer is of no use. An answer should be one's own. No one is going to test your knowledge of the scriptures; existence is going to test you existentially. No one is going to ask, "What did you hear? What did you read?" Existence will ask, "How have you lived?" If the answer comes from your life, then it means that it has come with your own effort. With outer wealth, if you earn it with your labor, with your hard work, then your life will be full of morality, and if you earn the inner wealth with your labor, then your life will be religious – it will be authentic religion. That is why Ramateertha called this real religion. Yes, there is borrowed religion and there is authentic religion.

Borrowed religion means the answers are correct but impotent. They are like empty, spent cartridges, they can't be used in a gun. People will laugh at you, but this is what most people are doing: they go on repeating others' answers. They go on repeating them mechanically. How can they get their own answers when they don't even have their own questions? They don't even know exactly what they want to know. They don't know the question which they go on seeking.

> Oh fool!
> Drop the desire of accumulating wealth,
> awaken right understanding...
> and be contented and happy
> with whatsoever you gain through your own labor.

THE SONG OF ECSTASY

> Oh fool! Always sing the song of the divine.
> Don't be infatuated by the beauty, the breasts,
> the navel and the waistline of a woman.
> These are nothing but the contortions of flesh and fat
> — contemplate upon this again and again.
> Oh fool! Always sing the song of the divine.

Man is attracted towards woman and woman is attracted towards man. The opposite always attracts, and this attraction is like hypnotism. Let us understand this.

When a child is born his first contact with this world is the breast of the mother; the first contact with 'the other' is the mother's breast. His journey in this world begins after getting acquainted with the mother's breast. That is why man is always obsessed with woman's breasts; that is the first impact, no other impact is deeper than this. That is why all painting, pictures, statues, films, stories, all go on revolving around the breasts of women. The breasts are the part of a woman's body which hypnotizes man's mind the most. Women keep trying to hide the breasts and men keep trying to uncover them. Women know what attracts men and men also know what interests them in a woman's body.

As civilization develops, this problem also goes on increasing. The fact is, that in the uncivilized tribes there is no attraction to the breasts because their women's bodies and breasts are not covered. Every child is free to suck the milk from the breast of his mother as long as he wants. He can even go on sucking them till the age of ten. In the civilized societies they try to wean away the child from the breast of the mother as early as possible. The sooner they wean the child away from the breast, the deeper becomes the attraction for it.

People go on writing poetry, painting pictures, making statues, etcetera, regarding the beauty of the breasts. Their mind is totally obsessed with breasts. This means that the child was not satiated, he remained dissatisfied. This dissatisfaction creates dreams. This dissatisfaction creates an inner hypnotism. But now there is no means of satisfaction till good sense awakens.

Shankara says to remember this continuously — the earlier impact can only be removed by remembering this again and again.

Scientists have made a few discoveries; one of them is very important. One scientist was experimenting with chickens. When a chicken was born out of a hen's egg he didn't let the chicken see the hen, but kept it with a duck. When the chicken opened its eyes it saw the duck, and this was its first imprint. And an interesting event happened: it would run after the duck and it would not recognize the hen.

The duck could not tolerate the chicken running after her all the time so she used to kick it, beat it, but in spite of this it would follow her everywhere. The hen tried her best to win it over, to get it near her, but it would be frightened of her and would stand far away. At night also, the chick wanted to sleep in the same place where the ducks were kept, but the ducks would throw it out. The hen wanted to take it to the hen house, but it was not ready to go there.

The first imprint, the first conditioning, is very important. It goes on haunting you the whole of your life. The first event of life, whatever it is, always haunts a person, and the mind keeps on dreaming about it. What is so attractive in a man's or a woman's body? Certainly there is something. Your body is built by a meeting of the bodies of a man and a woman — half is given to your body by the man and half by the woman. Every person is half woman and half man — it is a mixture of both. Your whole existence is half man, half woman; it is incomplete. The womanly half in you goes on yearning for the man and the manly half in you goes on yearning for the woman.

According to the latest researches in psychology, in the unconscious mind of every man is hidden the woman and in the unconscious mind of every woman is hidden the man. They go on searching outside till their inner man and their inner woman meet.

Until your inner man and inner woman unite, until your conscious mind and the unconscious mind become one by being united, the attraction for the opposite will always be there. A man will be attracted towards a woman and a woman will be attracted towards a man.

You must have seen the statue of Ardhanarishwar where Lord Shiva is shown as half woman and half man. Until the half woman and half man within you become the image of Ardhanarishwar, until you become whole within yourself, you will go on searching outside feeling lost and thinking that meeting a woman will bring fulfillment. But the woman is there in your unconscious mind.

That is why all the *yogas* and *tantras* are basically the process of uniting your inner energies. When you become united and one within you, then your outer desire ceases to exist. But at the same time, when the outer desire ceases to exist, only then can you become one. These two things are interdependent. That is why Shankara says:

> Do not be infatuated by the beauty, the breasts,
> the navel and the waistline of a woman.

Shankara is speaking to men, because in those days, especially in this country, religion was monopolized by men. But the same thing has to be told to women also, that there is nothing special in the body of man which should obsess or hypnotize her.

These words of Shankara, and other words of this type by other saints, have created a misunderstanding. It seems that there is nothing in the body of a woman, but there is something special in the body of a man. Actually, there is nothing in any body. Men look at a woman's body contemptuously saying, "It is nothing but bone and flesh and fat." But what about man's body? Is it made of gold, silver or diamonds? As long as you don't see the bones, flesh and fat in your own body you cannot see them in a woman's body. Because of the misunderstanding of these words, it has become a tradition to condemn women. Men think that women are the cause of their bondage. But who has put women in bondage? Men think that women are the main obstacle in their attainment of liberation. But the question is: If woman is the obstacle in the attainment of liberation, then who is the obstacle for a woman in attaining liberation? Then it means that women can attain without any obstacle. If there is no obstacle in their life, then they can directly attain without any difficulty.

No, it is not a question of a man or a woman. The attraction for the opposite is of no use. You must contemplate again and again that these are the perversions of flesh. It is necessary to contemplate again and again in this way to remove this imprint which is there in the mind. Continuous remembrance is like the waterfall which breaks the stone, a strong stone. Nobody can imagine that a small trickle of water falling for the first time will be able to break the stone. Eventually the stone turns into sand granules, and the water goes on falling in the same way. This imprint is very strong and very deep, but if the thought continues like the trickle of water, drop by drop, then one day the stone will break and disappear. And the day your imprints disappear, you become free.

Oh fool! Always sing the song of the divine. Shankara is saying: Go on being devotional to the divine continuously. Whatever you may do, you should always remember the divine. Don't ever forget the ultimate reality.

The bhajan, the song of the divine means that what is visible is not sufficient, is not enough, is not the whole, is not all. Remember that there is also that which cannot be seen. Let the invisible not get lost in the visible – always remember the invisible.

You are seeing me, I am seeing you. As far as you can see me, that is visible. When you come across men, animals, trees while walking on the road, whatever is visible is 'the world.' These things are visible. But if you can remember the invisible within me...the invisible hidden in the visible is godliness. The meaning of the bhajan of the divine is that the visible should not deceive you, you should not get lost in the visible; you should be able to remember the invisible always.

During the 1857 revolution a sannyasin was killed by a soldier by mistake. A silent, naked sannyasin was passing by the cantonment of an English battalion. The soldiers caught hold of him and asked him, "Who are you?" But as he was in silence he didn't reply.

Because of his keeping quiet they became suspicious of him and one English soldier pierced his chest with a spear. The sannyasin had taken the vow of speaking only once at the time of death: he had been silent for the last thirty years. When the spear pierced his breast and the blood gushed out, then he spoke only one sentence of the Upanishads: *"Tattvamasi, Svetketu"* – you are also that, Svetketu.

People gathered round him and asked him, "What do you mean?"

He said, "I mean that the divine can come in any guise, he will not be able to deceive me. Today he has come with the spear in his hand. The spear has pierced my chest, but I can see that inside the soldier it is only him. He cannot deceive me." The blood was oozing out of his chest, but the sannyasin was dancing because he could see godliness in his murderer.

> Oh fool! Sing the song of the divine,
> sing the song of the divine.

This means that whatever may happen, in all types of circumstances, the divine should be visible. He should be seen in the enemy, he should be seen in death too when it comes. He should be seen in a friend and in the enemy also. But at present you cannot see him even in a friend. At present you cannot even see him in the person whom you love; you don't see him even in your beloved or lover, what to say of others.

You don't see him in your own self, so how can you see him in the other?

Oh fool! Sing the song of the divine... means that whatever may happen, the divine is to be seen everywhere. He is there even in a rock — maybe in deep sleep. He is to be seen even in a tree — there he is dumb, but he is. Even in the lunatic — there he is mad, but he is. You should be able to recognize him in any form.

There is an anecdote in the life of Sai Baba of Shirdi. A Hindu sannyasin used to live about three miles away from the mosque where Sai Baba lived. This sannyasin used to come daily for Sai Baba's *darshan,* only eating his food after seeing Sai Baba. Sometimes there was a big crowd so he could not enter the mosque, the whole day would pass without his darshan. But the sannyasin never took food without first touching Sai Baba's feet. Sometimes he had to go to sleep without eating his food because he ate only during the daytime, that was his rule.

So one day Sai Baba told him, "There is no need for you to come here daily. I will come to you, but you must recognize me. Don't let it happen that I come and you don't recognize me. I will come just when your meal is ready, and you can have my darshan there where you are. Your coming here from a distance of three miles and then going back all that way is too much. It hurts me to think that sometimes you have to go without your food."

The sannyasin was very happy. He said, "It is my good fortune. Tomorrow I will wait for you."

The next day he cooked his meal early and was happily waiting for Sai Baba. Nobody came but a dog. The dog must have smelled the food. He chased the dog away with a stick and turned him out saying, "I am waiting for Sai Baba, get out of here." He struck the dog twice with his stick and made it run away. After that nobody came.

In the afternoon he ran to the mosque, where there was a

great crowd. He asked Sai Baba, "Why didn't you come? You are sitting here surrounded by people, but you had promised me you would come."

Sai Baba said, "I came but you didn't recognize me. You beat me with your stick."

The sannyasin was puzzled. He said, "But it was only a dog who came."

Sai Baba said, "Didn't I tell you that I will definitely come, but you must recognize me?" I can't say in what form I will appear, it all depends on whatever form is easily available, and at that time it was just appropriate to appear in the form of a dog. On this sunny day no other form was available. Only this dog was there, so I used him."

On hearing this the sannyasin started crying. He said, "It was my fault, but please give me another opportunity. You must come tomorrow, then I will definitely recognize you."

If the dog had come the next day he would have recognized him, but the dog didn't come. He kept on waiting for either of the two – either Sai Baba himself will come, or he may appear in the form of a dog. But the dog didn't turn up at all…well, dogs are not very dependable – they may come, they may not come.

The dog didn't come, but a beggar arrived who was a leper. He was stinking terribly. The sannyasin thought that the food would get spoiled by this stink, that nobody would feel like eating it. It was nauseating to see the beggar, so he said to him, "Please go away from here. Don't come in." For a moment he was doubtful, but then he thought, "How can this leper be Sai Baba?" Compared to this leper even the dog was better to look at, he looked nice and healthy.

In the evening he again went to Sai Baba and said, "I waited for you and for the dog, but you didn't come."

Sai Baba replied, "I came, but you couldn't bear the stink. You drove me away."

The man started crying and said, "Give me one more chance."

Sai Baba said, "Even if I come a thousand times you will not be able to recognize me."

You can recognize only when you are awake; only then it is possible.

Singing the song of the divine means that whatever you see will become a song of the divine. Anything from anywhere will become a message of the divine – when the breeze blows it will remind you, the sound of the waterfall will remind you, when the birds sing they will remind you, if it is silence it will remind you. The noise is the divine's, the silence is the divine's, the market is the divine's and the void of the Himalayas is the divine's. This remembrance, this message comes from everywhere – the flower, the leaf, the stone, everything will remind you of the divine. This remembrance will surround you from all sides; whenever you look into somebody's eyes you will be seeing the divine.

This is not imagination or poetry, this is a fact, because he is looking from every eye. If you have not seen, it is your fault. If you have not recognized, it is your stupidity, but he is seeing from every eye. Go back and look into the eyes of your wife or look into the eyes of your child. Soon you will realize that the child disappears and the formless is there. Wherever you see deeply you will find godliness. But you will go on missing the inner world as long as your sight is shallow.

> Life is as transient and unstable
> as a droplet on the lotus leaf.

This has to be understood properly – that the world is suffering from the disease of ego and is ill with unhappiness. So, *Oh fool! Always sing the song of the divine.*

Here nothing is stable. Everything is flowing, everything is changing. So don't make a building on what is unstable. Even sand is more stable than this. This world is like the flow of water: don't make a building on it, otherwise you will repent.

Look for the stable, the permanent. Always look for the one who is stable in this flow.

A wheel turns with the movement of the vehicle, but the axle doesn't move. So look at the axle, you will find the divine in the axle. The wheel means 'the world,' that is why we call it *sansar chakra*, the world wheel. The wheel goes on moving but the axle, on which the movement of the wheel depends, is stable. The existence of the unstable depends on the stable. Even a lie has to depend on truth for its existence. A seer is needed for a dream to exist, otherwise a dream cannot be dreamed.

> Life is as transient and unstable
> as a droplet on the lotus leaf.

Don't entangle yourself too much with life, otherwise you will repent and be unhappy. Nothing stops here; even if you want to stop it, it will not stop. Everything is flowing. You are young, but this youth will pass away. You will try to hold on to it, but you will not be able to do so. You will then repent because time will be spent in the effort of holding on to it. Today this body is; by tomorrow it will perish. Many such bodies have existed and perished. The world is transient, unstable and ever-changing. Don't make your home here, this is only a night's shelter. One stops here for the night and has to go away in the morning. If you have made a home here you will be unhappy – that is *why* you are unhappy.

People ask me, "Why are we unhappy?" You are unhappy because you are making your house where it cannot be made. You don't see where it can be built or where it is already built. You are unhappy because you are looking in the wrong direction. Unhappiness is the result of being associated with the wrong, being in the company of the wrong. To be in the company of truth is bliss.

Your family will love you as long as you have the energy to earn money. When you become old and the body becomes weak, nobody bothers about you. Therefore, *Oh fool! Always sing the song of the divine.* If you have to have a family, make it with the divine. If you have to marry, then marry the divine. The marriages of this world are nothing but divorces. All the relationships in this world are shallow. There is no depth in them.

Mulla Nasruddin was in love with the daughter of a multimillionaire. He used to tell her, "I may live or die, but I cannot leave you. If ever there is a need, I will die for you."

One day the girl was very sad. She told Nasruddin, "Listen, my father has become bankrupt."

Nasruddin said, "I knew that your father will create some trouble to stop our marriage."

The very reason why they were getting married was gone.

This is your sort of relationship. You don't mean what you say. You are deceiving most of the time and sometimes you deceive yourself also. You not only deceive others, you also deceive yourself. Man is very cunning; he deceives even himself.

The family members go on inquiring about your welfare as long as there is life in the body. When the body becomes lifeless, your own wife is scared of that body. Therefore, *Oh fool! Always sing the song of the divine.*

It is better to be in the company of the one who can be with you always. The company of those whom you meet for a short time while traveling together, or while crossing a river in a boat, doesn't count much. That company is momentary: for some time travelers are together, they move together, but soon each of them goes his own way. Don't give too much importance to this. In this world people are together for a short time. It is like meeting someone in a dream. When the dream is over the meeting will end.

> A child is obsessed with playing games,
> a young man is obsessed with young women,

the old are obsessed with worries.
Man never turns towards the divine.

So, *Oh fool! Always sing the song of the divine.* Childhood is spent in play, in games; youth is spent in the play named love; old age is spent in worries of older times, in thinking of the past, and the whole of life is wasted like this. The divine is never remembered. We go on postponing till tomorrow, and tomorrow brings death. We hardly ever remember the inner world until we die.

*Oh fool! Always sing the song of the divine...*before death arrives. Whenever you become a little conscious, awake yourself. Just think: What are you doing? What are you involved with? What is the result of your actions? Your actions, your money, your reputation will be of no use in the end. So don't spend too much time on what is going to be useless. The sooner you wake up the better it is.

You cannot be in love with the divine till your infatuation with life is over. If you are too infatuated by life you cannot recognize the divine. How can you recognize the formless if you are obsessed with the form? You cannot understand the formless with a materialistic attitude. If you are looking at the earth all the time how can you see the sky? You cannot get rid of your infatuation until you wake up and realize that this infatuation is the cause of your misery. The essence of life is misery.

All the temptations of happiness end up in misery. All hopes of happiness end up in misery. All the plans of getting happiness are as futile as the plan of getting oil from the sand. You remain empty-handed. If you are ready to go empty-handed from this world then there is no need to remember the inner world, but then you will leave crying.

If you want to go from here fulfilled, then the sooner you remember the divine the better it is. You should spend as much time and effort as possible in this remembrance; that is a virtuous act, and that's the only thing which can fulfill you. But you don't bother to remember the divine and you go on worrying about things which will never be able to fulfill you.

Mulla Nasruddin's wife was about to die. She was lying on the bed. She opened her eyes and asked him, "Do you really mean to say that you will go mad if I die?"
Nasruddin said, "Certainly I will go mad if you die."
The wife laughed and said, "You are lying, I know that you will marry again after my death."
Nasruddin said, "It is true that I will go mad, but not to the extent of getting married again."

If you watch this life carefully you will not want to be born again, you will not want to marry again, because out of them you gained nothing except misery. The quest of the East is how to get rid of this cycle of birth and death. Those who have seen life in the right perspective, their only desire is how to get rid of this life.
I have heard that when a unique sannyasin named Bodhidharma went to China with the message of Buddha, Emperor Wu told him, "I don't have much time. My kingdom is vast; I cannot spare time to be with you for a longer period. Please tell me briefly, what is the most valuable thing in life? What is the greatest good fortune?"
Bodhidharma said, "You will not be able to understand…. The greatest good fortune is if you were never born."
Wu was shocked — what a thing to say! Is it fortunate not to be born? But Bodhidharma is talking about good fortune. Buddhas certainly desire that they should not be born again.
Bodhidharma said, "But now this is not possible, as you are already born. But the next good fortune for you is to die as soon as possible." It is said that Wu never went to see him again.
I also want to say the same thing to you, that the greatest good fortune would have been not to be born, but since you

are already born, the next best thing is that you may die while living. The attraction for life should be over.

The meaning of dying while being alive is to live as if you are not. Sit in the marketplace, but as if you are not. Look after your wife and children, but as if you are not. Become absent, and soon you will find that your absence is not empty; godliness is appearing gradually.

Oh fool! Sing the song of the divine.

Enough for today.

SOWING
THE SEED

The first question:

> Beloved Osho,
> Shankaracharya teaches metaphysics and at the same time he sings the songs of the divine. Is there any interrelation between knowledge and *bhakti*, devotion?

Knowledge is negative, devotion is positive. Knowledge is like preparing the earth by removing the grass and the weeds and then putting in the manure, and devotion is like the sowing of the seed. Knowledge in itself is not sufficient. It cleans the earth, but the seeds cannot be sown. It is necessary, but not sufficient, because knowledge is of the mind and devotion is of the heart.

All the obstacles on the path of the divine can be removed by knowledge. But the steps of the stairs can be climbed only by devotion. That is why knowledge is negative. It is very effective in removing the meaningless but it is not able to create the meaningful.

Shankaracharya is talking about knowledge so that the layers of ignorance collected within you may be cleared away. And once the soil of the mind is cleared of all the unnecessary wild grass and plants, the seeds of devotion can be sown. Then it is possible to sing the song of the divine.

There is no contradiction between the two. Devotion is the culmination of knowledge and knowledge is the beginning of devotion, because man has both heart and mind, and both of them have to be approached, both of them have to be transformed. If you get stuck only in knowledge then you will be like a desert – very clean but nothing will grow there; clean but seedless; vast but without any height or depth.

Knowledge is dry and lonely. And if you remain a devotee, a *bhakta* only, then there will be trees, flowers and greenery in your life but you will not know how to protect that greenery. You will not be able to protect those plants. If anyone puts the seeds of doubt in your fertile soil, they will also sprout.

If a devotee has not passed through the process of knowledge then his building is going to be shaky. Anyone can put doubt in him. And he knows how to believe the believers, those who are leading him on the path, and he believes even those who are misleading him. He doesn't have the sense of discrimination and discretion. He gets hold of the wrong in the same way as he gets hold of the right. The devotee is like a blind man and the knowledgeable person is like a lame man. If they both get together then things work out beautifully.

You must have heard this story.

A blind man and a lame man were caught in a fire in a jungle. The blind man could not run away as he could not see. He had strong legs and feet and could save himself by running away, but he had no sense of direction. The lame person could see the path, he could see which part of the jungle had not yet caught fire, but he could not run away as he was lame. According to the story, both of them got together. The blind man carried the lame one on his shoulders. By becoming one, they overcame their shortcomings. With the joint effort of the blind man's feet and the lame man's eyes they could come out of the jungle safely. The fire could not destroy them.

You cannot save yourself from the flames of life until the intellect and the heart unite. Intellect has eyes but no feet; intellect is lame. Heart has feet, but no eyes; heart is blind. That is why they say that love is blind. When they meet, there is perfume. When they unite, there is attainment, there is enlightenment, there is *nirvana*. If they oppose each other, both will be destroyed. Then it will be impossible to get out of the jungle which is on fire. Alone, both are crippled. United, both become whole. And you have both, you have to use both. Hence make knowledge a support of devotion; make devotion a support of knowledge.

You can fly in this sky if you make both of them your wings. No bird can fly with one wing, no man can walk with one foot, nor can a boat be rowed with one oar; both the oars are needed. There is no contradiction, and those who have told you that there is a contradiction are wrong. They made this error because they didn't know this great harmony. They were either mind-dominated people who possessed only dry thoughts and logic and never experienced the dance of the heart, or they were heart-dominated people who could dance, but didn't have any understanding.

It will certainly be a fortunate moment when you can dance with understanding. That moment will be fortunate when you can love with understanding. And never refuse anything which existence has given you, because if you do so you will become disabled to that degree. You are whole, but everything has to be properly adjusted and made to coincide. It is as if there is a musical instrument, a *veena*: the strings are there, and the strings have to be fixed to the veena, they have to be tightened and adjusted. Everything is within you, but the coincidence is not there. The name of that coincidence which can adjust your inner veena and its strings, is *sadhana*.

Sufis say, that a man was dying of hunger. In his house there was flour, water, fuel, an oven, but he didn't know how to knead the flour, how to light the fire and how to bake the bread. Everything was there, but he was hungry. The uncooked food was there. But these things didn't coincide, so he died of hunger.

This story applies to everybody. You have all the means, but you are hungry. You have got everything; existence sends everyone with all the means. But these means are to be adjusted in the proper proportions, the proper harmony and music, only then the light of the divine will shine within you.

You are not to be dominated either by intellect or by the heart; your consciousness should flow like a river between these two banks. If you become the Ganges, then the sea is not very far away. But don't insist on flowing with the support of one bank only, because the support of both the banks is needed. In the end both the banks will be given up, but this end is possible only through that support. In the ultimate condition, in the ultimate realization, there is neither devotion nor knowledge. When a river flows into the sea then both banks disappear and the river becomes the sea.

Therefore, there are three types of people in this world. The first are the mind-dominated people — philosophers, metaphysicians. They go on thinking and arguing, but reach nowhere. Their life is full of the dry sand of logic.

The second type are the heart-dominated people. They sing and dance a lot, but their singing and dancing is without any understanding or discretion. They are not doing so out of freedom — it is a sort of madness or intoxication. Heart is like an intoxication for those who don't have awareness or discretion.

The third type are those who have made full use of mind and heart and have gone beyond both. Your aim should be the third. You must desire, you must aspire for this great transcendence.

Ultimately the Ganges has to leave both the banks and flow into the sea. But don't hurry, you have to reach the sea with the support of the two banks, and you can give up the banks as soon as you reach there.

The second question:

> Beloved Osho,
> Religions try to make us disinterested in worldly happiness by saying that it is temporary and transient. But is not this very transience the cause of its attraction?

Certainly it is so. Transience is the cause of attraction. And religions don't create nonattachment by saying that life is transient. Religions say that whatever is transient will be followed by misery. Transience is not the cause of nonattachment: misery follows transience like a shadow — the cause of nonattachment is misery. It is transience which attracts and invites.

As life passes, the mind says, "Enjoy it as much as possible, it may be over at any moment. No one knows when you will die, so make the best use of every minute by enjoying it. Live as intensely as possible — not a moment is to remain empty. Suck it in; enjoy every moment's possibilities."

Yes, transience is the attraction. Death is approaching, so we hold on to life. If death were not approaching then nobody would have held on to life. Nobody would have worried if happiness came and never disappeared.

The cause of attraction is transience. Anything which disappears quickly seems precious. The stone is not as precious as the flower because the flower blossoms in the morning and withers away by the evening. So you had better have a good look at its beauty and satisfy your eyes, because anything which has blossomed has already started withering. It will not take a long time to do so. The sun is already in the middle of the sky. The flower has started withering, half of its life has passed away. That is why there is so much attraction in beauty. If beauty could remain for ever then nobody would have bothered about it.

Another interesting point is that ugliness is more permanent than beauty. An ugly person remains ugly all his life, but a beautiful person doesn't remain beautiful all his life. He is beautiful for some time – during youth – and after that he withers away. Have you noticed that if a person is very beautiful, he withers away quickly? The more delicate the flower is, the more quickly it withers away.

The mind goes on saying: "Hurry up, don't waste time sitting and chanting in the temples. This can be done later on. Enjoy now as much as possible. Not only is the other changing, your capacity to enjoy is also becoming weaker day by day."

Certainly transience is the cause of attraction. If things were permanent then nobody would have worried about them. Perhaps that is why you are not worried about the inner world – it is eternal, so there is no hurry. It is not going to be lost, so we can easily go on postponing till tomorrow. If not in this birth then in the next one, and if not in the next one then still farther on. Whenever you will go the divine will be at home. The mind says, "But these transient flowers of life, the beauty of the eyes, the rosiness of the cheeks, this youth and your capacity to enjoy – all of them are withering away and weakening. So don't delay, enjoy them," the mind says to you.

Certainly this transience is the cause of attraction. There is no attraction for anything which is eternal. How can there be attraction in what always is and always will be? Dreams always seem beautiful – they are finished as soon as the eyes open.

Religion is not trying to create a feeling of indifference or nonattachment in you by saying that life is transient. By calling it transient, it is trying to point out to you the question: What will you do after that moment? After dancing for a moment you will cry. Life is transient; you will enjoy it for a moment, but you will repent it afterwards. You will be finished in this useless chase.

Just as children chase butterflies, you are running after small enjoyments which will tire you thoroughly, and one day you will fall down and die. Actually, you gained nothing by running after the transient, you have only wasted your time, because all the transient things wither away even before you get them, flowers are dead as soon as they are in your hands. By the time you bring it home, happiness turns into anguish.

The awakening of nonattachment is because of misery and anguish. Religion says that you must try to see that the momentary pleasure is followed by unlimited misery. You also know it very well that whenever you found happiness, misery followed. Whenever you were happy, later on your eyes were full of tears. You fell down whenever you were vain. Bad luck started as soon as you thought that good luck was smiling on you. Religion says that if you want a happiness which will not get lost and will not turn into misery, then look for the eternal, the immortal, and wake up from this transient world. Time spent in dreams is time lost. Seek the truth.

What is the definition of truth? The definition of truth is that which was always, which is always, and which will be always. The definition of untruth is that which was not yesterday, but which is now, and which will not be tomorrow. Untruth means the existence of that which is momentary between two 'nots'— the illusion of being, between the two 'nots.'

Just think it over: if it is not on both sides, then how can it be in between? That is why Shankara says that the world is *maya*, an illusion. The meaning of maya is that it was not yesterday, it is today and tomorrow again it will not be. So what is not on both ends cannot be in the center either, though it appears to be so. How can 'is' be born out of 'is not'? And that which is, how can it not be?

There was a time when you were not. Where were you before your birth? Where will you be after death? It is only a dream of short duration. You see the dream while sleeping, but it is lost as soon as you wake up. Sahajo has said that this world is like the morning star. Yes, the morning star is there for a short while and it soon disappears. It will disappear whilst you are watching it. Yes, the whole of life is like the morning star.

Mahavira has said that life is like the dewdrops on the grass leaf. Have you noticed the dewdrop on the grass? It is about to drop at any time — it will drop while you are still watching it, a whiff of breeze is sufficient. It will evaporate with the sunrise. A small push by the breeze and it is gone. But during its existence it is so beautiful even pearls are no match for it; even the pearl envies its luster. But its existence is momentary, it is like nonexistence.

If life is transient then it cannot be true. Whatever you have known, if it is later lost, then it cannot be truth. It must have been the imagination of the mind or the projection of the mind. It is not the truth, but you believed it to be true. That is your belief. Belief is illusion. You go on watching the projection of your inner desire on the screen of life.

Have you ever noticed that a woman or a man who seems very beautiful at one time doesn't seem so after a few days? It is the same woman or the same man...what happened? Actually, a few days before you had projected your own desire. That desire has now disappeared, so there is nothing on the screen, there is no picture on the screen. With the mind full of desires you just cannot see that which is; you just go on seeing what you want to see.

Only the pure eye can see that which is. The impure eye sees whatever it wants to see. If you are in search of beauty, then you will see beauty. Everyone has his own definition of life. Because of this definition, life is an illusion.

Mulla Nasruddin makes and sells medicines. On one packet he has written that the price of the medicine will be returned if it is not beneficial. I was sitting in his shop when a man came —

he was very annoyed. He said, "I have been taking this medicine since last month but it has done no good to me, it was of no benefit to me. So give me back the money I have paid for it."

Mulla said, "It is written on the packet that the money will be returned if it is not beneficial. Well, you may not have benefited but I have, so why should I return the money?"

It all depends on one's own definition. You see life as you want to see it. Accordingly, the meanings of words change and the meanings of truths change. You build up a world of your own beliefs and you go on living in it, and to keep up those beliefs you go on finding your own reasons to strengthen them so that they may not break.

Mulla Nasruddin quarreled with someone in the market. That man was very angry and he told Mulla, "I will give you such a slap that all your thirty-two teeth will fall out of your mouth."

Mulla was also enraged. He said, "What do you think of yourself? If I slap you, all sixty-four teeth will fall out."

A third person who was watching this fight said, "My dear fellow, you should surely know that a man doesn't have sixty-four teeth."

Mulla said, "Well, I knew that you would interfere. That is why I said sixty-four teeth! With my one slap all the sixty-four teeth of both of you will fall out."

Man is like that. You cannot accept your own mistakes. You find reasons and logic to justify your mistakes. Actually, it needs great courage to admit one's own mistakes. If you admit the mistakes then gradually the mistakes disappear.

You are in love with a woman — you dream of heaven, you write poetry and you think that you have attained heaven, but in a few days the heaven disappears. You don't realize that it was you who had made a mistake, you think it was the woman who has deceived you. You don't see that your imagination, your conception has broken. You don't realize that your idea, which was like the morning dew, has disappeared. You think that this woman has deceived you, this woman was wrong. So now you will look for another woman. You start looking for a new woman again. You will go on projecting your ideas, and again you will make the same mistake, the same hangover! Again the same dream which will again break in a few days.

There is a very old and sweet story in the Mahabharata. The four Pandava brothers were living deep in a forest. One day they lost their way; it was afternoon and they could not find water anywhere. One of the brothers went in search of water and he came across a lake, but as he bent down to take the water from the lake a voice said, "Stop! You cannot take the water till you answer my question." It was a *yaksha*, a spirit, who possessed the lake.

"What is your question?" asked the Pandava.

The yaksha said, "If you don't answer the question or if you give the wrong answer then you will die immediately. But if the answer is correct then you will get water as well as innumerable presents from me." The question was: What is the greatest truth of man's life? But the answer — whatever the answer was — was not correct, so the first brother fell down and died.

One by one all the four brothers went looking for water and died. In the end Yudhishthira followed them wondering what had happened to them all. He found all the four dead.

Then the yaksha called out, "Be careful! First answer my question, otherwise you will also die like them. You can take water only on one condition — that your answer has to be correct, because my salvation depends on that reply. I will be free the moment I get the correct reply; the bondage of my being a yaksha will break. The question is: What is the greatest truth of man's life?"

Yudhishthira said, "The greatest truth is that man doesn't learn from his experiences."

The yaksha got free of the curse. All the four brothers came back to life – the yaksha was so happy to be free that he brought all four of them alive again.

Yes, man never learns from his experiences. He is hardly free from one woman when he starts running after another one. One trouble is over and he is ready for another. He is always running after something or other. After the fulfillment of one desire he will be wanting ten more. He cannot see the illusion of desire. He never realizes his mistake and justifies every one of his mistakes with reason and logic. He makes someone else responsible for his own fault, and then happily again indulges in the same mistake.

Making the other one responsible for your mistake is preparing to repeat it again and again. Whenever you make the other responsible for your mistake, you are refusing your own responsibility. That responsibility could have awakened you, because in that moment of responsibility you could have realized that you were making a mistake.

There is no fault in any woman or in any man; fault is in the desire or imagination which you projected on that man or woman. That desire is transient, that desire will break. Just think, how long can you keep a thought in your mind? Even the morning star remains for some time, even the dewdrop remains for some time. But how long can you hold a thought? It is there for a second and it disappears. Even if you try to hold it, it is gone, you cannot catch it in your fist. Even if you run after it you cannot find it. It comes and goes like a whiff of a breeze. The life that you live in this world on the basis of such a mind is transient. Don't think that the world is transient, it is only a way of speaking. The world is not transient. The world was when you were not, and it will remain when you will not be. The world is eternal. But the world that you make on the basis of your mind is transient. In fact, the world doesn't exist, only godliness exists.

These pictures of your own desires which you make on the screen of existence, these pictures are the world, and that world is full of misery. Every day you get misery, but you go on hoping for the happiness which tomorrow will bring. Many times you fall down, but you stand up again. Many times life says that you will never get what you are looking for, but you always find some excuse or the other saying that now you will not repeat the same mistake again; no longer will you commit the same mistake.

I have heard that a prisoner was released from prison. He was there for the thirteenth time. The jailer felt pity for him – half of his life had been spent in the prison – so while setting him free the jailer told him, "Be sensible now and don't come to the prison again."

The prisoner replied, "Every time I try not to come here, but I come again and again. But this time I will not come back."

The jailer said, "I am happy to hear this."

The prisoner said, "From your happiness it seems that you have not understood me. I am saying that now I will not make those same mistakes that allowed me to be caught. I am not saying that I will not steal – but I will not repeat the old mistakes which were the cause of my getting caught. I will not repeat these mistakes which I have made thirteen times. I will steal, but now there will be no mistakes on my part."

Stealing is not the mistake; the mistake is in being caught! The people who are sent to prison come back as hardened criminals because there they meet even greater criminals. They learn all the tricks from them, they gain from their experience, they get trained by them and then again indulge in crime.

It seems that stealing is not the wrong thing, the wrong thing is in being caught. Yes, just think about it: if you are sure of not being caught then will you steal or not? Your mind will say, "Why not? Stealing is not bad, but being caught is bad." You will be in misery if you go on thinking this way. But, actually, misery is not in being caught but in being a thief; misery is in stealing and not in being caught.

But if you could see that misery is in your wrong-being, then you will realize that misery is *because* of your being wrong. This is the meaning of the theory of karma. It means that if you are in misery it is because of your own actions, and if you are happy it is because of your own actions.

If you want bliss, then you have to go beyond actions – where there is no happiness and no misery, you are beyond both. There, there is utmost peace and your inner balance is absolutely correct, just as when both sides of the scale are even, they stand in one line. Similarly, when you have the capacity to go beyond happiness and misery, then you gain the ultimate bliss.

Religion is not trying to make you unattached to the world by calling it transient. By calling it transient is meant: Don't get lost in happiness; anguish is fast following it. As soon as happiness comes, misery enters from the other door and you are bound to meet misery sooner or later.

The attraction is to the transient, not to misery. If you are able to see misery behind every happiness then a revolution will occur. You will try to be free not only of misery, but also of happiness. If every pleasure is definitely followed by misery, then one has to be free of misery as well as of pleasure. This is the difference between a *sannyasin* and a householder. The householder wants to be free of misery and wants to hold on to pleasure. The sannyasin has understood that every pleasure is followed by misery. He wants to be free of misery and pleasure both.

And whosoever wants to be free of both can certainly be free of them, but whosoever wants to be free of only one of them, he cannot be free of it. It is just like if you have a coin in your hand and you want to get rid of its one side and keep the other. That is not possible. Either the whole of the coin with both sides is kept, or you lose the whole of the coin. Either happiness and misery both will disappear, or both will remain. If this

kind of clarity comes into your life only then will there be
unattachment, only then will there be sannyas.

The third question:

> Beloved Osho,
> You have said that when the self surrenders, the
> whole of existence then protects. Then why was the
> fakir who could see the formless everywhere, or
> who could feel the presence of godliness
> everywhere, murdered by the English soldiers?

It appears like murder to you, but not to him. You see it as murder because you are under illusion. He saw only the divine in that spear; he saw that the death was a meeting with the divine. Existence protected him in the sense that even death didn't seem like death to him. Death became the door of the ultimate bliss. To you it seems that he died, he was finished.

When the Ganges flows into the sea, to you it seems that it is finished. But ask the Ganges: it will say, "I have disappeared and thus become the sea." The Ganges will say, "The fear of annihilation was there before, but now it has disappeared. Before this I was very narrow, bounded by the two banks. I could have been finished. I was limited, so I could have died. But now I have become unlimited, now there is no death." The Ganges has become the sea.

Ask that sannyasin: he saw godliness even in that soldier, even in that murderer. Even in that spear he saw the arrow of the divine piercing his heart. It seems death to you, but not to that sannyasin. He attained the ultimate life.

You have asked, "You have said that when the ego surrenders then the whole existence protects." Really, it will not protect you, and if you try to surrender yourself to get this protection then this surrender will not be true, it will not be real. Surrender means, that there is nobody left in me who can be protected.

If you think, "Existence will protect me so I will surrender," then you are not surrendering at all, you are only appointing the divine in your service. Surrender means, "Now I am not, only you are; now there is no question of my protection." Now you are just a plain sky, an empty house. "There is nothing left to be finished. I finished myself long before you." The meaning of surrender is, "I am finished; now there is no need for you to finish me. I will not give you that trouble, I will do it myself."

The actual meaning of surrender is suicide. The suicide which you think of as suicide is only the killing of the body. The soul doesn't die, only the body dies and a new body is acquired. But actually, surrender is suicide. You destroy your ego. You tell it, "Now I am not, only you are." Now there is no question of your protection. Now who are you? Whose protection do you want? And when you don't exist, only then does the whole of existence protect you. Now there is no fun in annihilating you – what is the point? When you annihilate yourself, death becomes meaningless.

When the spear pierced the chest of the sannyasin, the soldier must have thought that he had killed him. It must have appeared to the onlookers also that he had died, but ask that sannyasin: he announced, "*Tattvamasi* – you are also that." He said, "You may come in any form but you cannot deceive me, I will recognize you. Today you have come with a spear and played the drama of death, but I recognize you, I am looking at you. You may come in the garb of an enemy or in the garb of a friend – I will recognize you in every situation."

The sannyasin did not die. His Ganges had become the sea.

But I understand your difficulty. Even when you do right things you do them for the wrong reasons; your reasons are not right. Even if you go to the temple it is for the wrong reason. Someone goes there asking for a job, someone goes there asking for money, someone goes asking for a wife and someone goes asking for a son. You don't realize that you never step out of the market. Is this the way to go to the temple? You are taking the whole of the market with you to the temple. If you are like this, then the temple cannot purify you, you will pollute the temple.

The temple is not a place, it is a state of mind. There can be no temple as long as there is a demand. You go on asking for the petty things which are available in the market — as if it were a supermarket. You couldn't get these things in the shops, so you want to get them in the temple. You couldn't get them in this world, so you will get them in heaven! But why do you ask?

Only that person can reach the temple who has understood that asking for anything is in vain, who has understood that by asking one doesn't get anything except misery; who has understood that in spite of all efforts the beggar's bowl remains empty — it is never full.

Only that person reaches the temple who goes there not for asking, but for thanking. The day you are full of gratitude — flowers blossom and you are thankful, it rains from the clouds and you are thankful, a child shouts with joy and you are thankful, even your breathing, your being is so peaceful that you feel thankful — this state of gratitude, this feeling of thankfulness which is within you day and night is actually the song of the divine. There is no need of chanting, one doesn't become devotional by chanting. It is the continuous, inner state of mind. The day you realize that existence has given you more than you deserved, will you go to thank him or ask him for more? You have not even earned what you have got. He has showered his grace on you, he is in abundance so he has distributed it, but he hasn't given it to you because you deserved it.

People ask me, "Why did God create the world?" They think that this creation must be out of some desire, because we don't make anything without desire. Even an ordinary man has a reason for making a small house. So why has God made this whole world?

And it is not that only ordinary people think like this. Somebody had asked the great German musician Wagner, "Why did you create such wonderful music?"

He replied, "I was unhappy. So to keep myself occupied, involved, I created this music." And Wagner said, "I say to you that God also must have been unhappy, so he created this world." What Wagner is saying, is true about man. Man writes poetry to cover up his wounds; to hide his tears he sings; he smiles so that he doesn't cry; he walks merrily on the road because his inner poverty hurts him.

Others should not know about your inner poverty, so to deceive them you smile. When anyone asks you, "How are you?" you answer, "I am fine, I am happy." Have you ever thought over what you are saying? You, and happy? But of course you have to say this, otherwise it doesn't look nice. To say this is only a formality. Truth is not to be uttered. Only those words are said which are appropriate and not the truth.

Everyone has different masks on his face, and he is hiding the deep anguish and hell behind them. A thousand and one things have to be done to forget that hell. Someone paints... look at Picasso's paintings. It seems as if anguish and misery are spread all over them. There is a very famous painting by Picasso named 'Guernica.' It is nothing but madness spread out. You will go mad if you keep looking at it for half an hour.

Wagner is right in saying this about man – that man is in misery, that is why he creates. But this is absolutely wrong regarding existence. The world was not created for any reason. That is why we in this country call creation *leela*. Leela means, without any reason; leela means play; leela means that there is so much energy – what else to do? The is so much bliss that it is overflowing, so it has to be distributed. There is so much water in the lake that it is overflowing! But not because of any reason, only because it is too much so it has to be distributed. When the flower is full of fragrance, it opens and the fragrance flows out. In the same way, godliness flows in this world: he has so much in abundance, he has so much surplus, that there is no other way but to distribute it.

Creation is bliss and not anguish, but you are miserly even in giving thanks. He has flowed in you so much, he has given you doors with such unique possibilities – he has given you eyes so that you can see beauty; he has given you ears so that you can hear music; he has given you hands so that you can feel the touch of life; he has given you a mind so that you can understand; he has given you a heart so that you can be overjoyed; he has given you life so that your life can become a big festival. But you are miserly even in feeling thankful. When you go to the temple you cannot even say, "You have given me so much, and without any reason! And if you had not given this, there would have been no way I could even complain. Had you had not created me, in which law court could I have complained about you not creating me? What you have given me is too much. I don't deserve it."

The meaning of prayer, the meaning of Bhaj Govindam – singing the song of the divine – is that you are singing out of your happiness. You are saying, "You have given us too much and it will be a discourtesy on our part if we cannot even thank you."

But whenever you go to the temple you go to complain: "My son is ill, why hasn't he recovered yet? My son is not employed, are all our prayers and devotion in vain? Why don't you hear anything – are you deaf?"

Whenever you go to the temple you go to complain. Going with a complaint means that you have never really entered the temple, you remained outside. If you are asking for something then you cannot go in; only those go in who go there to thank. Even your surrender is with the motive of asking for protection. Who are you, that you need protection? You want to make even the divine your bodyguard! You want him to stand near you with a gun to guard you!

Surrender means: "I have nothing worth saving in me; I surrender my emptiness at your feet." And while surrendering, that you don't feel that you are doing something great. You are simply returning to existence what he has given to you: "Your gift is returned to you." But what else do you do? You are just returning it after making it a little dirtier.

There are very few blessed people like Kabir who are able to say that they have returned the cloak just as clean as it was. It is certainly very difficult to keep the cloak clean, because it always gets a little stained. So when you offer yourself at the feet of the divine, you don't do so with the hope that he will be made happy by this act and will be thankful and grateful to you. In fact, you will feel sorry for making the cloak dirty; you will feel bad for not returning only what he gave you. You will say, "I am not even returning just what you gave me, I could not add anything to it, I could not fill that cloak with pearls and diamonds." In that moment the whole of existence protects you.

Don't surrender to seek protection. The essential result of surrender is protection.

The fourth question:

> Beloved Osho,
> There is such an intense emptiness within me that in my own eyes I feel even more insignificant than dust. And when there is no feeling of any worthiness left, I cannot trust that God will ever come and sit on this empty throne. Because of this feeling, life seems insecure. It seems I have reached nowhere. I am neither here nor there.

"There is such an intense emptiness within me that in my own eyes I seem worse than dust." If emptiness becomes so intense, then you will not be conscious of your being. Then you will not be able to say that "emptiness has become intense within me," you will only be able to say "emptiness has occurred." You will not be able to say "within me," because as long as you are, emptiness cannot be. You are full of yourself.

And you say that "in my own eyes I feel even more insignificant than dust." Who told you that dust is insignificant? Who taught you this condemnation? You are made out of this dust and eventually you will go into this dust, and you say that dust is insignificant!

Man's ego is wonderful! Just because dust remains under his feet he thinks it is insignificant. But this very dust is your heart and your mind. Every particle of your body is made of this dust. Earth is the mother. You came out of it and you will go back to it.

"More insignificant than dust" – this language of 'great' and 'insignificant' is the language of the ego. The day you become empty you will see the divine in every particle of dust and it will no longer seem insignificant to you. Then nothing will be insignificant because he is great, he is present everywhere and in everything and in every way. Then you will even kiss the dust and you will see his feet there.

Dust is insignificant? This is your ego speaking. There is no emptiness within you yet, you have only thought about it. Man is very clever in thinking. If one becomes empty, then there is nothing left to be done.

And you are asking "when there is no feeling of any worthiness left..." What kind of worthiness can there be? To attain the divine the question of worth doesn't arise. If worthiness is needed for the attainment of the divine, then it is like getting a government job. Then Kabir could never have got it; he was illiterate and didn't possess any certificate. Even Mohammed could not have got it; he could not read or write.

When Mohammed heard the echo of God for the first time he became nervous. He started shivering and had a fever, because he thought, "How can God shower on me? Impossible! There are so many more worthy people in this world, how can he choose me? Impossible! I must be in some illusion."

Just then a voice echoed, "Read."

Mohammed said, "This is sheer madness. I am not literate." He came home, covered himself with a blanket and went to sleep.

His wife asked him, "What happened? When you left here in the morning you were all right."

He said, "I am under the illusion that God's voice has spoken to me. But it cannot be – I am not worthy."

But this was real worthiness. As long as you think that you are worthy, you are not. There is an obstacle, there is ego. To feel worthy, in other words, means ego. You are standing in front of the temple, not in front of the employment office. Here certificates will be of no use. In fact, the more certificates, the more difficult it will be to enter the temple. Only those who feel unworthy can enter there.

You must understand properly what I am saying, because you are in so much illusion that you can even mistake a false unworthiness to be a real unworthiness. You say, "I am unworthy, so why has God not come to me yet?" You can also turn unworthiness into some kind of worth.

No, the meaning of not having any feeling of worthiness is that you cannot demand to attain the divine; you cannot ask the divine why you have not yet been able to attain him. Any demand is ego. If you don't attain him, know that there is a reason why you have not attained him. But if you do attain him, then you will dance out of gratitude – that you attained him not because of any cause, but just by his grace.

To feel worthy, means that you have confidence in yourself and not in the divine. To feel worthy, also means that you are ready to buy him. It means you are saying: "I have acquired all the virtues, so why is there any delay? I have prayed, I have worshipped, I have lit so many earthen lamps, burned so many incense sticks, offered so many flowers at your feet. I have fasted, meditated and undergone a lot of austerity. I have done all this, but you have not yet come."

"You have not yet come" – through these words your ego is

announcing, "I have earned him and he is being unfair to me. You are coming to other people who have done nothing. You have come to those who have no claim on you, and you haven't come to me!" This very claim is the obstacle.

Only those people have attained godliness who have given up all their claims. They say, "We are insignificant, very small, so whatever we do will be insignificant, very ordinary; we are just ordinary. We realize we can't attain by our own effort or by doing anything – all our doing is like trying to grasp the whole of the sky in our hands. Such a vast sky and such a small fist! It is so ridiculous."

You can attain godliness only when you accept your insignificance and helplessness, in its totality. Then you become an empty vessel which doesn't make any claim. Only a person who is not harassing the divine to come to him and who just goes on waiting can attain to godliness. Even to say "you must come to me" is egoistic.

You write, "And when there is no feeling of any worthiness left I cannot trust...."

If there is no feeling of worthiness, trust that the divine will come, will emerge at that very moment. Even now there is some feeling of being worthy. Actually, you are thinking that your so-called intense emptiness makes you worthy. You say that you have become more insignificant than dust; you think this makes you worthy. Now you are waiting for him, and if he doesn't come to you, you think he is being unfair. "I have done so much, and still you haven't come. It is too much!"

Remember, the divine only dawns in your emptiness. That is the basic condition. When you are totally empty, then there will be no delay. As soon as you become empty the divine appears. These two things happen simultaneously.

So what you think to be emptiness is just a thought of your mind. Beware of the mind's tricks. Mind is very cunning, very efficient, very calculating. It does everything calculatedly, and it keeps account of everything – even of religion. Beware of this mind. It is this mind which is saying, "I am neither here nor there."

Well, what is the need of being either here or there? What is wrong in being in the middle? But you think that you have neither gained the divine nor this world. I have understood your meaning. The ambition of achieving in this world is still suppressed in you. That's why you are "neither here nor there"... otherwise, the freedom exists in the middle. What difference does it make to the laundry-man's donkey whether he is tied up at home or at the riverside? In fact, there is some freedom in between: from there he can run away, because the washerman is at home in both places.

The mind says that if the time devoted to meditation had been utilized in doing business, you could have earned some money, or "I would have become a leader by contesting an election. The whole world is busy doing something or the other and I am doing meditation! I am not attaining the divine and am losing the world as well."

This thought arises only because you still have attachment to this world. Therefore it will be better if you go back to the marketplace because your sannyas will not be real and your meditation also cannot be real. Your attraction to money is still there. You are only curious about meditation. You are not thirsty, you are not a seeker yet.

That is why I say that you had better return to the marketplace instead of sitting and thinking that existence is being unfair to you. Perhaps it is not the right time yet; you are not yet ripe. You are raw. To become ripe, mature, you will have to undergo a lot of misery and anguish. You have not suffered so much yet.

When a person has suffered all his life, when he has experienced only unhappiness in life, then he arrives at the conclusion that there is nothing worth gaining in this world. Then he says, "Now it doesn't matter whether I find the divine or not, but one thing is clear, that I will not get anything out of this world. Now it doesn't matter about attaining godliness, and the possibility of returning to the world doesn't arise — that gate is closed, that bridge is broken, that ladder has been thrown down, so the question of being able to climb down doesn't arise."

The fifth question:

> Beloved Osho,
> Shankaracharya emphasizes the sense of indifference, nonattachment towards the bodies of man and woman. But in this ashram you approve of free mixing of men and women.
> Please say something on this.

So that you may become ripe, mature... I don't want to break you off from the world, I want to make you free of this world.

To break off and to be free are two different things. Breaking off is like plucking the raw fruit and to be free is like the falling of the ripe fruit. Outwardly these look alike because in both of them the fruit separates from the tree, but there is a basic difference between them. When a raw fruit is plucked, the pain of being plucked remains in the fruit and a wound is left in the tree also. There is no need to pluck the ripe fruit; the ripe fruit falls down by itself without any pain, without any yearning to be with the tree for a little more time. When the fruit ripens the work of the tree is complete, so there is no pain left in the tree. A ripe fruit forgets the tree absolutely, it doesn't look back. And after the fall of the fruit the tree also becomes lighter, it is not wounded.

I don't want to break you away from this world because whosoever is deliberately plucked from the world remains attached to this world. You are to be free of this world and you are not be plucked from it. And where can you go after a forcible breaking away? You have your wife, children, family, a shop. Even if you leave them, where will you go? You may go anywhere, but if the shopkeeper remains in your mind then you will open a new shop! It will not make any difference.

If the attraction for women remains in the mind, then running away from your wife is not going to help you, some other woman will attract you. If you are interested in money, giving it up will not make any difference. You will start collecting coins in some other sense – maybe this time the coins are of renunciation and austerity, but coins are coins. You will start amassing the other kind of wealth. First you used to announce about the amount of money you possessed, now you will announce about how much you have renounced. Your vanity will remain just the same. I want to free you from the world; I don't want to break you off from it. In this commune I am trying to make you free to live.

If you can be free while living in this life then that is the real freedom. You walk in water, but your feet should not get wet. You should become like the lotus leaf: you may touch the water, but the water will not touch you. You live in the water but you are free from it.

The ultimate conception of sannyas is: Sannyas is not nonattachment, *vairagya*, as the opposite of attachment, *raga*. Sannyas is beyond attachment and nonattachment. It is *veetragata*, beyond both attachment and nonattachment. §§

The sannyas about which Shankaracharya is talking is nonattachment. But the sannyas about which I am talking to you is veetragata, beyond attachment and nonattachment. Shankara's sannyas will not take you very far. After Shankara's sannyas, you will still have to search for the sannyas I am talking about. Shankara's sannyas can be the beginning of the journey, not the end. What I am telling you is the end.

I don't tell you to run away from a woman; I say, "Wake up from the attachment to women." I don't say, "Give up money"; I say, "Understand money." In that understanding is freedom.

Money is not holding you, you are holding it. It is your inner condition, it is your attraction. You can be free of this attraction only when the experience of life will tell you that this is useless. If you don't learn from the experience of life, then you may go on thinking in your mind that "it is useless, what is there in the world?" but deep down somewhere in the mind you will think, "Who knows, there may be something worthwhile in this world and I left it. I might have made a mistake."

Many sannyasins have been coming to me – some as old as seventy or eighty years. They say, "Sometimes we wonder if we have wasted our lives because we have not attained the divine and we gave up the world also." So now this doubt wavers in the mind. This doubt arises because you ran away from the world when you were still attracted towards it. You didn't leave the world because of your own experience, you left it because you were influenced by somebody.

When people like Shankaracharya and Buddha are in this world their influence is unlimited, their influence is all pervasive. They attract thousands of people like magnets. Their life is beyond attachment and nonattachment.

They are quite right when they say, "This world is meaningless; there is no meaning in man, in woman or in children." They are like the ripe fruits on the tree. But by listening to their words the raw fruits start thinking that when there is no meaning, let us give up this world. They break away from the tree, then doubt arises because they don't even have the fragrance of the ripe fruit.

The ripe fruit has a fragrance, its own smell; even that they don't have and they have already broken away from the tree. They have neither related to the earth nor connected with the sky. They are hanging in between.

This was exactly the meaning of the previous question: "I am neither here nor there, I am hanging in between." This hanging in the middle is a very miserable condition. That is why I tell you that there is no need to run away from anything. Wake up wherever you are. Forget about leaving the world; call the divine, ask him to come, and let him appear in your innermost space. As soon as his rays start penetrating you, you will begin to become ripe. The sun ripens the fruits, existence ripens you.

Don't run away from life, because if existence has given you life there must be some reason for it. It is not a coincidence. There is total planning behind this, because nobody can be free without going through the experience of life.

There is a great statement in the Upanishads which says: *Ten tyakten bhunjeethah*. I have not found a more revolutionary sentence than this in any scripture of the world. It is a unique statement. It has two meanings. The first meaning is: Those who have renounced, only they have experienced it. The second meaning is: Only those who experience a thing can renounce it. Both meanings are very valuable; both meanings are actually like the two sides of a coin. Only those who renounced, experienced – how can you renounce unless you have experienced it? The understanding of renunciation can come only by going through the experience. The lotus of renunciation can bloom only out of the mind of experience, there is no other way. So don't denounce the experience of pleasure, because the lotus will grow out of it. Don't condemn experience, don't run away from the mud, otherwise you will remain without the lotus. And how different is the lotus from the mud!

Godliness will arise in you, the lotus will blossom. How different the divine is from you! Even where you are living with your wife, your children, the shop, the market, one day, all of a sudden, the divine nectar will start flowing in you. All that you have to do is to make yourself empty for his nectar. When you receive diamonds and precious stones, then you will automatically throw away the pebbles and the rocks. Don't insist on renouncing, insist on receiving. Of course it is not certain that you will get diamonds and precious stones just by throwing away the dirt and pebbles. But one thing is sure, that after getting diamonds and precious stones nobody hoards dirt; they are given up automatically – and that giving up has a beauty of its own, it has a different music. Why? – because when you give up without knowing that you are giving it up, then no imprint of the giving up is left – then there is no claim of renunciation.

Every morning you sweep the house and throw the garbage away outside. Do you inform the newspapers that you have renounced so much rubbish today? If you do, then people will laugh at you. They will think that you have gone mad. If it is rubbish, then throwing it away doesn't mean renunciation. And if it was not garbage, then why did you renounce it?

When you announce your renunciation, you are actually saying that I had money, but I renounced it under the influence of someone. You were not ready yet, you were not ripe yet; you were still raw and you took the step in a hurry. No one ever becomes transformed through hurry. I don't want you to hurry at all. If you have an attraction for women, then go through that experience. Indulge in it thoroughly. *Ten tyakten bhunjeetha* – renunciation will be born out of that indulgence. When you go on indulging and find that you gain nothing out of it, then you realize that by this indulgence you only get misery, nothing blossoms in life. Then the indulgence has given you the key of renunciation.

Indulgence is not your enemy; it is your friend. My only condition is that you go through the indulgence with awareness. You should not go on experiencing without learning anything, experience should teach you a lesson. Experience is always worth going through. Even going through hell is useful if you go through it fully awake, because in that wakefulness you find the path to heaven.

That is why I don't want to cut you off from life at any level. Remain where you are and sow the new seeds of awareness in your heart. That is why my emphasis is not on renunciation but on meditation. I don't say anything against the world, but I say a lot in favor of godliness. Shankaracharya's emphasis is against the world.

The old conception of sannyas was that people should give

up the world so that they can attain the divine. My idea is that people should be brought near the divine so that the world just drops away.

The last question:

> Beloved Osho,
> My mind is extremely skeptical. That is why, in spite of all my efforts, it doesn't settle anywhere. Since my birth I have only known the material — and you say that everything is godliness. So should I believe it? Will it be honesty?

Just understand these words, "My mind is extremely skeptical...." It may be skeptical, but not *extremely* skeptical, because an extremely skeptical person starts doubting the doubt. That type of doubt has not arisen in you yet. Your doubt is lame, quite impotent. You have doubted, but you have not yet reached the climax of doubt. The climax of doubt is faith... because when you go on doubting everything, then in the end you start doubting the doubt. You start thinking, "Will I get anything out of this doubt? Has anyone ever gained anything through this doubt?"

When you start doubting the doubt, then it is the extreme of skepticism. But at that moment doubt cuts off the doubt and a virgin faith is born.

You are skeptical but lame; you have not traveled the whole path. If you were not lame you would not have come to me. There was no need to come to me for doubting, the whole world is there for doubting. Actually, you are tired without completing your doubt, and now you want to have faith so you have come to me. But you have come a bit too soon, you should have waited a little longer. Go on doubting a little longer and remember, just as a thorn is taken out by a thorn, in the same way doubt is removed by doubt.

"My mind is extremely skeptical. That is why in spite of all the efforts it doesn't settle anywhere."

No, it will not settle. Has any skeptical person ever attained renunciation, ever attained meditation or ever realized the divine? No, because a skeptical person cannot do anything. What he does with one hand, he removes with the other hand.

I have heard:

A great thinker joined the army during the first world war. It was a compulsory recruitment where everyone had to go to war, so he also went. But it became a problem because he was a great thinker, a philosopher, and was always doubting. When his commander would order "Left turn," the whole regiment would turn left, but he would remain standing as he was, thinking whether he should or should not turn.

His commander asked, "Why do you take such a long time? Are you deaf? All the lines have moved, but you remain here!"

He answered, "Excuse me. But I don't do anything without thinking first, and it takes time to think. First of all the question is: Why turn left? What is the necessity of turning? What is the harm in turning to the right? Just because you have said, "Left turn," why should we turn left? I don't understand the purpose of all this turning left and turning right. What is the use of this parade? In the end we come back to where we were standing before. But I am already standing there! All these people will also come back here after all their left turns and right turns."

He was a famous thinker. So the commander understood that this sort of doubting was his old habit and he wouldn't be of any use in the army, so he was sent to the army kitchen. The very first day he was given some peas and was asked to separate the big ones from the small ones. When the commander came after some time he was sitting lost in thought near the peas — they were just as they were given to him. The commander said, "You couldn't even do this?"

He said, "It is very difficult. There are big peas and small peas, but there are medium ones also. Where should they be put? I don't start any work until everything is very clear. I was waiting for you to tell me what to do with these medium ones."

This type of personality cannot do anything. He cannot accomplish anything. Even a simple act is not possible because doubt surrounds his every act like poison. Meditation is beyond his reach because meditation is the ultimate act, meditation is a great matter. Right now you are wavering. When you even doubt about turning left or right, then turning in is going to be very difficult.

"Since birth I have known only the material." Your saying this is also wrong. If you really were a doubting person then you could not have said that you have known only the material. Real skeptics say, "No one knows whether matter exists or not." And it is not certain.

I am sitting here and you are listening to me. You may be dreaming: "Is it definite that I am here and you are sitting there?" In your dreams you have also seen people many times, so this can also be a dream. And have you ever seen matter? You are hidden behind the brain, and matter is outside of the brain. Have you ever taken matter inside the brain? You have never seen matter; only the pictures of matter go into the mind. Do you see the tree there? No, you have never really seen it. The rays which come out of the tree fall on the eyes; these rays carry a picture inside. Just as a picture is created in a camera, the same way a picture goes into your brain. You have only seen that picture. It is not certain that there is a tree just like that picture. There is no proof; there is no proof that the tree exists outside.

A doubting person cannot even believe in matter, to say nothing of the divine. But I am telling you that it is difficult to know matter, but easy to know the divine, because matter is outside and the divine is inside. The divine is near and matter is far away. You yourself are godliness, and matter is the world.

SOWING THE SEED

The divine is not a thing to be known. He is not an object to be known, he is the knower. You are that; he is your consciousness. The one who is doubting is that same godliness. Try to understand this. If the one who is doubting is the divine, then how can you doubt him? – because the one who is doubting is inside. Even if you doubt he is there, because even for doubting he is needed. If he is not, then who will doubt? Try to understand.

One evening Mulla Nasruddin came home with his friends. When they were sitting in a hotel one of them remarked, "You are a great miser."

Mulla said, "Who says that? I am a charitable person!"

Hearing this the friends said, "Well, if it is so, then you had better invite us home to your house today."

On hearing this Mulla replied, "Yes, come on, let us all go." And a crowd of thirty to thirty-five friends went with him. But by the time he arrived at his house he had realized his mistake. In the excitement, he had forgotten about his wife sitting at home – his wife didn't like even one guest coming to their place, and here were thirty-five people! So he told his friends, "You are all men with families, you know a man's reality; you must understand my problem. My wife is inside. You had better wait outside and I will go in first, explain to her, then I will call you all inside. He went inside and closed the door, leaving them outside.

His wife lost her temper when she came to know that he had brought so many people home with him. She said, "There is no food, no vegetables, nothing to eat. Where were you the whole day? You have not brought the food from the market."

Mulla said, "You had better tell me what to do. It is night-time, even the market is closed. How am I to deal with these people?"

She said, "You have brought this trouble, so now you had better deal with it."

He said, "Go and tell them that Mulla is not at home."

She went out and told them that Mulla was not at home.

"How can that be?" they argued, "He came with us. He went inside and we never saw him come out."

Mulla was listening to the arguments and in his enthusiasm he forgot that he was inside. He peeped out of the window and said, "Well, he could have also gone out from the back door."

You cannot deny yourself. Back door or front door, you cannot say that you are not in. If somebody knocks at your door you cannot say, "I am not at home." If you say so, it will mean that you are, because even to deny you, you are needed.

The divine is not a thing, not a commodity. He is not outside you, he is your inner being, your inner nature. He is your innerness. He is your *svarup*, your being. But don't believe this just because I am saying so; that will be dishonesty. You yourself should go in search of him. And you know, yesterday I was reading the words of a poem which I liked:

Ages passed; I did not even remember you,
But it is not that I forgot you.

"Ages passed; I did not even remember you, but it is not that I forgot you." The divine is just like this. Ages might have passed, you might not have remembered — but you have not forgotten him!

It is only a question of sitting down with peace within you and that is meditation. The meaning of meditation is: be peaceful within and know the one who knows all. Be conscious of your consciousness.

The divine is not sitting up in the sky. He is surrounding your inner sky. "You *are* the divine" — this is the announcement. You have to search the essence of this sutra within yourself. You don't have just to believe in me. When you find it, only then you will have faith in me. Your experience will give you the faith. Your faith in me cannot give you the experience.

When you have a little fragrance within you, then you will have faith in me, because then you will be able to understand what I am saying.

Ages passed; I did not even remember you,
But it is not that I forgot you.

Enough for today.

3

THE SEARCH FOR NIRVANA

Who is your wife? Who is your son?
This world is very strange.
Whose are you? Who are you?
From where have you come?
Do think over these essential questions.

From satsang comes aloneness,
from aloneness comes nonattachment;
because of nonattachment mind becomes stable
and because of a stable and unwavering mind
liberation is attained.

What is sexual desire once old age has set in?
What is a pond once its water is dry?
Who is the family once your wealth is finished?
Where is the world after self-realization?

Do not be proud of wealth, people and youth,
because death takes them all away
within a moment.
Dropping all these illusory matters,
know the divine and enter into it.

Day and night, evening and morning,
winter and spring come and go again and again.
Thus the play of time goes on and one's life is over.
And yet the breeze of hope
does not leave one alone.

Oh, you madman!
Why are you caught up in the worries
about your wife and your wealth?
Don't you know
that even a moment's company with good people
is the only boat there is to take you
across the ocean of this mundane world?

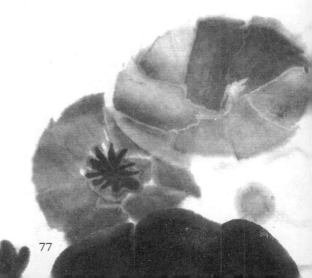

Before starting the sutra it is necessary to understand an essential complex of the human mind. Because of this complex many people, in spite of understanding, miss the point. Because of this complex they are saved from the abyss but they fall into a pit. The mind stops itself from going to one extreme, but in that process it goes to the other extreme.

Someone eats a lot, he is a glutton, his only interest is in food. But one day or other, without anybody's telling him, he will understand that he is torturing his body. The body will become sick and will be in pain. It will not be difficult for him to realize that eating too much is not healthy, but then the danger is that he may start fasting – from eating too much he may go to the extreme of giving up food altogether.

If there is too strong an attachment with the world and with money, then it is easy to run away from the world. Instead of interest there may be disinterest. Attachment may create detachment. Those that are near and dear to you may appear to be enemies rather than one's own people. There is hardly any difference between the two conditions. This is what is meant by falling into a pit while saving oneself from the abyss.

These sutras of Shankara's are not meant to help you understand detachment, they are meant to explain to you the uselessness of attachment. If attachment becomes meaningless it is enough; if attachment is over, it is enough. The disappearance of attachment is detachment – nothing else is needed except this. But the reverse always happens. After reading these sutras many people, innumerable people, have caught hold of detachment without giving up attachment. Attachment continued, but now in the guise of detachment. First you were standing on your feet, now you are standing on your head – but nothing changes by standing on your head, things remain just as they were. But when attachment stands on its head it becomes detachment – ordinary people's detachment, the so-called *sannyasin*'s detachment. But when attachment disappears, then the detachment of Mahavira, Buddha and Shankara is born.

Mulla Nasruddin was suffering from a mental disease. Whenever his telephone rang he would get scared that it was his landlord ringing about the rent, or that it may be his boss, sacking him from his job – thousands of anxieties. Because of these imaginary fears he couldn't even lift the telephone. So I told him to consult a psychiatrist. He took the treatment for two or three months.

One day, when I went to his house, I saw him speaking on the phone and he was not shaking. He was not feeling scared at all! So I asked him, "The treatment seems to have done you good. Now you are not scared anymore?"

Mulla replied, "Well, the treatment has helped me more than was necessary."

I asked, "What do you mean by 'more than was necessary'?"

He said, "You know, I have become very brave now. I pick up the phone and start talking even when it doesn't ring. Earlier I used to be scared of the ringing of the phone. But just now the phone didn't ring, so I picked it up and I started scolding the landlord. He got so scared that he kept absolutely quiet on the other end of the phone — I couldn't even hear his breathing."

This is the irony of human life! It is easy to go from one extreme to the other.

There is a Hindi proverb that a person whose mouth was burned while drinking hot milk is afraid even to drink cooled buttermilk, having first blown it cold. In the same way, a person who is scared of the world is scared of the divine also. One who is burned by the world is afraid of drinking the divine.

One has to be detached from the world — but not out of any fear. If you give up anything out of fear it will not really be given up, it will chase you, it will follow you. If you are scared of anything, it will scare you more. If you run away from anything, it will follow you because the fear is inside you. Where will you run away to? From whom will you run away? If the world were outside you could run away, but wherever you go you will find the world.. Even in a cave in the Himalayas it will be the same 'you' who will be living there, the same 'you' who lives here. So the real question is not of changing the place or the way of living, the real question is to change the inner state of the mind. At present the state of your mind is too bent to one side. So don't bend it too much to the other side: the extreme is the disease. One who becomes balanced in the middle is free, that is why Buddha has called his path *majjhim nikai,* the middle path. One who stays in the center reaches. A person who is in the middle, who doesn't lean to this side or to that side, has reached.

As long as you lean to one side there will be no stability, you will not be healthy, and you will go on wavering. Just as the flame of an earthen lamp burns steadily without being disturbed by the breeze, in the same way, when the light of consciousness becomes steady in the middle, when neither desire nor detachment are able to shake it, in fact when nothing shakes it — when it is neither this side nor that side, when it is stable just in the middle – then Krishna calls it *stithapragya*, one who has stabilized in his wisdom. You sit, you stand, but within you nobody sits or stands. You eat or you fast, but within you nobody eats or fasts. You may live in the world or in *sannyas*, but there is neither sannyas nor the world within you. This ultimate, middle condition is detachment.

If detachment is seen as being the opposite of attachment, then it is wrong. But if detachment is freedom from attachment, then it is right. This is a very delicate difference. If detachment is the opposite of attachment then there is something wrong somewhere, because that which is the opposite of attachment is definitely connected with attachment. All opposites are interconnected. If you love anyone, you go on remembering him. If you hate anyone, even then you go on remembering him. Hate and love are opposites, but they are connected. A friend you can perhaps forget, but you cannot forget your enemy; it goes on pricking you like a thorn. You are related with the friend; similarly you are related with the enemy too.

Don't ever think that an enemy is one with whom all kinds of relationships have been broken. No, if all relationships were broken altogether, then he would not be the enemy. You don't have a friendly relationship with the enemy, but you do have a relationship of enmity with him – the relationship is not broken. If the relationship is really broken, then the friend is not a friend and the enemy is not an enemy. If the relationship changes, then a friend becomes an enemy and an enemy becomes a friend.

How long does it take for a friend to become an enemy? It can happen in a moment. How long does it take to make an enemy a friend? Why doesn't it take long? – because both are relationships. It is just a question of changing the direction a little. You were going to the east – you turned to the west. You were going to the west – you turned towards the east. Both are movements – just the direction has changed a little.

I have heard that there was a great thinker in England by the name of Edmund Burke. Once he was invited to give a lecture in a church in a small village near London. But he was known as an absent-minded person; very often he used to forget the time and date of his lectures. Sometimes he used to arrive at the place on the following day. But this time the host had urged him over and over again to arrive at the church in time and on the right date, so he also tried to be extra careful about this invitation. It was some anniversary of the church and he had to be there at seven in the evening.

He started at two o'clock from his house. He was riding his horse and it was hardly one hour's journey, so he arrived at the church by three o'clock – but there was nobody in the church at that time because the function was to start at seven o'clock in the evening. What was he to do? He took out a cigarette, put it in his mouth, and tried to light a match, but because of the breeze he could not. So he turned the horse so that he could light the cigarette. The cigarette was lit – and the horse started trotting.

At four o'clock he was standing in front of his house. He looked at it very carefully. What had happened to the church? Where had it disappeared to? Then he remembered that to light the cigarette he had changed the direction of the horse. He had started smoking, and the horse had started going towards his house.

This is just the difference in changing the direction. Any small incident like lighting a cigarette can be the reason for changing the direction. Then a friend can become an enemy and an enemy can become a friend. You can turn to the west from the east, or turn from the east to the west. Any small incident – one becomes bankrupt or the wife dies or a child dies – can make a person renounce the world and become a sannyasin. These incidents are of such little value as lighting a cigarette, but they can change the direction. But this type of renunciation will be false. This renunciation will be full of hatred and not full of understanding. It will have a sense of failure, agony, and will be devoid of understanding and freedom.

There is another type of renunciation in which the direction is not changed. You don't turn your back towards the world, you look at the world carefully, attentively, and in looking at it carefully, the world disappears. In that understanding, in that state of meditation, we realize that all the relationships of the world are meaningless. Then we don't create any new relationship with the world — until now our relationship with the world was that of attraction, but now it will be of detraction; until now we were running towards the world and now we start running away from the world in the opposite direction.

No, this type of detachment is wrong. This becomes the new disease and you have to get rid of it also. This is not health. This is just like a sick person who has recovered from his illness, but has become dependent on the medicines. He carries his medicines with him wherever he goes; he is not ready to give them up.

Buddha used to explain this situation by narrating the story of the five stupid men who crossed the river in a boat, and then carried the boat on their heads. People asked them why they were doing so. They said, "We are very grateful to this boat. We crossed the river because of it, so now how can we give it up? We are not ungrateful."

They carried the boat to the market on their heads. People said, "This boat has taken you across the river, but now it has become a load for you which you will carry on your head all of your life and you will not be able to do anything else."

The so-called sannyasins, *mahatmas* and saints, whom you know — if you look at them carefully you will find them carrying a boat on their heads! They gave up attachment, but caught hold of detachment, because they aroused the opposite of attachment.

What Shankaracharya is saying is a different thing entirely. He is saying, "Watch the attachment carefully, with discretion." In that state of knowing the actual reality, the clouds of attachment will disperse — not that detachment will take their place.

Detachment is the absence of attachment; it is not the opposite of attachment. It is not that attachment will disappear from your heart and detachment will take its place — attachment will disappear and nothing will take its place. This is the ultimate detachment.

So don't make a mistake in understanding these sutras, because this mistake is very easy to make.

> Who is your wife? Who is your son?
> This world is very strange. Whose are you?
> Who are you? From where have you come?
> Do think over these basic questions.

Shankara is asking you to think over, to contemplate, to wake up and to watch, with awareness. Don't be in a hurry to borrow detachment. The borrowing of detachment will be of no use.

If right thinking creates the light of understanding in your heart, then attachment will disappear. So don't try to throw out the darkness — just light the lamp.

So Shankara says, *Who is your wife?* Yes, who is your wife? *Who is your son?* They are just like strangers who meet on the roadside. Did you know your son before he was born? Did you call this son to be born out of you? You didn't even know him, how could you call him? You didn't know his address. You didn't even recognize his face.

This is just a chance meeting of strangers. But the human mind creates illusions — "This is my son, this is my wife, this is my sister, this is my brother." How do you create these relationships? How? This is a very strange occurrence. It is like two unacquainted persons walking on the same path. They will walk together for a short time and then each one will go in his own direction after saying goodbye, but all sorts of relationships will be made in that short time. There must be some other deep reason for this. These relationships are not true, because all of us are strangers. In spite of living together for years we don't know each other.

Do you know your wife? You have lived with her for thirty or forty years, but do you think you know her well? Can you make a prophecy of what she will do tomorrow? Even after living with your wife for forty years you cannot make a prophecy about what she will do the next moment. Just a minute before she was smiling, she was happy, and now she is annoyed. It is difficult for you to say what her mood will be the next moment!

Does your wife know you? This 'knowing' is just on the surface. Nobody can peep inside the other person. It is so difficult even to go into oneself, how can going into the other be easy? But there must be some deep reason for our making so many relationships — because man is alone; because he is afraid to be lonely; because he gets frightened and worried when he is alone. It is very painful to be alone.

We are alone. The whole earth may be crowded, but still every individual is alone. Even when you are in a crowd you are alone. This loneliness is unbearable and you want to get rid of this loneliness, so you create these relationships to forget yourself and your loneliness. For some time you feel that you are not alone.

Have you ever noticed? If you are walking along a dark street at night the loneliness frightens you, so you start singing a song. You don't usually sing when people ask you to do so because you feel shy, but at night, in a lonely street where it is absolutely dark, you start humming a song or you start whistling. What is the reason for this humming or whistling? While humming you listen to your own voice and you feel that you are not alone, somebody is with you. Your own song creates this illusion that there is nothing to be afraid of. The song gives you the courage.

In loneliness a person starts talking to himself. Psychologists say that if a person is kept absolutely alone for three weeks he will start talking to himself. You also talk to yourself, but you don't talk aloud. If you watch someone carefully, you can even see the slight movements of the lips, because when you are talking inside your lips move a little. But if you are kept in a lonely place, the loneliness is so frightening – being alone in this vast world, to be alone in this great void – one starts shaking. So you start talking to yourself.

Have you seen mad people talking to themselves? They are the enlarged copy of yourself! The difference between you and them is only of quantity and not of quality. You talk softly – they are a bit more courageous, so they talk loudly. The madman also talks to himself because he is frightened, he is nervous. He forgets by talking to himself. These are methods of forgetting oneself, of self-forgetfulness.

I was reading the memoirs of a German writer, of his time in Hitler's prison. He has written that he was alone in his prison room, but there was also a lizard. He used to be scared of lizards. He used to get the creeps looking at them, but now in the prison he was quite happy to see one. Looking at it he thought, "I am not alone, there is someone with me," and gradually he started talking to the lizard.

Sometimes he used to laugh at his own madness. But he became so used to it that he felt as if the lizard was also replying to him. Then he was speaking for himself and also on behalf of the lizard.

Man is lonely, very lonely. With this loneliness you can do only two things: either you make a world of your own or you enter sannyas. Making a world, means making relationships so that loneliness can be forgotten. And the meaning of entering into sannyas is, accepting this loneliness, because this is your nature. Don't run away from it, don't avoid it; accept it, embrace it. This is your nature. You will not get anywhere by running away from it. You have done this in innumerable lives and you have failed. You have gained nothing except failure.

Sannyas means, one who has accepted his loneliness – now he doesn't whistle, he doesn't sing, nor does he make any relationship – he is absolutely satisfied with himself.

It is very interesting to note that the more you run from yourself the more you will have to run – the more you will get scared of loneliness. The more you accept to be with yourself the more you will be able to find that the loneliness is not loneliness, but aloneness. There is a difference between loneliness and aloneness. Loneliness means, that you miss the presence of the other. To be alone, means that being by oneself is enough. Loneliness is painful; but there is bliss in being alone. When Shankara is alone he is by himself, but when you say that you are alone you are lonely.

Being lonely, means that you feel the absence of the other. Aloneness means that you are happy to be with yourself. Aloneness means you have fallen in love with yourself. Meditation means to be in love with yourself. Meditation means to make such a relationship with yourself that there is no need to have a relationship with anyone else.

Meditation means to be fulfilled in oneself. Your world, your whole world is in you. There is nothing lacking. You are complete, you are whole, you are the divine, there is no need for you to go anywhere. This inner state means sannyas.

We make our world because the loneliness hurts: we try to fill this loneliness with money, with friends, with family, with religion, caste, nation. We make so many efforts to fill this inner void because this wound is painful. But it is wrong to think of it as a wound, it is not a wound.

Last night a sannyasin came to me and said that since she has started meditating her heart seems to have died. There is no desire to make any relationship with anyone, there seems no interest in love; even friendship seems meaningless. She was very sad... because she has come from the West, and in the West if love starts disappearing then people think that the whole of life is finished; if feelings disappear and relationships break, then people think that now there is no meaning in life. This is their definition. So she was sad.

We in the East have done a deeper research. We have discovered that when a person stays wholly within himself, then all relationships dissolve. It is a very fortunate thing to happen; it is not something to be unhappy about. When a person becomes stable within himself, sex dissolves and the keenness to make relationships with others also disappears. The feeling of gratitude is so much that one doesn't want to make any relationship with anyone. No longer will that person beg of others to have some relationship with him, no longer will he say, "I cannot live without you." Now he can live alone. And the person who can live alone, *really* lives! The other type of living is only a deception, an illusion. If you cannot live alone, how can you live with others?

So I told that young woman, that sannyasin, "Don't be scared, don't be unhappy. This definition of yours is wrong. This definition of the West is wrong. Be happy, be blissful; how fortunate you are that you no longer desire any relationship."

Relationship only gives you pain and anguish. This is quite natural also, because when two unhappy persons meet how can they give happiness to each other? The mathematics is quite clear: when two unhappy persons meet, then the unhappiness doesn't just become double, it multiplies many times more. You are looking for the other person because you are not happy. You are not happy alone, so you are looking for the other. The other is also not happy to be alone, and he is also looking at you with the same expectation. Like this, two unhappy people meet in the hope of getting happiness. But they don't get happiness. It is not possible, because two beggars are begging from each other and neither of them is a giver – both of them are beggars. Both of them go on expecting from each other. Whenever you love anyone you expect him to return your love.

People tell me, "We give lots of love to others, but others don't love us." How can you love? Love can flow only from the heights of bliss. The river of love only comes out of the peak of bliss. You are not happy, you are not blissful, you are begging, and the other person is also begging. Neither of you has anything to give to the other, but you go on waiting to receive some love in charity! As you go on waiting, the disappointment starts. Until a person is happy within himself no one else can make him happy.

There is a very old story.

God made man. Man was alone, and became fed up with his loneliness. He prayed to God to give him a companion as he was alone. But God had utilized all the materials, everything was finished. He had made forests, mountains, birds and animals and in the end he had made man – now there was nothing left. But man cried and cried, so he asked him to wait and he tried to make a woman. However, no material was available at that time, so God asked the animals, birds, flowers and plants to give something back. He told the moon to give a little of its light, told the peacock to give its arrogance, told the pigeons to give their sweet murmur, asked the parrots to give their voice, asked the rivers to give their restlessness and movement, asked the flowers to give their delicacy – like this he made woman!

After seven days man came back and said, "This woman is a nuisance. I thought I would get a companion, but she goes on quarreling all the time. The voice given to her by the parrots is very sweet – no doubt it is very sweet when she is loving, but she is arrogant like the peacocks. She is very kind and very cruel at the same time. She is very contradictory. I am fed up! It was better to be alone. You must take her back."

God took the woman back, but after seven days the man came again and said, "She made my life miserable but now I miss her. During these seven days I could neither eat nor sleep. I keep remembering her. Please return her to me."

After seven days he was again standing at God's door. He said, "I can neither live with her nor can I live without her."

God turned his back on him and said, "How long am I going

to listen to your nonsense? You cannot live with her and you cannot live without her, so you had better sort it out yourself."

Since then man has been trying to sort it out, but has not been able to do so up till now. It is not possible, because when you are alone then you are afraid of the loneliness. When you are with someone else, then you are disturbed by his or her presence. When you have company you want to be alone; when you are alone you want company. When you are with someone, then you start observing the bad points in him or her. When you are alone, the loneliness frightens you like death. Both the company and loneliness are troublesome for you.

That is why man makes many relationships. He brings a wife home so that he is not left alone. Then, in his effort to be away from his wife, he sits in the hotel or in the club. Becoming a member of a club means that he is trying to escape from his wife. He makes one mistake, then he tries to rectify it by making another mistake. Thus starts the chain of mistakes. And you call this life!

> Who is your wife? Who is your son?
> This world is very strange.

All of you are strangers here. You don't know each other. You don't know yourself, how will you know the other? One who has known himself will know the other also. But if one doesn't know oneself he cannot know anyone else. You have made relationships without knowing. All relations are coincidental. Your whole life, your whole world, is based on coincidence. When you fall in love with a girl you say that God has made both of you for each other – but it was because of the coincidence of living in the same building or going to the same school. It was just a coincidence that both of you met – not that you were made for each other. In fact, nobody is made for any other. But man tries to justify a mere coincidence with the theory of destiny.

THE SEARCH FOR NIRVANA

Mulla Nasruddin went to Africa on a safari. When he came back, all his friends gathered around him to listen to all his adventures. He was narrating with great enthusiasm and exaggeration, saying "There is a certain animal over there. When the male animal has to call the female he screeches and the female animal, wherever it may be in the forest, comes running to him."

A friend asked him to copy the sound of the screeching of that animal. He copied it, screeching loudly. Just then the door of the next room opened and his wife asked, "Well? What is the matter?"

He told his friends, "See, now you understand the theory."

It is only a coincidence. There is no theory in it. But if a person thinks that his love is mere coincidence, then there is no place for poetry. If you tell Majnu that his meeting with Laila was a coincidence then the poetry dies, the romance dies. Majnu will say, "No, this is not possible. Laila was made for me and I was made for Laila. And even if the whole world puts obstacles in our path we will definitely meet." If Majnu had lived in some other village, then some other girl would have been his Laila. Majnu would have definitely found some Laila who would have been different from this one.

What you think to be the structure of life is not a structure at all, it is only a coincidence – a few incidents, a few coincidences. You have a son. Don't be under the illusion that you have given birth to your son. While you were having sexual intercourse a soul was waiting eagerly for rebirth. You were nearby, you were available, so that soul entered your womb. You had dug a pit, it was raining, so the water which was near entered that pit. The water which was farther away entered other pits. It is a coincidence.

It is a coincidence to be a mother, it is a coincidence to be a father, it is a coincidence to be a son; friendship is a coincidence and enmity is a coincidence. If you can see this properly, then all at once your deep relationships will become weak, their depth will disappear.

> Who is your wife? Who is your son?
> This world is very strange.
> Whose are you? Who are you?
> From where have you come?
> Do think over these essential things.
>
> Oh fool! Always sing the song of the divine.

...Because nothing will happen only by thinking: thought alone is lame. You must think, but you will not be able to reach only by thinking. All the obstacles will be removed by thinking, but you will not be able to travel. The journey is possible only by *bhajan*, devotion. The journey is possible only by feeling and not by thinking. *Always sing the song of the divine.*

> From satsang comes aloneness,
> from aloneness comes nonattachment;
> because of nonattachment mind becomes stable
> and because of a stable...mind
> liberation is attained.

Try to understand this. It is a very valuable sutra: *From satsang comes aloneness.* This is the definition of satsang. Satsang is that which creates aloneness. The satsang which creates relationship and attachment cannot be satsang. The meaning of satsang is that you start seeing truth. The meaning of satsang is that your eyes should be open and your dreaming is over.

The search for the master is meant to wake you up from your dream. The master will wake you up and tell you that all the relationships which you have made are illusions — don't waste your life in these dreams and don't let your soul be lost in them. These relationships are just formalities to be observed in this world, so don't attach too much importance to them — don't give importance to them to the extent of destroying yourself. They can be necessary in this world, but for the inner world they are not at all necessary. You cannot take your father with you into the inner world, nor your son, your brother, your wife, your friend — there you go alone. Therefore, in spite of living in all the relationships, you must know that your real self is in being alone. Don't forget it. Don't let the sun of aloneness become covered with the clouds of relationships.

> From satsang comes aloneness,
> from aloneness comes nonattachment...

And when you find that you are alone, then there is no attachment.

> ...because of nonattachment mind becomes stable...

And when there is no attachment mind doesn't waver.

I have heard that a house caught fire and the owner of that house was watching and crying. But then somebody from the crowd told him, "Don't cry. There is no need. Perhaps you don't know, but your son sold this house yesterday."

That man at once stopped crying. The house was still on fire, the flames were spreading everywhere, but the man was not crying anymore because now the house didn't belong to him. Just then his son came running and said that the preliminary discussion about selling the house had started, but the final sale was not done yet. Hearing this, the man again started crying loudly.

The house is still the same. He is not crying because of the house being on fire, he is crying because of his relationship with the house. If it is not his, then it makes no difference to him whether the house is on fire or not.

If someone's son dies but he is not *your* son, then it doesn't make any difference to you. It effects you only if he is 'yours.' You cry because of his being 'yours,' not otherwise. If you come to know that nobody is 'yours,' then there will be no anguish. As attachment disappears, misery too disappears. If it becomes clear to you that nobody is 'yours,' then you are alone, the mind becomes stable. Then the mind is not restless; then you become stable, unwavering. That stability, that unwavering condition is the ultimate experience. In that unwavering condition you come to know who you are. Then the ultimate question of life, "Who am I?" is solved. As soon as the flame becomes unwavering one gets the answer, one gets the solution. This stability, this unwavering condition, is called *samadhi*. Samadhi means the solution to all.

> ...because of a stable and unwavering mind
> liberation is attained.
>
> Oh fool! Always sing the song of the divine.

Where is the desire for sex when the time for sex is over? Where is the pond when the water dries up? And nobody is close to you when you have lost your money.

In the same way, after the realization of truth, where is this world? Try to understand this. Whenever Shankara, Buddha or Mahavira talk about the world, you make the mistake of thinking that they are talking about this expansion which is spread all around. No, they don't mean this expansion. Whenever they talk about the world they mean the world made by your attachment, created by your attachment; the world made by your unconsciousness, the illusions that you have created. Even when you wake up these trees will be there; they will not disappear.

People often ask, "When a person is enlightened and this world disappears for him, then what happens to these trees, mountains, the moon, the stars, the sun?" These don't disappear. In fact, for the first time they appear in their purity. That purity is the divine. Then you don't see the moon, then you see the light of the divine in the moon; then you don't see the trees, you see the greenery of the divine in the trees; then you don't see flowers, you see the divine blossoming. Then this all becomes unlimited godliness.

Just now you don't see the divine. You see the world and the world is not one. There are as many worlds as there are different minds, because every individual has his own world. If your wife dies you will cry – nobody else. Others will try to explain to you that the soul is eternal, it doesn't die, so don't cry. They will make the most of this opportunity of showing off their knowledge. They will see you in a pitiable condition and will start preaching to you. They will say, "Why are you crying? Who really belongs to us?" Tomorrow, when their wives die, then you will get your chance, then you will go and preach to them that this world is an illusion, that all these relationships are an illusion.

Every individual's world is his own. Your attachment, your unconsciousness, your ignorance, your infatuation, your love – this is your world. What you have seen through the medium of this infatuation, love, attachment, unconsciousness is not true, it is all false. It is as if your eyes are covered with clouds of smoke.

Shankara says: After knowing the essence, the reality, there is no world.

> Where is the world after self-realization?

Truth remains, but whatever was added to truth by you is lost.

> Always sing the song of the divine.

> Do not be proud of wealth, people and youth,
> because death takes them all away
> within a moment.
> Dropping all these illusory matters,
> know the divine and enter into it.

THE SONG OF ECSTASY

I was reading a song this morning and a few lines of that song appealed to me. *Jor he kya tha jafa-e-bagvan dekna kiye ashian ujra kiya hum natwan dekha kiye.* The meaning is: The garden was being destroyed and I watched it helplessly. Yes, your whole life is the same story. Daily your garden will be destroyed. The spring will soon be over, youth will also pass away. This speed and this energy will gradually become less and less. The house will be destroyed and death will come nearer and nearer. Life is only a momentary dream; death is approaching every minute. You are dying from the day you were born – a birthday is actually the deathday also. You cannot postpone death, you cannot run away from death, it is coming nearer and nearer.

> Do not be proud of wealth, people and youth...

This ego is shallow. In fact, all egos are shallow; shallowness is the nature of ego. It thinks as its own that which is not its own. The transient seems permanent, and that which is flowing seems static to it. You fool not only others, but also yourself.

One day Mulla Nasruddin came home. He knocked at the door, but there was no reply. He again knocked, but nobody replied. So he shouted, "I am Nasruddin, not the landlord who asks for the rent, nor the milkman, nor the vegetable vendor."

Even then there was no reply. So he shouted again, "I say I am the *real* Nasruddin."

He must have told his family not to open the door when somebody knocked because he must have owed money to lots of people. So when he himself knocks at the door of his own house nobody opens it. He then has to explain that he is the real Nasruddin. But in spite of it nobody believes him.

We go on deceiving others and we create a world of deception around us. Then we deceive ourselves, and in this way we become unauthentic. Then whatever we do in life is false.

The person who wants to wake up should stop sowing lies and should say good-bye to all his false beliefs. He should know that this body is not permanent, it is not static, it is dying every moment, and death is not going to occur tomorrow, it is occurring now. We are dying. Death isn't going to occur after seventy years – we are dying gradually and there will be nothing left after seventy years.

Life goes on finishing, drop by drop. Don't call it life, it is a lie. You can call it a gradual death. Don't celebrate birthdays, all are deathdays. The day you see death in your birthday and you hear the footsteps of death in life, you will know the truth. That truth will give you freedom.

As soon as you know that truth you will start a new search – money will seem meaningless, the body will seem meaningless; the relations of body and money will become meaningless and even the world based on money and body will seem meaningless. And before knowing the truth it is necessary to know the untruth as untruth, the false as false.

> Day and night, evening and morning,
> winter and spring come and go again and again.
> Thus the play of time goes on and one's life is over.
> And yet the breeze of hope does not leave one alone.

Hope is poison, and because of this poison you have mistaken death to be life. Today you are unhappy, but the mind says that tomorrow everything will be all right. Today there is no happiness, but the mind says, "Wait, tomorrow everything will be fine." This is the way the mind has led you up to now – it has been giving you hope. The day you give up hope you will wake up. Hope is a dream.

Have you ever thought how hope affects you in life? Hope says, "Don't worry about today. Whatever happens doesn't matter. But tomorrow you will definitely attain heaven." This very hope has made you understand that there is nothing to worry about even if this life is lost, because you will get heaven after death. This is the expansion of hope. Hope says "tomorrow." Hope says "future." Hope says "more life!" But if the revolution of life is to occur, it will occur just now and here.

Don't depend on tomorrow because tomorrow never comes. Tomorrow is a lie. And the hope which is giving you the assurance about tomorrow is the cause of creating these dreams in you. Whatever is to be done is to be done today; whatever is to be, is to be today. Don't hope for more than today.

It will be quite shocking at first. With the disappearance of hope you will become absolutely dejected. You will feel that you have become totally hopeless. But if you are ready to live without hope you will find that if there is no hope in life, then there is no hopelessness either.

Hopelessness is the reverse of hope and it will disappear with hope. Life without hope, is life without hopelessness. Then there is neither hope nor hopelessness. That is the stability. The flame stays in the middle. Then there is no wavering. That is the condition of unwavering consciousness.

> Day and night, evening and morning,
> winter and spring come and go again and again.
> Thus the play of time goes on and one's life is over.
> And yet the breeze of hope does not leave one alone.

So,

> Oh fool! Always sing the song of the divine.

> Oh, you madman!
> Why are you caught up in the worries
> about your wife and your wealth?
> Don't you know that even a moment's company with
> good people is the only boat there is
> to take you across the ocean of this mundane world?

Who is a saintly person? The one in whose company you wake up. An unsaintly person is the one in whose company you go into deep sleep and who helps you to increase your illusions and attachments.

But just the opposite of this happens in this world. The person who tries to wake you up doesn't seem friendly to you. The person who puts you to sleep seems a friend to you. The one who gives you alcohol to drink seems a friend to you, and the one who tries to bring you back to consciousness seems an enemy to you. That is why the wine shops and the bars are crowded and the temples are empty. There are long queues in the bars, and God goes on waiting in the temple but nobody turns up. Yes, the priest comes, but he is already a servant; he gets his pay so he comes to worship. His worship is not from the heart – it is professional. He is not a lover. What is the reason?

Wherever there is intoxication there will be crowds of people. There is a crowd in front of a cinema – people are intoxicated for three hours. They are lost in the movie for three hours – they forget their miseries, their pains, their worries and anxieties. For three hours they forget themselves. This type of intoxication is not the solution to your problems. After three hours the movie is over, the lights are on, and you are where you were – full of worry and misery. Alcohol makes you forget yourself for two or three hours, but after its effect is over you are again unhappy and in pain.

Your going to the temple is also going with the expectation of getting some sort of intoxicant. This is the difference. You can sing the song of the divine in two ways. One is like alcohol – to be lost in it. For the time being you forget the worry, the misery; you forget that you have to return home – that you have a wife and children; that the wife is ill, the children have to be admitted in a school and you don't have the money. You forget your worries as long as you are lost – if you are getting lost in singing the song of the divine, then this is also like alcohol. If it wakes you up, only then is it the song of the divine.

Even the temples are like bars, and on the pretext of religion people go on looking for unconsciousness and not consciousness. It is very difficult to wake up. Sleeping is very soothing; you go on dreaming beautiful dreams. You will resent being woken up and being brought to consciousness.

To know the truth of life is a great challenge. You will have to struggle for it. You will have to work hard for it. You will have to go through *sadhana* and spiritual practices and make an effort towards self-realization. This journey can be undertaken only with open eyes as the path is very difficult and full of thorns. It can mislead you also. Those who never walk on the path can never be afraid of being lost. Those who are always lying down on their bed will never meet any accident.

But those who tread the path can be lost on the path or can have an accident and can face many difficulties. This journey is laborious, because you have to climb the mountain. Going towards the divine, means going towards the summit. It becomes more and more difficult. Only those will attain the bliss of the summit who are ready to cross all these difficulties.

One doesn't get bliss for free, you have to earn it, you have to labor for it. Of course, it is not attained by labor alone, it is attained by grace, but this labor *you* have to do. Godliness can shower only on the person who has labored and who has prepared himself.

> And yet the breeze of hope does not leave one alone.

You start hoping in the divine also. When people come to me I tell them to give up hope and to meditate. They say, "If we give up hope, then why would we meditate? It is because of hope that we have come to meditate – hoping that by meditation mind will be at peace, that we will attain samadhi and we will realize the divine."

Now this is very complicated. Hope will create the obstacle, because when you are hoping you are not meditating – you will only hope. You cannot do both of them together. Even if you meditate for a little while you will go on wondering why you have not yet found peace – "Three days have passed and nothing has happened yet, there is no experience of bliss."

Try to understand it this way. If I tell you to come to the river to swim, as swimming is very enjoyable, you will come. But if from the very start of swimming you go on expecting and waiting for the enjoyment then you will not get it.

Because of your eagerness, your anxiety to attain it, you will not get it; the very nature of bliss is that it looks for you when you are not looking for it. You will not get it as long as you are in search of it, because when you are searching for it you are not in the present; your mind is in the future hoping to get it. And it is now!

You get it when you are purely in this moment without any hope, without any expectation, without any desire or wish. When you are present in this moment you find that it has showered all over. It has always been showering, but you were not present. You were absent, you were lost in the future because of your hope – and here bliss was being distributed. You were wandering somewhere else so you couldn't receive it. You receive it the day you are in the present, and to be in the present, means to be without hope and without desire.

So I tell them, "Meditate. Don't hope. Meditation is not the means but the end. Meditation in itself is joy, bliss, and don't ask for more bliss, don't look forward to the result. If you can do any action without expecting any result, then that very action will become meditation."

In the Gita, Krishna has told Arjuna only this. He has said this repeatedly, in different ways: don't expect any result. This desire for the result, the expectation for the return, is 'the world.' The giving up of the desire for the result is the salvation. There is no need to run away from the world – only the expectation for the result should end. Then you will live here, but the world will disappear for you.

> Oh, you madman!
> Why are you caught up in the worries
> about your wife and your wealth?
> Don't you know that even a moment's company with
> good people is the only boat there is
> to take you across the ocean of this mundane world?

But people go on worrying about nothing till the last moment of their lives. All worries are meaningless. The meaningful has to be contemplated and not to be worried about.

I have heard that a Marwari merchant was dying, he was on his deathbed.

He asked his wife, "Where is the eldest son?" The wife told him that he was standing beside the bed. "Where is the middle one?" he asked. She said that he was also near by. "And where is the youngest one?"

She said, "Don't worry! He is standing at your feet. Relax and sleep with peace in your mind."

The Marwari merchant got up and said, "How can I sleep peacefully? Who is looking after the shop? All of them are here!"

Their father was dying. Thinking this, all the sons had gathered there. They had closed the shop. But death is not the concern of the dying father – "Who is tending the shop?" He is not asking for his sons out of love: where is the oldest one, where is the middle one, the youngest one? He is asking to find out who is tending the shop. All of them are present there – does it mean there is nobody in the shop?

Yes, even at the last moment your mind is full of the shop. It will be so, because whatever you have done in your whole life, you will also think of it while dying. You cannot suddenly change yourself at the time of death. Don't believe in the false stories.

A man was dying, his son's name was Narayan – which is

another name for God. So he called for his son Narayan, and God thought that the man was calling him. Such stories are created by *pundits* for the consolation of sinners. On the basis of such stories, the pundits are able to take some money from the sinners – nothing else is going to happen.

If God gets deceived, then surely he is not God. This man went to heaven just because he called out "Narayan" while dying. Such a cheap God is not worth obtaining! This type of heaven or salvation is absolutely false. This story cannot be true.

Death is the summing up of your whole life; at the moment of death your mind will be full of what you have done during your life. If for the whole of your life you have been counting money, then you will be counting it while dying also, because death is the essence of your life. If you have been restless all your life, then you will be restless at death also. If you have been peaceful, then your death will be very peaceful.

Every individual dies a different death because everyone lives a different life. Neither your life nor your death can be the same as that of someone else.

When a buddha dies, the grandeur of his death is different – the grandeur of his death is much more than your so-called life. Your life is just nothing compared to his death. The grandeur of his death is a million times more than your life, because in that moment of his death the whole of life shrinks and comes near, the music of his whole life becomes condensed – as if the essence of all the flowers of his life has been taken and made into a fragrance. At the moment of death, the fragrance which comes out of a buddha is the essence of the flowers of his whole life. The stink which will come out of you will be the essence of all the dirt and trash of your whole life.

You cannot suddenly change at the time of death. So don't believe the pundits who tell you to become religious at the end of your life. If you want to be religious, you have to do it here and now; don't postpone it to the end. If you are careful now, you will be able to take care in the future. If you wake up today, then gradually you will become wakeful. If you sing the song of the divine from today, then perhaps at the moment of death the divine will hear you.

Don't think at the time of death that a borrowed pundit will save your soul by reciting mantras in your ears, by pouring the water of the Ganges in your mouth, by reading the Gita near you. That pundit will go on repeating the Gita, but you will not be able to hear it within you at that time. Only that person can hear the Gita at the time of death who has learned the art of listening properly the whole of his life. If one has sung the song of the divine all his life, then at the time of death he will not have to listen to it by a borrowed servant or pundit; every breath, every beat of his heart will be singing the song of the divine.

In that moment of death you will go dancing toward the divine full of gratitude. Your death will become the gate to a greater life; you will change death. Death kills you now, then you will kill death. And religion is the art of killing death, it is the science of becoming nectar.

Therefore,

Oh fool! Always sing the song of the divine.

Enough for today.

4

EVERY STEP IS THE DESTINATION

The first question:

> Beloved Osho,
> It is said that Shankara was a Hindu Vedantin, and you have said that Shankara is a hidden Buddhist. Please clarify this.

Shankara is a hidden Buddhist, a hidden Jaina, and a hidden Mohammedan...in the same way as Buddha is a hidden Hindu, a hidden Jaina, and a hidden Christian...in the same way as Christ is a hidden Hindu, a hidden Mohammedan, and a hidden Buddhist.

Those who have known, have known only the one; there are not two to be known. Hindu, Mohammedan, Christian — these are just the names on the surface, the outer identity; the inner truth is one. Language may be different, but what is said is not different. The style of saying will be different, the process of explaining will be different, but there is no possibility of the taste being different – it is the same. This has to be understood properly. This misunderstanding, this stupidity creates a lot of unpleasantness. Hindus fight with Mohammedans, Jainas fight with Buddhists – and you must understand that truth is lost whenever and wherever there is any type of conflict. Truth is murdered in your fighting, untruth is created in your conflict, because conflict means violence. Then it doesn't matter whether the violence is expressed in physical conflict or mental conflict. Violence is violence – it makes no difference whether the effort to destroy the other is physical or mental. The desire and the mentality to find fault in the other is the expansion of violence.

You must know that until you can see yourself in the other you have not gone beyond mind, nor have you entered the temple of consciousness. That temple has many doors and entry is possible from every door. Whosoever enters the temple, forgets the door. Nobody remembers the door after entering. Before entering, the door seems to be very important because one has to enter through it, but after that it becomes useless. Before entering one was facing the door and after entering the door is behind your back.

All the creeds are doors. You must know that you have not entered the temple if the creeds – Hindu, Mohammedan, Jaina – if they still seem very important to you, that means you are still looking at the door. After you have entered the temple and your back has turned towards the door, then the words Hindu and Mohammedan will become meaningless.

The great meaning which will appear in the inner recess of the temple will not only destroy your creed, your scripture, but it will also destroy you, and in that flood everything will be drowned. Whatever is left after that flood is your very nature. In that flood whatever was the other element will be swept away; in that flood whatever were the outer coverings will be lost; in that flood your relations will break with whatever was foreign to your nature and only you will remain in your pure virginity, in your innocence.

You cannot understand that inner being without having experienced it; you have to taste it, you have to drink it and get intoxicated. Until you get drunk, until you get lost in it after losing everything, the world will remain as long as you remain. Only then godliness will begin.

The divine is not, until you are not. And the divine begins only when your ego, your separate identity is dissolved. Shankara is a hidden Buddhist because he is saying the same thing which Buddha said. Buddha was also a hidden Vedantin because he was saying the same thing which the Upanishads had said. The garments are different, and sometimes the garments even seem contradictory.

Try to understand this. Buddha opposed the Upanishads and the Vedas, and still he propounded the Upanishads and Vedas. One has to oppose. When the Upanishads were born, when the Ganges of the Upanishads was born, then the Ganges was very clean, pure; it was the Gangotri, the source. Then the Ganges flowed on — thousands of people bathed in it, it passed by thousands of villages — it became dirty, trash got into it, rivers and rivulets joined it. In Varanasi, the Ganges doesn't have the piety which it has at Gangotri. It cannot be so. With the passing of time the original source loses its purity.

Two thousand five hundred years before Buddha, when the Upanishads were born, their grandeur was unique. Each and every word contained in them was luminous, every line was full of the divine. But that grandeur was lost by the time of Buddha — the mirror was there but lots of dust had gathered on it. Now the mirror had become blind and nothing could be reflected in it. A big belief system stood in front of the mirror. Even if Buddha tried to clean the mirror that creed would not let him do so, because what is called dust by Buddha is said to be religion by the masses. The communal mind doesn't know the mirror, it only knows the dust gathered on it and it thinks that this dust is the decoration, the jewels. The communal mind cannot agree to the dust being wiped away; it thinks that by this its religion will be destroyed.

It was because of this dust that Buddha had to deny this mirror. People couldn't accept another mirror until this mirror was denied. But the other mirror is exactly like the first one; the only difference is that the first one had become old, dilapidated, and dust had gathered on it.

When truth gets organized it dies. Now the other truth is again new – newly born, fresh like the morning dew. The new truth will also become old in a few days.

Buddha's truth had become old by the time Shankara was born. Time doesn't forgive anyone and covers everything with dust. The thing which is new today will become old tomorrow, the newborn baby of today will become old tomorrow; today he is being welcomed into this world, tomorrow good-bye will be said to him when he dies.

Just as men are born and die, in the same way religions are born and die. With time everything becomes old, weak, dilapidated and useless. When somebody dies in the house – your mother dies; how much you loved her… but when she dies you have to take her to the cremation ground. If some foolish person keeps the corpse of his mother in the house, then it will be difficult for the living people to live there. It may be very painful to cremate your mother whom you loved, but there is no way out. A dead body cannot be kept in the house, it has to be cremated.

But we don't deal with belief systems with this understanding. Religion means *living* religion; when it becomes a creed it becomes a dead body. But we keep the corpse very carefully: because of the stink of the creed it becomes difficult to breathe. Religion unites, but creeds fight and make others fight. Creeds break and make others break. There is a lot of enmity between a temple and a mosque, but there cannot be any enmity in the divineness of the temple and of the mosque. There is a lot of enmity between the worshippers of the temple and of the mosque, but the one who is being worshipped in the temple and in the mosque – someone calls him 'Rama' and someone calls him 'Allah'... these addresses can be different, but the one who is called, is one.

By the time Buddha's stream reached Shankara it had became dirty, it had lost its purity – the Ganges had reached Varanasi. Shankara had to oppose it, because now there were lots of Buddhists, followers of Buddha, and it was a large creed. They would not allow the dust to be cleaned, so again a new mirror had to be made. Today the condition is just the same: dust has gathered over the mirror of Shankara. It will always be thus.

Don't worship the dust. Always look for the mirror. Then you will find the same mirror in everyone. When you can see the same mirror in everyone, only then wisdom is born in you.

This is the only difference between intelligence and wisdom. Intelligence criticizes, opposes, debates; but wisdom communicates; intelligence tells where the difference is, and wisdom shows where the unity is. Intelligence analyzes, wisdom synthesizes; intelligence draws boundaries, wisdom destroys boundaries.

When all boundaries disappear, then the unlimited is obtained. Don't think that you can know the unlimited while remaining limited. Who will know? If you are bound and limited, then who will know the unlimited? Whatever you will know will be limited. For knowing the unlimited, you will have to break all your limitations. If you see the sky from the window you will see only that much which is visible through the structure of the window, not more than that; the window limits the sky also. If you want to see the whole of the sky then you have to come out. Be under the open sky where you will be neither a Hindu nor a Mohammedan, because these are the names of the windows. Only you in your purity will remain under the open sky, and this is pure isness.

There is a way to know the unlimited. To know the unlimited one has to *become* unlimited – this is the only condition, because only the like can know like. How can you, the limited one, know the unlimited? If you try to see the unlimited you will only see what your limitations can show you.

Not only Shankara is a hidden Buddha, Buddha also is a hidden Vedantin. Anything which is polluted has to be destroyed; that which has become perverted has to be destroyed. Anything which has become dilapidated has to be put on the fire so that there can be space for the new. The mind says, "Save the old." Mind says, "Look after the old." But if you go on looking after the old too much then there will be no space for the new. The old man has to go so that children can come in. The old, rotten tree will fall down so that a new seed may sprout.

I have heard that there was a very old, dilapidated church – it was in such a bad condition that it could fall down at any moment. People who used to pray in it were also afraid to go in. Then at last the trustees called a meeting to decide what to do about it, because now even the priest was afraid to go in. People were afraid, and even passers-by were afraid of its falling down at any moment – anyone could get killed. So now nobody passed by on that road – it became quite lonely. So they passed three resolutions.

The first, was that the old church had to be demolished. It was passed unanimously with great sorrow.

Second, was that a new church had to be constructed. This was accepted with a lot of heartache, because the attachment for the old is always there. The new is not born yet, the new is not known yet, so there cannot be any attachment with the new – attachment is always with the old. That is why if a small child dies then the anguish is not much. But the anguish goes on increasing with age, because relationship, attachment, increases proportionately. The old one has to be demolished – with great sorrow. The new has to be constructed, just out of sheer helplessness.

And they passed a third resolution, that the new church will be constructed on the same site where the old church is, "And until the new one is built we will go on using the old one. For the new church we will use the stones of the old one. And while the new one is not yet built we will continue to use the old one." This was also passed unanimously! That church is still there. It cannot be demolished, because there is deep attachment to it.

I call only that person religious who, after giving up the old, is always moving towards the ever new, and thus is able to retain his innocence and purity – one who is coming out of the past every moment, just like the snake coming out of his skin, and doesn't look back. If you get attuned with that which is ever new, if you live in that which is always new, if you refuse to carry the old garbage, then you will find in the new that which is eternal. In that eternal, godliness is hidden.

The second question:

> Beloved Osho,
> Before telling us to sing the song of the divine, why do you and Shankara address us as 'fool' every time?

Because you are! To call you anything else will be a lie! When Shankara says, "Oh fool! Sing the song of the divine," he says this with great love, he says this because of his compassion. He is not cursing you, he is not calling you names, because Shankara just cannot curse or call names; it is impossible for him. He is shaking you, he is waking you up. He is saying "Get up! It is morning and you are still sleeping." He is calling you 'fool' because until he uses some strong words your sleep is not going to be disturbed and you are not going to wake up. He is calling you 'fool' because this is true, this is a fact.

Foolishness means unconsciousness. Foolishness means to live in sleep. Foolishness means to be without discretion. Foolishness means not being wakeful, not being conscious when you are angry. Then you become even more foolish because then you lose consciousness even more. But sometimes, when you are conscious, then you are not too foolish. And you also know that sometimes you are less foolish and sometimes you are more foolish. When the mind is full of attachment then foolishness increases. When there is passion you become more foolish.

In the life story of Tulsidas, it is said that when his wife went to her parents' home, he followed her at night. It was raining and dark. He climbed up to her room by holding onto a snake. He must have been in a very deep, idiotic state to mistake a snake for the rope. It must have been a very strong passion. That passion made him almost blind; he couldn't even see the snake!

Generally, people mistake a rope for a snake because of fear. Death scares a man. A rope on the road always appears to be a snake. But this was just the opposite: Tulsidas thought that the snake was the rope. He caught hold of it and climbed! He didn't realize it even by the touch; he must have been absolutely unconscious. Passion must have made him mad.

Seeing his condition his wife said, "If you had loved God the way you love me, then by now you would have attained salvation!" He turned back and saw the snake and realized that passion had made him blind. A revolution took place in his life. The wife became the master. The passion had pointed out to him the nonpassionate state. He became a *sannyasin* and went in search of the divine – the energy which was being spent in passion turned towards Rama. The energy which was expressing itself in sex started turning into Rama.

Foolishness is that energy which is asleep today, but will wake up tomorrow. It is hidden today, but it will be revealed tomorrow. This foolishness will become your wisdom. Your sleep will become your awakening. So don't be angry with it, don't condemn it, and don't try to hide your foolishness. Most people are doing this. They are trying to hide their foolishness – so they are even bigger fools! You collect information, and then you try to cover up your foolishness with this information. You cover up the inner wounds with flowers.

Knowledge borrowed from scriptures is like these flowers, the borrowed information from others is like these flowers with which you cover your foolishness to help you forget it. Foolishness is not to be forgotten. Foolishness is to be remembered, because it can be destroyed only if it is remembered. That is why Shankara goes on repeating: *Sing the song of the divine, sing the song of the divine, Oh fools!*

Seeing your unconsciousness, he goes on repeating it out of compassion so that you may not forget that you are a fool. You try your best to forget it. You make every effort to forget that you are an idiot. You believe that you are a very knowledgeable person – only a really knowledgeable person knows that he is not knowledgeable. All the ignorant people believe that they are knowledgeable. The ignorant person is not ready to accept that he doesn't know. Only the most knowledgeable person is ready to question his own knowledge.

Edison has said, "People say that I know a lot. But the reality is, that a child on the seashore who has gathered a few seashells... My knowledge is only that much – a few seashells in my hands and there is this vast sea which I do not know."

Your little knowledge seems great to you. You have lit a small lamp; its dim light is able to light up a small place and you think it is great knowledge. But you aren't aware of the unlimited darkness surrounding you. When you understand your foolishness then you will say, "Is this knowledge, this dim light? I have gathered a few seashells in my hand and I think that I have become knowledgeable, but the journey of knowledge is endless, the search is unlimited." Then you will give up that knowledge also.

The day you become aware of your idiocy, the day you are aware that you are a fool, your foolishness will start dissolving, because that awareness will bring you out of it. Foolishness is unconsciousness; it will start dissolving with awareness.

Psychologists say that a madman will become alright if he

realizes that he is mad. A mad person never knows that he is mad, he thinks that the world is mad.

Kahlil Gibran has written that one of his friends became mad, so he went to visit him in the mental asylum. The friend was sitting on a bench in the garden of that asylum.

Gibran sat down near him and said, "I am very sorry to see you here."

The friend looked carefully at Gibran and said, "Sorry for what?"

Gibran replied, "To see that you had to come to this mental asylum."

That mad friend started laughing and said, "You are mistaken. Since I have come here I have found the company of sane people. Outside, all of them are insane; I am fortunate to get rid of them. You think this is the mental asylum? No, the mental asylum is outside these walls. Only a very few wise people live here."

An insane person cannot understand that he is insane. If he had that much understanding, he would not have gone insane. If he understands that he is insane, then insanity will disappear. If at night in your sleep you realize that you are dreaming, then the dreaming will stop. To dream, it is necessary that you don't remember that you are dreaming. In the morning when the dream is over you will remember it. As long as you are dreaming it will seem real to you. But if right in the middle of the dream you remember that this is a dream, it will be over.

Gurdjieff used to tell his disciples that before shattering big dreams they should learn how to shatter small dreams. This big world is an illusion, a big dream; you cannot break it till you break the small dreams. How can you stop the daydreams when you cannot stop the nightdreams? So Gurdjieff used to tell his disciples that while going to sleep at night they must go on reminding themselves that whenever they start dreaming, they must remember at once that this is a dream. It takes about three years to break the night dreaming. For three years continuously, every night while going to sleep, if you go on thinking, contemplating, meditating on this thought then that moment comes – that fortunate moment – when suddenly you remember that this is a dream. And this remembrance breaks the dreaming, consciousness even enters your sleep. From that moment dreaming stops.

Then there is no more dreaming. Only after this can you wake up and see the big dream – this dream that you see now with open eyes is the big dream. The night dreaming is personal, private – alone. It is absolutely private. A husband cannot call even his wife into his dream. Even a friend cannot call a friend into his dream. This dreaming is alone; nobody else can participate in this dream.

But this big dream is collective, public. It is very difficult to break it because it is not only yours, it is everybody's collective and joint dream. But if the first dream can be broken, then that remembrance can break this dream also. That remembrance is enough. Even while awake one should be able to remember that this is a dream.

Just think, if somebody has cursed you or called you names and you remember that this is a dream, then it will be impossible for you to lose your temper. If anything valuable of yours breaks and you remember that this is only a dream, you will not be unhappy. If your wife or husband or son dies, then it will be difficult to remember that this is all a dream, but if you can do so, then your agony will disappear.

The person who has realized that this is a dream becomes a buddha, a *jina*; neither death nor life is able to waver him. Then happiness doesn't seem like happiness to him and unhappiness doesn't seem unhappiness. This is the ultimate wisdom: neither happiness nor agony affects you!

Shankara is reminding you again and again that you are a fool – so don't get annoyed. If you get annoyed, then you are proving that Shankara is right in calling you a fool. Perhaps you are a big idiot and Shankara is calling you just a fool, he is hesitant. Don't insist on proving that you are not an fool, otherwise this insistence will strengthen your idiocy. You must accept it. Your acceptance will dissolve your idiocy. Not only should you accept it, but you should also remind yourself every moment that you are a fool – that you are unconscious, ignorant, insane. Then your consciousness will move into a new direction, your inner quality will change, your actions will change. If you could only remember that you are not sensible, then that will be the beginning of your becoming sensible.

Realization of one's ignorance is the first step towards knowledge. The effort to kindle the fire, the light, starts only after understanding the darkness. If you don't know darkness as darkness and blindness as blindness, you will not try to heal your eyes. When you go to a doctor he doesn't give you the medicine at once. First of all he tries to diagnose the illness, then he gives the medicine. If the diagnosis is correct, then it is easy to give the treatment. That is why all the great doctors take the fee for the diagnosis and not for the treatment, because after the diagnosis anyone can give the medicines. Once the illness is diagnosed, its treatment will be easy.

Shankara is telling you again and again: *Oh fool! Sing the song of the divine.* He has diagnosed your sickness. Foolishness is your sickness and singing the song of the divine is the treatment. But if you think you are not a fool, then why would you sing the song of the divine? If you don't consider yourself ill, then why would you take the treatment? If you go on protecting your illness, if you go on claiming that your illness is your health, then of course you are incurable, nobody can treat you.

The third question:

> Beloved Osho,
> During catharsis I express only negative emotions, anger, jealousy, anguish, etcetera. Why do I not express love, devotion, bliss and religious emotions? Do I not possess them?

They are in you, but they are a little deeper. When a well is dug, first of all it is stones, pebbles and mud which come out and not the water. It depends on the land also. Somewhere the water is at thirty feet and somewhere the water is at sixty feet deep. Water is certainly there. Every land has water underneath it, but the difference is of depth.

A simple person will find the water soon – maybe at two, three or ten feet, and if a complicated person digs then he may get it at fifty or sixty feet. An innocent-minded person will get it quickly, but a violent, angry man will take a long time to reach the water level. The difference is in the layers in the ground; water is underneath all land. The soul is there in everyone, godliness is there in everyone – the difference is in the layers of past actions. When you start digging you cannot achieve the divine straightaway, you will get only the layers of actions, because these surround it. When you first start digging the well you only get stones and pebbles. Don't be dejected by this. In fact, this is a good beginning; these things give the signal that the journey has started. Yes, first of all stones and pebbles will come out, then garbage, then good earth, and then wet earth. You are coming closer and closer every day. When you see the wet earth you must know that water is not very far away.

Water is inside everyone, because you cannot live without water. Life is inside everyone, how can you exist without life? You may have hidden it, you may have covered it, but you cannot destroy it. The soul can be covered with your activities, but it cannot be destroyed. We have suppressed the soul in birth after birth, so the catharsis has to be done according to the degree of suppression. Therefore, don't be disheartened.

"During catharsis I express only negative emotions, anger, jealousy, anguish, etcetera."

It is alright. These are good signs. Throw them out. When you cathart absolutely, then you will come across the other hidden streams. The day anger is plucked and thrown out of you, from that day you will get compassion, because compassion is the other side of anger. The moment violence is finished in you, nonviolence will be born in you.

Go on digging as long as you go on having these negative emotions – the positive emotions are hidden somewhere underneath these. But the digging has to be done and you cannot be lazy. Continuous labor is necessary, continuous watchfulness is necessary, because it is possible that you will go on digging with one hand and putting back the stones and the earth with the other hand. In the morning you will throw out anger while meditating, but you will gather anger the whole day in the market. Then this digging will be useless. It will be like digging a well during the daytime and getting it filled up with stones at night and you again start digging the next day.

There is a story of Jesus:

A man sowed wheat in a field but someone put the seeds of wild plants and weeds into it to destroy the field. The servants were very worried. The head of the servants called a meeting to think over what to do and how to save the crop. They asked the master. He said, "If you start uprooting the wild plants, then the wheat plants will also die. The two can be separated at the time of the harvest." But this thing didn't appeal to the servants. They said that the field should be weeded soon. The evil should be destroyed as early as possible. They decided to look for the person who had done the mischief. "Who could be the enemy of our master, who is a thorough gentleman?" They tried to find out, but couldn't succeed.

Then one evening a servant came to the head servant and he said, "Forgive me, but I cannot hide this secret any longer. I know who has thrown the seeds of these wild plants into our field. I myself have seen that person because I was awake at that time and I saw him going into the field. But perhaps he was not conscious at that time, because I was standing in front of him but he neither saw me nor recognized me; perhaps he was asleep. I have kept this secret so long, but now it is difficult to keep it."

The head servant was very annoyed and asked him why he had kept this secret until now. Why hadn't he told him about it earlier? The servant said, "Even now I don't have the courage to tell you, but I cannot keep it with me any longer. So you had better listen to the whole story first."

The head servant said, "You must tell me the name of this man. He will be punished." The servant sat down and bowed his head. The head servant asked him, "Why don't you tell me his name? Why are you afraid?"

The servant replied, "You won't believe me. It is our master who has thrown the seeds of the wild plants in the field. It is our master." Then both of them decided to keep this secret to themselves.

This story, told by Jesus, says that whatever you build in the day you demolish at night. Whatever you make during the daytime when you are conscious, you destroy it at night when you are unconscious.

There are some people who walk in their sleep. There have been cases in the courts – a woman gets up at night, sets fire to her clothes and goes back to sleep. She is not trying to deceive anyone, because these are her own clothes which are very valuable and she likes them immensely. But in the morning when she gets up she cries that somebody has burned her clothes. But nobody has entered the room; only the husband and the wife are sleeping in that room and nobody else has come in. The husband couldn't burn them and how can the wife do such a thing? Yes, it could be the mischief of some ghosts! After a lot of investigation it was found that it was the wife who was burning her own clothes; she had the habit of sleepwalking.

There are some people who go to the kitchen in their sleep, eat something and go to sleep again. If you ask them about it in the morning, they will deny this and say that they never got up during the night. At the most they may remember that they had a dream; that too they cannot remember clearly.

Actually, every individual suffers from this disease. What you make with one hand you destroy with the other hand. You hate the very person whom you love. You have disrespect for the person whom you respect a lot. You are contradictory; you are divided into many pieces, into many parts within yourself. You destroy your love with your hatred, and you destroy your compassion with your anger. You go to the temple to remember God and you start remembering the market, the shop! There was no need to go to the temple, you could have sat in the market. But the trouble with you is that when you are sitting in your shop you go on remembering the temple, and when you are in the temple you go on thinking about the shop.

I have heard that a sannyasin died. That very day a prostitute also died. They had lived in houses facing each other. When the angels came to take them, they were taking the sannyasin towards hell and they were taking the prostitute to heaven. The sannyasin said "Stop it! You seem to have made some mistake. You are doing just the opposite – taking me, the sannyasin, to hell and taking this prostitute to heaven! You must have misunderstood your instructions. It is quite natural, even ordinary governments make mistakes, so there can be a mistake in the administration of this universe. You had better find out first."

The angels also became doubtful. They said that there has never been any mistake..."but it is quite clear that you are a sannyasin and she is a prostitute." They went and checked that there was no mistake – that the prostitute was to be taken to heaven and the sannyasin was to be taken to hell. "If he insists on knowing the reason then tell him this reason...."

The reason was that the sannyasin was living in the temple, but was always thinking about the prostitute. While worshipping God, his mind was thinking of the prostitute. And when at night there was singing and dancing, drinking and merrymaking in the house of the prostitute, this sannyasin would be missing all that and thinking that he had wasted his life sitting in that empty temple. He would say to himself, "What am I doing sitting in front of this stone image? I don't even know whether God exists or not." He was doubting God! He couldn't sleep the whole night, he kept on dreaming about having a good time with the prostitute.

The mental attitude of the prostitute was just the opposite. She was a prostitute, so she had to entertain people by dancing, but she was always thinking of the temple. When the temple bells used to ring she would think, "When will that happy day come when I will be able to enter the temple? I am the most unfortunate person. My whole life is wasted, it is dirty. Oh God, please make me a priestess in my next birth. I will consider myself very fortunate even if I become just the dust on the steps of the temple so that people who come to worship will touch me with their feet. That will be more than enough for me."

When the fragrance of the incense of the temple would come her way she would be lost in ecstasy. She would be thankful to God for keeping her near the temple. She would think, "There are many people who live far away from the temple, but I am lucky to be so near – though I am a sinner." She would sit down and close her eyes whenever the priest would worship.

The priest was thinking of the prostitute and the prostitute was thinking of worship. So the priest went to hell and the prostitute went to heaven.

Man is always in a dilemma. You think of the temple when you are in the market. The householder, the family man, thinks of becoming a sannyasin, and the *sadhus* go on repenting and thinking that they may have made a mistake in renouncing the world: "This life may be the only one, and we are dreaming about the next life. Heaven and salvation, who has seen it?"

Sometimes some old sannyasins come to me – the honest sannyasins, because the dishonest ones never say this to anyone, they keep it to themselves. Yes, the *honest* sannyasins sometimes come and tell me, "We are now seventy years old and it is forty years since we became sannyasins, but up to now we have not attained anything. Now we have started doubting whether there is anything that is worth all this trouble, or have we wasted our lives? We didn't enjoy what we had and we have wasted our lives in the hope of getting something which is not." These are honest people. What they are saying is authentic, they are not hiding anything.

If you come to know the inner stories of your sannyasins you will be surprised, and it will be difficult for you to bow down your head at their feet. You are thinking that they have attained bliss, they have attained peace, they have attained God, but most of them have attained nothing, they are in a worse condition than you. There is no doubt that they have lost their world and have also not attained God.

Now this is a complicated matter. By renouncing or giving up the world one doesn't attain the divine. The fact is, that if you realize the divine then the world is lost. Light cannot be created by removing the darkness; the arrival of light removes the darkness.

Sannyas therefore is not negative, it is positive. First one has to attain, then one gives up. And this is right, too. How can you give up the futile till you have seen the meaningful, the significant? The glimpse of the meaningful gives the courage to give up the nonessential. After seeing the meaningful, automatically the nonessential is given up. You will not have to make the effort of giving it up, you will not get the pain of giving up; your steps will go towards the significant with great joy, you will never look back. Only he who doesn't look back is a sannyasin. Looking back, means the sannyas is immature.

In the beginning you have to take out the negative emotions which are hidden in you. In the beginning the disease has to be thrown out. When the disease is thrown out – the catharsis has been done – then health will appear. Don't be afraid. You are fortunate – you have had the opportunity to throw out the disease. If the disease is thrown out then the water of health is not very far away. You have dirt in the upper layer; once that is removed the water within you is as pure as it is in Mahavira, in Buddha and in Shankara. Your innermost nature is exactly the same, there is no difference at all. There cannot be. The meaning of nature is that there is no difference.

But to reach that nature you have to do a lot of digging. The earlier you do it, the better it is. And you must be careful about one thing, which is, that whatever you throw out should not be put in the pit again. Otherwise you will be laboring your whole life and you will attain nothing. Many people start digging many times.

There was a great Sufi *fakir*, Jalaluddin Rumi. One day he took his disciples to a nearby field to show them how the field had been spoilt by the owner; it was full of big holes. This man had started digging a well, but he hadn't found any water after having dug fifteen or twenty feet deep, so he began to dig again at another place. He didn't find water even at the second place, so he began digging at a third place. In this way he dug in eight places, and was now digging the ninth. He had spoilt the whole field.

Jalaluddin said, "Look at this man! If he had concentrated on one place and worked hard only on one place, he would have surely come across water, however deep it might have been. But he digs only ten or twenty feet and thinks that there is no water there, so he tries at another place. He has dug eight holes, and in all he has dug one hundred and sixty feet deep, and even then he couldn't find water. But if he had dug one hundred and sixty feet deep in one place, he would have definitely found water."

You will also start digging many times in life. Sometimes you start meditation and out of enthusiasm you do it for fifteen days or a month and then forget about it. Then you think about it again after four years and you start digging and become a bit peaceful, and then forget about the meditation again. Like this you will dig many holes, but you will not reach the level of water. Your field will be spoilt.

If you get into the habit of giving up after digging for a few days, then it would have been better if you had not dug at all because that labor is wasted. If you don't reach the water level, then all the labor is wasted. Continuity is needed. And remember, that as the continuous trickle of water breaks stones, the continuous trickle of meditation will certainly break the big rocks around you.

Today it may seem that your anger is so very strong, how can meditation break it? But it breaks – it has always broken. Rock is very strong and meditation is very delicate, but this is one of the mysteries of life – the continuity of the delicate can break the strongest and the hardest.

The fourth question:

> Beloved Osho,
> You say that to get lost in singing the song of the divine is an intoxicant. You also say that joy is lost if you are seeking joy while swimming, playing, meditating, and joy seeks you when you are immersed in them. Please explain and clarify the boundary lines of immersion, consciousness and unconsciousness.

Singing the song of the divine in order to get lost is an intoxicant, but to get lost while singing is not an intoxicant. Let me repeat it — it is a little complicated. It is subtle, but it can be understood. For getting lost, singing the song of the divine is an intoxicant. If you only want to get lost.... Life is full of worry, anguish, pain, tension, disturbance, misery; to forget this, to save oneself from all this, you have to become busy or involved somewhere so that you can forget yourself. So somebody sits in the movie house and forgets himself; somebody sits in the wine bar and forgets himself for two hours; somebody goes to the temple, starts singing the song of the divine and forgets himself. These are all different methods of forgetting oneself. But the aim of the three is the same — to forget your worries. But the worry is waiting for you to come home. After you return home you will be the same. Those two hours were wasted, they were futile. The worry is not going to disappear just because of these two hours.

The search for something which can make you forget yourself is an intoxicant — like alcohol. For this you can even make religion your alcohol. But to get lost while singing the song of the divine is an entirely a different thing. You didn't go there to get lost, you didn't have any wish to forget yourself, you didn't go there to save yourself from worry, you had gone there to awaken from the worry.

The worry is not to be forgotten, but to be destroyed. You went to destroy the worry, to understand the essence of life; you went to create such a moment in life where worry would become impossible, a moment where there is no disturbance, no restlessness; you had gone in search of nature. You had gone in search of deep sources of water. You had gone not to forget, but to awaken. But you got lost while meditating. This type of getting lost is not an intoxicant. If this is an intoxicant, then this intoxicant is of consciousness. In this you will be lost and yet you will remain awake. You will find yourself absolutely finished, and at the same time, for the first time you will be. On one side you will find that everything is lost and on the other side you will find that everything has become new. You are, and yet you are not. This thing you can understand only by experience.

In meditation there is a moment when you are not – there is no 'I' at that moment, only existence is, only your being is. 'I' is lost, only existence is. There is no thought, no ego; the mirror of mind is absolutely clean, there is no dust on it. The divine is reflected in that clean mirror. This is a wonderful moment of peace, this is the unique experience of *samadhi*.

But you didn't go there to get lost, you went to get transformed, you went to change yourself. You didn't go to get lost, you went to be finished; you didn't go there to rest for a while, you went for a revolution to happen in your whole life. Meditation can be done in two ways: the first is that you only want to forget yourself, the second is that you want to transform yourself. And you will gain the fruits of the real reason that is within you. You will reap whatever you sow.

If you sow the seed of erasing yourself in your meditation, then in the harvest you will find that you are finished; only godliness remains. If in meditation you sow the seed of forgetting yourself, then you will find that even meditation has become an intoxicant; you forget yourself for a moment but afterwards remain just the same. You go back to your original condition, maybe worse than before, because even that moment was wasted, was futile.

So I definitely say that to get lost in singing the song of the divine is an intoxicant – if you do it to get lost. But if you do it to erase yourself then it is not an intoxicant, it is an awakening, it is consciousness.

Always remember that if you go in search of joy, of ecstasy, you will not find it because that very search will become an obstacle. You will miss joy whenever you are hankering for it, because you get joy only when you don't ask for it. Joy and bliss go only to emperors and not to beggars. When you go with a begging bowl you don't get joy; it comes to you when you stand like an emperor. You will not get it as long as you ask for it. You will get it only when you give up asking for it, then it will come running to you from all sides. The most important rule of life, the most ancient religious law of life, is that you will not be able to attain joy and bliss while you go on running after it.

Try to understand it like this: you have forgotten somebody's name. You say, "I know it, but I cannot remember it. It is just on the tip of my tongue." But if it is on your tongue, then why don't you say it? The harder you try to remember, the more difficult it becomes to do so. The more you try, the more you forget – and you know that you know it! You try hard; you begin to perspire. What is the problem? Actually, when you go on trying to remember you create tension within yourself, and that tension affects the mind – it becomes narrow, it shrinks, no space is left in it. Then you give up and start reading the newspaper, or you go into the garden or start sipping your tea. Just when you forget to remember the name, all of a sudden like a flash the name appears in the mind – you remember the name. When you are making an effort you become disturbed, restless. This effort causes tension. When you give up the effort and you are at peace with yourself, then automatically the name is remembered.

Ecstasy, bliss is your nature. You shrink when you make any effort for it. It is within you, it is not to be brought from anywhere. But you shrink so much that there is no space left. You must have seen sometime that the more you try to hurry, the more you get delayed. If you are in a hurry to catch the train, then you go on putting the buttons in the wrong buttonholes. In your hurry you cannot close the suitcase properly. When you leave in a hurry you either forget the key or the ticket at home; thus your reaching the station in time becomes useless.

You also know that if you had done all these things without tension, without the hurry, then everything would have been done very conveniently. Every day you button up your coat properly, there is never an error in it; but the day you hurry the button is in the wrong hole. The coat is not your enemy, the coat is not trying to take any revenge on you; the coat has nothing to do with you. But your hurry upsets you, makes you worried, and your hand becomes unsteady. When you do things with confidence and certainty then everything is done in time. But because of the worry you get delayed. If you try to run fast, you will reach late; the slower you go, the earlier you will get there. It sounds paradoxical, but it is not so, because patience is a great strength, and not to ask for anything is a great self-confidence.

You get joy, bliss, ecstasy when you are not looking for it. Then the festival of ecstasy, of joy starts coming from every side – from within and from outside. Give up the search for it. Don't ask for it. Don't make meditation the means, make it an end. Don't think that you are meditating to get bliss. No, the meditation itself is a bliss, a joy. You should not do it with the idea of attaining bliss. The bliss, the joy, is in doing it. When the means becomes the end, then you have attained the destination. You do not have to go anywhere, your godliness appears wherever you are. Where can you go? You don't know his address, you don't have any inkling of its whereabouts, where will you look for it? Where will you search for bliss? Where will you search for truth? Where will you search for salvation? You had better sit down quietly.

You must have seen the statues of Shankara, of Mahavira, of Buddha. They don't seem to be walking, running or going anywhere, they are just sitting quietly. On their face there is no expression of any search. Look at Mahavira's face carefully: there is no hurry on the face. Does the face show the expression that he is searching for something? He is just sitting. There is no search, no desire, no expectation and no future – only here and now.

If you have seen the statues of Buddha, Mahavira and Shankara, then you will find that their whole message is: "Now and here." They are sitting peacefully, they are not going anywhere, they are not becoming anything, they are not attaining anything, there is no running for any desire. And then everything happens in that moment! The sky showers.

The last question:

> Beloved Osho,
> Is singing the song of the divine, like prayer, also an expression of thanks?

Prayer is the seed; *bhajan*, singing the song of the divine, is the tree. Prayer is hidden, not expressed; bhajan is the expression. Bhajan is the dancing prayer, the singing prayer. Bhajan is the expression of prayer. If you want to see prayer, you will have to look at it in Mahavira and Buddha. If you want to see bhajan, then you had better look at Meera and Chaitanya. Bhajan is the prayer expressed. What remains within Mahavira and Buddha flows out of Meera and Chaitanya. What is static within Buddha and Mahavira has started dancing in Meera and Chaitanya. Bhajan is the expression of prayer.

You can understand it like this. Supposing you are in love with someone. You can just keep it to yourself; there is no need to say anything about it. It doesn't matter even if you don't say, "I love you." You can keep your love within you. Usually women don't tell about their love to anyone, they keep it to themselves. There is no need to say that love is, because the very experience of love is sufficient in itself. But love gets expressed — sometimes in a song, sometimes in the touch of the hand, sometimes in the expression of the eye, and sometimes in silence also. But whenever love is expressed flowers blossom, the seed doesn't remain a seed. Both are beautiful.

There are two types of people in the world. For some prayer is enough — for those who will attain godliness in their emptiness, in their silence, there is no need to say anything. But this is not enough for the other type of people. Unless it is more than enough, it is not enough for them — they have to overflow. They have to go on flowing, expressing their inner ecstasy. So Meera dances. Buddha did not express himself in this way, but Meera did; and both are beautiful, both ways are good. You must know your own nature. If you want to keep it to yourself it doesn't matter, and if you want to distribute, even then it doesn't matter. And I don't compare the two. The seed is beautiful because the flowers bloom out of it, and the flower is beautiful because it becomes the seed. They are interconnected. The expressed and the unexpressed, the manifest and the unmanifest, both are connected. You must find out your nature, your temperament and choose whatever appeals to you. But remember that bhajan is an expression and prayer is silent.

The question is: "Like prayer, is singing the song of the divine also an expression of thanks?"

No, prayer is thanks and bhajan is gratitude with ecstasy. Prayer says: "Whatever is given to me is enough; I am fully satisfied and contented with what is given to me." But bhajan says: "Whatever is given to me is more than necessary, it cannot be contained within, it has to be distributed." Bhajan expresses itself by dancing; it is not silent, it speaks. It has its own beauty.

Prayer is an unsung song – the picture hidden in the mind of a painter which has not taken the form on the canvas. It is the statue hidden in the stone which has not been carved out with the chisel. Bhajan is the visible statue. The stone has been cut, the chisel has done the work. Bhajan is the song which is being sung.

When Rabindranath was about to die, a friend came to see him just two days before his death. He said, "Yours has been a very successful life. There is nothing to worry about or to regret now." They had been friends since their childhood and now both of them were old. He said, "You can die peacefully. I did not attain anything in this life, I have wasted it, so I will not die peacefully. You have sung so many songs!"

Rabindranath has sung six thousand songs. No other poet in this world has sung so many songs. The poet Shelley is very famous in the West, but his songs number about three thousand, while Rabindranath's are six thousand, and all these six thousand songs can be put to music.

The old friend said, "You were given the Nobel Prize; honors have been showered on you, you can die peacefully. Of course I will die without peace, but you can thank God while saying good-bye to the world."

Rabindranath listened to what his friend was saying. Then he said, "Well, I have not been able to sing the song which I wanted to sing, it is still within me like a seed. These six thousand songs are the unsuccessful efforts to sing that one song. Many times I have tried to sing that one song which is in me like a seed, but I have failed every time. You may have liked those songs, but they are the stories of my failure. My song has not been sung yet. I have not sung it yet, and God has come to take me away. I was just tuning my instruments; with great difficulty I was able to tune my sitar... All people thought I was singing. No, I was tuning my instruments. Now I have become mature enough, the instruments are ready, my spirit is ready, now the moment of singing has come, but now it is time to go. Yes, I am complaining to God."

Rabindranath could not sit like Buddha under a tree, he wanted to sing the song of the divine. Rabindranath has criticized Buddha a lot – not out of any dislike, but out of love and gratitude. But Buddha never appealed to Rabindranath: he had regard for him, but Buddha's sitting silently like a stone statue did not appeal to him. The Baul fakirs appealed to him – the fakirs, the sadhus dancing with the *ektara*. This is the difference of individuals. Rabindranath had respect for Buddha, he had nothing against him, but they were two different types.

The personality of bhajan is different and the individuality of prayer is different. Prayer is silent, bhajan is speech, words, expression. Prayer is silent, quiet.

The people who pray have said, the Sufis have said, if your left hand is praying your right hand should not know about it. It should be done in the darkness of night. If a husband prays, the wife should not know about it, otherwise it will be showing off, and showing off means ego. The person who prays is afraid that others may come to know about it.

But the one who sings the song of the divine dances in the middle of the road. He is just not bothered about other people coming to know about it. He says that it doesn't matter whether people know or don't know. He destroys his ego in dancing. His ego is lost in his dancing. These are two different ways. Prayer is only thanks, bhajan is the expression of gratitude.

You should understand your inner condition. You can reach the divine through prayer or through bhajan. The paths are different, but the destination is the same. And you must always choose the one which suits you, the one which you can enjoy. Always think of yourself, observe yourself...because it is possible that something in the other person is very appealing to you, but it doesn't suit you. So you should not go for it even by mistake. What is good for the other may not be good for you. The other person's medicine can be poison for you. Your medicine also can be poison for the other person. Actually, medicine is not medicine, poison is not poison – the poison which suits you becomes the medicine for you; the medicine which doesn't suit you becomes poison for you. So you should always go on observing what suits you, what is harmonious to you, and then choose the one which is meant for you.

If you want to sit quietly like Buddha, if you want to go deep in silence without any movement of the body....We have made the statues of Buddha and Mahavira out of marble. The reason is, they were sitting like this marble. When they were living they were unwavering. But a marble statue of Meera will not be appealing. People have made it, but it doesn't appeal. Meera's statue cannot be static, it has to be made of water – dancing, liquid, not static. Meera is a movement, a physical expression of emotion, a dance. Mahavira is static. He is like a pond without any ripple. Meera is like a waterfall – like the water falling from a hill, where every drop dances.

These are the big differences, but these differences are of the paths. Ultimately the still pond also gets lost, evaporates in the sky by riding on the rays of the sun, and the river also gets lost in the sky by riding on the rays of the sun after it flows into the ocean.

The destination is one, but the paths are many. The temple is one, but the doors are many. Choose your own door, don't follow the other. A creed is created by following, and religion is born by going according to your nature.

Enough for today.

5
THE BONDAGE OF HOPE

One who has long hair on his head,
one who has shaved his head,
one who has pulled his hair from the roots,
one who is wearing ochre robes,
or is dressed up in a variety of ways,
that fool, in spite of having eyes, is blind.
Just for the sake of his stomach
he dresses up in different ways.

All limbs have become infirm,
all hair has turned white,
there is not a single tooth in the mouth anymore
— such an old man walks with the help of a stick;
even then he is bound down with the mass of hope.

Struck by the cold,
in the morning he warms himself
by keeping the fire in front of him
or by keeping his back towards the sun.
At night, he sleeps with his chin between his knees,
he takes alms in his hands and lives under a tree;
even then he does not drop the bondage of hope.

He may undertake the journey
to the Ganges or to the ocean,
he may undertake many austerities and fasts,
he may give away in charity,
but if he does not have self-knowledge
he will not be liberated
even in hundreds of lifetimes.

One may be residing in the temple of God
or under a tree, the earth may be his only bed,
deerskin may be his only robe,
he may have dropped all kinds of
possessions and indulgences
— who would not be made blissful
by such a renunciation?

He may be absorbed in enjoyment of the senses
or in yoga, he may be engrossed
in somebody's company or he may be alone,
but if his heart dwells in the divine,
then it is he who is blissful, it is he who is blissful,
it is he alone who is blissful.

There is an old story about an ascetic who was doing *sadhana* in a dense forest. He was sitting with closed eyes and was praying to God continuously. He wanted to gain heaven. Hunger and thirst didn't worry him.

A very poor young woman used to come to that forest to collect firewood. Out of kindness and consideration for the ascetic she used to pluck some fruit, bring water from the pond in cups made of leaves and to put them near him. The ascetic was able to sustain himself on these things.

Gradually his asceticism became even more intense. He forgot about hunger and thirst and he neither touched the fruit nor the water. That poor young woman felt very unhappy and sad about this, but there was no way out. Lord Indra also became worried and said that this person was going beyond the limits: did he intend to get hold of the throne of heaven? It was absolutely necessary to disturb his sadhana.

It was not very difficult to do so, because Lord Indra knows the mind of man. A breeze came from heaven and turned that poor, dark, ugly young woman into a stunning beauty. It seemed as if a ray had come down from heaven and turned her ordinary body into a golden one. When she was collecting some water for the ascetic from the pond she saw her reflection in the water and couldn't believe it, she was looking like a fairy. She became fascinated by her own reflection.

She continued to look after the ascetic. Then one day the ascetic opened his eyes and told the young woman that he wanted to leave that place and to go to some other mountains, as he had to walk on a more difficult path and that he cannot rest until he has conquered heaven itself.

The young woman started crying, the tears fell from her eyes. She said, "What have I done wrong that you are stopping me from serving you? – and I have never asked you for anything."

The ascetic looked at her face and thought he had never seen such beauty – not even in his dreams! The woman looked familiar and unfamiliar both. The face was just the same, but now there was a glory in it. The body and the features were the same, but now they were radiant. She was like some forgotten song, played again on a flute by some musician. The ascetic sat down and again closed his eyes. He didn't go.

That night the young woman couldn't sleep because she felt so happy at her victory, but also repentant for polluting the *sadhu*. She was happy that she had won, but felt unhappy for being an obstacle on the path of the ascetic. She felt sorry that because of her he couldn't continue the journey upwards. That night she couldn't sleep. She laughed and she cried. In the morning she made a decision. She touched the feet of the ascetic and told him, "I have to go. My family is going to another village." The ascetic blessed her so that she would be happy wherever she lived, and the young woman went away.

After many years the asceticism was complete. Lord Indra himself came down, bowed and said, "The doors of heaven are open to welcome you."

The ascetic opened his eyes and said, "I don't want heaven."

Indra was very surprised. He couldn't believe that any human being can say that he doesn't want heaven. Then Indra thought that maybe this ascetic had the desire of attaining salvation. So he asked, "Do you want salvation?"

The ascetic said, "What would I do with salvation?"

Lord Indra was highly impressed by this attitude. He thought to himself that this is the height of asceticism – there is not even the desire of attaining salvation. Out of regard he wanted to bow down in front of that ascetic, but before doing so he said, "But there is nothing beyond salvation. What else do you want?"

The ascetic replied, "Nothing except that young maiden who used to collect wood in this forest. I want her!"

Don't laugh. This is the weakness of man. Don't laugh, but think over it, because the gravitation of earth is so strong! Don't think this story is just a story – this is the whole agony of the mind of man. And don't think that this alternative was only before that ascetic, that it was only he who had to choose between the young woman and heaven. You also have the same alternatives. In fact, everyone has the same alternatives: either you choose the pleasures which are transient, or you choose the eternal. Either you lose the eternal for the transient or you dedicate the transient to the eternal. And of course most of the people will choose what that ascetic chose.

Don't think that you have done anything different. Whether Lord Indra has stood in front of you or not, whether someone has given you the alternative of heaven and earth or not, the fact is that the alternative is always there for you, and when you choose the one you miss the other. One whose eyes are filled with the intoxication of the earth remains deprived of the heavenly awareness. The heavenly gold cannot shower into hands that are full of earthly dust; heaven can shower only if the hands are empty. The divine can descend only if you are empty within.

If you are filled with some infatuation the throne of your soul is already occupied. Then don't say that the divine has been unfair to you – this was your choice. Don't blame the divine if you don't find him – it means that you have not chosen him yet, because whenever someone chooses him, he finds him immediately. It doesn't take even one second. But if you yourself don't want him, then the divine will not force himself on you.

Truth doesn't force itself upon you. You have the freedom to refuse the truth birth after birth, life after life. This is the glory of man, but it is the misfortune of man as well. The glory is because of the freedom – the freedom to choose. The misfortune is that we make the wrong choice. But the choice of choosing wrongly is included in that freedom. A freedom which can choose only the right and not the wrong cannot be called freedom; then that is not freedom. The meaning of freedom is that you have the right to go astray, to go on the wrong path. The meaning of freedom is that you have the freedom to sin. The meaning of freedom is also that you have the freedom to refuse godliness.

Buddha was born, and the fifth day after his birth, according to the custom, the best of the *pundits* got together and gave him the name Siddhartha. The meaning of Siddhartha is: fulfillment of desire, fulfillment of hope, attainment of wealth, attainment of destination. After waiting his whole life, after hoping and dreaming and going through many disappointments, at last a son was born to Shuddhodana in his old age – certainly he was a 'Siddhartha'! The pundits had given him the correct name.

There were eight great pundits. The king asked them to tell him the future of the newborn baby. Seven pundits raised their hands and pointed two fingers. The king did not understand, he said, "I don't understand these gestures so please tell me clearly."

The seven pundits said that there are two alternatives: either he will be a great emperor or he will renounce everything and be a great sannyasin. Only one pundit kept quiet. He was the youngest of them all. His name was Kodanna. But he was the most intelligent. The king asked him "Why are you quiet? You haven't raised the two fingers!"

Kodanna said, "The two fingers can be raised at the birth of everyone, because these two alternatives are for everyone: either this world or sannyas — these two alternatives are for all. These pundits, therefore, have not said anything important about Buddha by raising two fingers. Well, I raise only one — he will be a sannyasin!"

On hearing this Shuddhodana started crying.

The unfortunate mind of man always behaves like this. He knew that Kodanna was an all-knowing astrologer. He was young but very luminous, his words, his prophecy, would certainly turn out to be true. The other pundits had talked about the possibility of his being a great emperor, but Kodanna had disregarded that alternative. He said that the boy will definitely be a buddha. The king had felt happy when these pundits said that he will be an emperor. He didn't give any importance to the other alternative of his becoming a sannyasin — because if one can be an emperor then why should one think of becoming a sannyasin?

But Kodanna destroyed this hope by raising one finger. The king tried to console himself by thinking that Kodanna was just one person and there are seven pundits opposing him. Man always goes on consoling himself like this: seven will be right and one will be wrong. But only that one proved to be right — and it is good that only that one proved to be right.

At the time of your birth also, whether the pundits are called or not — nature raises two fingers. Nature puts forward two alternatives: either to be lost in unconsciousness or to be awakened in consciousness. Either collect the outer wealth, run the race of becoming a great emperor; or collect the inner wealth, rest in your being. Always remember Kodanna's one finger. In real life no Kodanna will meet you with a raised finger. You yourself will have to raise your finger.

These sutras of Shankara's are most subtle gestures of renunciation and detachment.

> One who has long hair on his head,
> one who has shaved his head,
> one who has pulled his hair from the roots,
> one who is wearing ochre robes,
> or is dressed up in a variety of ways,
> that fool, in spite of having eyes, is blind.
> Just for the sake of his stomach
> he dresses up in different ways.

Always remember that man's mind is very dangerous. Even in sannyas it looks for the world. It finds hypocrisy even in the temple; even in sadhana it finds the enjoyment of the senses. Whatever the outer activity, the mind goes on acting according to its old habit.

So Shankara says: Don't get deceived by someone who has long hair on his head. Long hair doesn't make any difference. Don't get deceived by anyone whose head is shaven. The shaving of the head, keeping long hair or pulling out the hair doesn't make any difference, it just doesn't matter. So don't get deceived by seeing such people. Jaina Digambara *munis* pull out their hair – don't get deceived. There are people who wear ochre robes – don't get deceived by them. Don't worry if the other is deceived, but you should not get deceived, because it is very easy to wear ochre robes or to pull out one's hair; only a little experience is needed. What is the difficulty in shaving the head or in keeping long hair? Only a little experience is needed. But try to see what is going on inside the mind. Under these various garbs of sannyas they are just carrying on business to fill their stomachs.

Ninety percent of *sannyasins* are only filling their stomachs. If only the stomach had to be filled up then the world would be a better place. Then at least one would be honest – then your shop could be run as a shop without any deception; there would be no need to pollute the temple. Ordinary clothes would be alright, there would be no need to pollute the ochre robes. What would be the need to pull your hair out? – the barber could have cut your hair. All these outer things don't matter if your mind is involved in doing business: if your mind is involved in "running the shop," then this is just a deception.

I received the news a few months before that two Jaina munis – they live naked, they have given up everything and possess nothing – went out of the village to answer the call of nature and they started quarreling. They were master and disciple. They attacked each other. Because of this quarrel and fighting their secret was out. Both of them had hidden money in the hollow stick of the *pichie* they were carrying; the fight was over the distribution of the money. Both of them were caught and brought to the police station. Their disciples in the village became worried and were unhappy, because it was also a question of their prestige. Somehow they quieted the matter down by bribing the police so that this news didn't spread to other places.

The naked man is also doing the same thing as the shopkeeper is doing. Then isn't it better for him to sit in a shop? Then at least the nudity will not be polluted.

Nobody is forcing you to give up the world. Give it up only when you feel like it. Otherwise this pretense of giving up the world is nothing but deception.

> One who has long hair on his head,
> one who has shaved his head,
> one who has pulled his hair from the roots,
> one who is wearing ochre robes,
> or is dressed up in a variety of ways,
> that fool, in spite of having eyes, is blind.

Why does Shankara say, ...*that fool, in spite of having eyes, is blind?* Whom is he deceiving? It is not a question of deceiving others; the other is not concerned about him. He is only deceiving himself. The final conclusion is based on what you are inside, it is not based on what you are outside. Life is motivated with what you are inside, not with what you are outside.

Inside you are continuously counting money, outside you are chanting "Rama, Rama." This chanting is futile. Your counting the money is meaningful – the judgment will be based on that; because there is no one else making the judgment, the judgment is being made every moment by what you are doing within yourself. If it had been someone else who was making the judgment then you could have asked his forgiveness, you could have asked him to relent. But there is no judge. There is no God sitting somewhere who can be pacified by you. Whatever you have done, your action is your destiny. The result is hidden in your actions. Your thinking is the basis of your being.

There is a very sweet story about Mahavira's life. Mahavira was standing in a forest engrossed in meditation. A king who was a childhood friend of Mahavira's was coming to him for his *darshan*. On the way he saw another king, who had become Mahavira's sannyasin, standing near a rock doing *tapasya* – making effort towards self-realization. These three were childhood friends.

The first king felt very repentant for leading the worldly life. He thought, "Look at this king, Prasenchandra, how peaceful and silent he is. How blissful he is. How unfortunate I am. Mahavira has attained salvation and I am still counting money." The thought of renunciation arose in him.

When he met Mahavira he said, "I want to ask you a question. On the way here I saw Prasenchandra doing spiritual practices, tapasya. He is your disciple. Seeing him, I feel like renouncing this world also. And I want to know something: if Prasenchandra had died at the moment when I was standing near him, where would he be reborn?"

Mahavira said, "If Prasenchandra had died at that time he would have been born in the seventh hell."

The king was shocked to hear this. Prasenchandra was standing so peacefully, so silently, merged in meditation – and if he dies now he will be born in the seventh hell! Mahavira said, "Don't be worried. But if he dies now" – only a few moments have passed between the two events – "he will enter the seventh heaven."

The king said, "This sounds like a riddle. Please explain it to me."

Mahavira said, "Before you came soldiers had passed by Prasenchandra. They saw him and remarked, 'This fool is standing here with closed eyes. His sons are too young yet, and the ministers to whom he has entrusted his kingdom are busy looting his wealth and he is standing here like a fool!'

The soldiers said this while passing him, and when Prasenchandra heard this, that the ministers were looting his wealth – that the people whom he had trusted were deceiving him – for a second he forgot that he had renounced everything. He forgot, he was not conscious, and the thought came to his mind, 'I am alive yet, you fools. What do you think? I am very much alive yet and I will sever the heads of these ministers from their bodies!' Unconsciously his hand tried to get hold of his sword which is not there now, but due to the old habit he tried to draw the sword from its sheath! And another old habit was that when he used to be angry he used to adjust his crown...."

Many of you are also in the habit of scratching your head or scratching your brow. So now in his anger, when he tried to adjust his crown, there was no crown, and he could touch only his shaven head. At once he became conscious: what am I doing? I am no longer King Prasenchandra, I have renounced everything. How could I think of killing people?

Mahavira said, "When you were standing just near Prasenchandra, within him the sword was drawn, so if he had died at that moment he would have gone to the seventh hell. But now he has become conscious, he is laughing at his own foolishness. If he dies at this moment then he will be born in the seventh heaven."

Every action is the judge, and the decision of the action is within you, not outside you. You can stand silently outside, while a storm may be raging within you. You may look very peaceful from outside, while you may be restless within. You may be quiet outside, while within you may be ready to explode at any time.

Your outside is not valuable. Your inside is your existence. Every action of yours decides the nature of your soul. Every action of yours creates you. There is no other judge except you.

That is why Shankara says: ...*that fool, in spite of having eyes, is blind* – because he thinks that he is deceiving others. But all deception is deceiving yourself. You are fooling yourself. You cannot make others lose anything, it is you who will lose. You may be able to get hold of some money from the other's pocket, but with that money you will lose your soul. You will lose a lot and gain nothing.

Even if you are able to deceive others, what will you receive? At the most you will snatch some money from the other person. That money is going to remain here – neither you can take it with you nor can the other person take it with him after death. It doesn't matter whether the money is in this pocket or in that pocket. But by snatching it, by desiring it, you became perverted, your mind became dirty, you sowed the seed of sin within you. Then you should not hope to get any tasty fruit or any fragrant flower from this seed.

> ...that fool, in spite of having eyes, is blind.
> Just for the sake of his stomach
> he dresses up in different ways.

Therefore,

> Oh fool! Always sing the song of the divine.
>
> All limbs have become infirm,
> all hair has turned white, there is not a single tooth
> in the mouth anymore – such an old man walks

> with the help of a stick; even then
> he is bound down with the mass of hope.

Even to the last moment of death hope is not given up. You die, but hope doesn't die. Even in death hope lives, remains alert and young. Even the man who is dying thinks that tomorrow everything will be alright. He dreams about tomorrow even when he is dying: people die dreaming.

One must understand hope. What is hope? It's the illusion of getting what you don't have; this dream of what is not now, of what will be there sometime, is hope. And what is waking up from hope? The awareness of what is. Hope disappears when you become aware of what is. Hope exists in the demand of what is not. The poor live in hope and the rich also live in hope.

When Alexander the Great was coming to India he went to meet a *fakir* named Diogenes because he had heard a lot about him. And many times it so happens that even emperors become jealous of fakirs.

Diogenes was also such a fakir. He used to live naked, just like Mahavira. He was a unique fakir, he didn't even keep a begging bowl with him. In the beginning when he became a fakir he used to have a begging bowl, but then one day he saw a dog drinking water from the river. He said, "I must be mad! Why am I carrying this bowl with me? This dog is drinking water without any bowl. The dog is more sensible than me – if he can do without the bowl then why can't I do without it?" So he threw the bowl away.

Alexander heard that Diogenes lived in ecstasy, so Alexander went to meet him. When he saw Alexander, Diogenes asked him, "Where are you going?"

Alexander said, "I have to conquer Asia Minor."

Diogenes asked him, "What will you do after that?" Diogenes was lying down on the sand of the river. It must have been a winter morning like this. He was taking a sunbath. He stayed lying down, he didn't even get up and sit. He again asked, "What will you do after that?"

Alexander replied, "Then India has to be conquered."

Diogenes asked, "Then?" And Alexander said that after that he will conquer whatever is left of the world. Diogenes asked, "And then?"

Alexander said, "Then what? Then I will rest."

Diogenes started laughing. He said, "I am resting now. You will rest then! If you want to rest in the end, then why go through all this trouble? I am resting now. You can also rest on this river bank, there is a lot of space here. There is no need to go anywhere, you can rest here right now."

Alexander was definitely very much impressed by this. For a moment he felt embarrassed, that what Diogenes was saying was correct: if he is to take rest in the end, then why is he planning for it in this way? And Diogenes was certainly resting; it cannot be said that he was saying something wrong – he was resting and was happier than Alexander. His face was like a fully blossomed lotus.

Alexander possessed everything, but there was nothing inside him. Diogenes had nothing outside, but had everything within him. Alexander told Diogenes, "You make me feel jealous of you. If ever I am to be born again I will ask God not to make me Alexander but to make me Diogenes."

Diogenes said, "You are again deceiving yourself. Why are you bringing God in? If you want to become Diogenes, then what is the difficulty in your being Diogenes right now? It is difficult for me to be an Alexander because I may or may not be able to conquer the world. I may or may not be able to collect such a big army. But there is no difficulty in your being Diogenes: just throw away your clothes and rest!"

Alexander said, "What you say appeals to me, but it doesn't appeal to hope. I will come back. I will definitely come back. But now I have to go as my journey is incomplete. What you say is one hundred percent correct."

This is most interesting. What he says seems right and yet hope goes on pulling you. Just a few days before I was narrating the words of a great Japanese poet named Issa. His wife had died, he was very unhappy; then his daughter died, and when he was thirty-three years old all of his five children died and he was left alone. He was in great agony. His was a poet's heart, he was completely shaken. He couldn't sleep at night; he was not in his senses during the daytime. He went on asking the question, "Why is there so much agony in this world? What did I do? Why did I have to face this misfortune!"

Somebody suggested to him to go to the temple as there was a monk there who may solve his problem. He went to the temple. The monk said, "The question, 'Why is there so much agony?' is meaningless. Life is like the dewdrop which will disappear at any moment. You will also go. Your wife has gone, your five children have gone – you will also go. Now don't waste time. Life is like the dewdrop on the grass leaf which will fall down any moment." Issa came back home. The monk's words appealed to him. Life is like this. He wrote a small *haiku* which is:

Life is a dewdrop,
yes I am perfectly convinced.
Life is a dewdrop, and yet and yet....

"And yet," is hope. Even if you understand the fact, hope doesn't let you do it. Even when the intellect understands, it doesn't affect life. At the most thinking may get an inkling of it, but it is not reflected in the emotions. And hope goes on weaving its net.

> All limbs have become infirm,
> all hair has turned white, there is not a single tooth
> in the mouth anymore — such an old man walks
> with the help of a stick; even then
> he is bound down with the mass of hope.

THE BONDAGE OF HOPE

Hope is the thread with which we live. It is a very thin thread, it can break at any moment. But it doesn't break. It has become a very strong shackle. If it breaks from one end we hold it from the other. If it breaks from the world we start hoping for heaven, for liberation. Hope continues. Hope is bigger than the world.

When the agony of the world is realized and one becomes detached from the world, then one starts hoping for heaven. Hope drags you on even when you are tired and fall down. Many times this question must have arisen in you. When you see a beggar on the roadside who is without hands, feet, eyes – whose whole body is wasted – you also start wondering why he is living. What is he living for? But he is not the only one who is making the mistake. If you were in his place what would you do? You will also continue to live. You will hope that tomorrow everything will be alright on account of some miracle.

Man goes on living in spite of suffering any amount of misery and anguish. I want to tell you a unique thing: man doesn't give up hope even in great misery. Logically it seems that anguish will kill hope. But no, anguish cannot destroy hope. The greater the anguish, the greater the hope man has. Anguish doesn't destroy hope, it kindles it. Yes, sometimes hope is destroyed in happiness, but not in misery.

That is why the hope of princes like Mahavira and Buddha was destroyed, but the hope of beggars is never destroyed. All the twenty-four *tirthankaras* of the Jainas were princes, all twenty-four buddhas of the Buddhists were princes, all the *avataras* of the Hindus were princes. What can be the reason?

The irony is that hope can disappear in happiness but it does not disappear in unhappiness. Hope *should* disappear in unhappiness, hope should disappear in misery, but the fact is that as the misery increases the mind goes on creating more and more hope. Hope sprouts in misery, hope blossoms in misery, but is destroyed in happiness.

That is why the society which is happy becomes religious. The society which is unhappy can become communist, but it cannot become religious. There is a possibility of America becoming religious, but India cannot. India was religious when it was happy, when the country was happy. When its people were satisfied and contented hope disappeared.

When you have everything then you realize that it is all futile. And this is right, because how can you see the futility of something which you don't have? The person who has money can see the futility of money. But the person who doesn't have money, how can he see its futility? To realize the futility of anything, one has to have it first.

A person who has knowledge can see the futility of knowledge, but a person who doesn't have knowledge cannot see the futility of it. If you have the Kohinoor diamond in your hand you realize its futility – you cannot eat it or drink it. But if you don't have it, then you can go on dreaming about it. Dreams are never futile – you have no way of discovering their worth. You cannot see the uselessness of anything until you possess it.

Hope lives in unhappiness, gets nurtured by it, but is destroyed in happiness. That is why a man on the roadside may be suffering and going through hell, yet he goes on hoping. If you ever visit hell you will find there the most hopeful people in this world. In spite of their agonies they go on hoping that they will be free of this tomorrow.

I have heard that a new prisoner came into a prison. He was taken to a cell where another prisoner was already living. That person asked him how long he was going to be in the prison. The new prisoner replied, "For ten years."

He said, "Then you had better stay near the door, because I will be imprisoned for thirty years. I will stay near the wall. You be near the door as you will be going soon. You are here for only ten years."

Even in prison one goes on hoping for the day when he will be set free. People go on living hoping for that day.

THE BONDAGE OF HOPE

You must understand one thing in life: watch carefully the happiness which you have, for it is only out of happiness that you can be free. If you have a beautiful wife then you must enjoy beauty thoroughly; if you have money then you must taste it properly; if you have position, observe it from all sides. You must watch carefully whatever you have, only then can hope be destroyed. And if you observe what you don't have, hope will never be destroyed.

Religion cannot enter into the life of a person whose hope is not yet destroyed. Hope is the door of irreligiousness; the annihilation of hope is the entry of religion. And you should also know that the annihilation of hope is not hopelessness. The loss of hope is hopelessness: hope is still quite alive in hopelessness. One may feel hopeless now, but after a moment he will again be hopeful. Hopelessness is the defeated aspect of hope. It is the tired, exhausted hope. It is not destroyed hope, it is fallen hope. When hope is destroyed, then hopelessness also disappears.

Because of this Mahavira and Buddha seem to be pessimistic to the Western mind because they ask you to give up hope. They are being misunderstood. Mahavira and Buddha are not pessimistic; they are neither optimistic nor pessimistic. They say that when hope gets annihilated, hopelessness also disappears by itself because hopelessness is the shadow of hope.

Your shadow is cast when you walk in the sun. If you don't walk in the sun then the shadow will not be cast. When hope is not there at all, hopelessness disappears automatically. The more you hope, the more hopeless or disappointed you will be, the more unhappy and miserable you will be. Then new hope is born out of hopelessness and this game goes on like day and night.

If hope breaks, then there is neither hope nor hopelessness. Then you are at peace. The light of your consciousness goes on wavering with the strong wind of hope and hopelessness. When there is no hope and no hopelessness, then the strong wind stops blowing and the consciousness becomes stable, unwavering and steadfast. That stability, that steadfastness is very fortunate.

That steadfastness is *samadhi*.

> Struck by the cold,
> in the morning he warms himself
> by keeping the fire in front of him
> or by keeping his back towards the sun.
> At night he sleeps with his chin between his knees,
> he takes alms on his hands and lives under a tree;
> even then he does not drop the bondage of hope.

Therefore,

> Oh fool! Always sing the song of the divine.

> He may undertake the journey
> to the Ganges or to the ocean,
> he may undertake many austerities and fasts,
> he may give away in charity,
> but if he does not have self-knowledge
> he will not be liberated
> even in hundreds of lifetimes.

Try to understand this:

> He may undertake the journey
> to the Ganges or to the ocean,
> he may undertake many austerities and fasts,
> he may give away in charity,
> but if he does not have self-knowledge
> he will not be liberated...

...Because it is easy to do these things – to fast, to give in charity, to live in discipline, to live by rules and regulations and in austerity. They are easy because actions are always easy. You don't change and the action is done.

THE BONDAGE OF HOPE

Self-knowledge is difficult because knowledge means transformation. Knowledge means that you have to change, the way of consciousness has to change. The meaning of knowledge is that the movement and the direction of your consciousness should change. The meaning of meditation, the meaning of knowledge, is that your consciousness should not waver; it should be unwavering, stable and steadfast. It is difficult.

It is easy to *do* something. If you eat more, then you are troubling your body; if you fast, even then you are troubling your body. There is no difference between these two conditions. First you were troubling the body by eating more, now you are troubling it by fasting. You go on collecting money, you can give it up also. You will know the futility of money only after you have collected it. Is it very revolutionary to give away in charity something which is useless?

There is a story in the Kathopanishad – because of that story, that Upanishad is called Kathopanishad; *katha* means story. Nachiketa's father performed a big *yajna*, a religious ritual. After the yajna he gave away many gifts.

Nachiketa was a small child. He was sitting near and asking his father again and again, "Will you give away everything?"

The father said, "Whatever I have I shall give. Everything will be given in charity."

Nachiketa saw that his father was giving away only the cows which were incapable of giving milk. People usually give away such things in charity which have become useless. The father was distributing with enthusiasm and pleasure things which were of no use. Nachiketa's intellect was fresh, the father's intellect was old. So what Nachiketa could see, the father couldn't see. Nachiketa said, "What is the use of giving these cows who stopped giving milk long ago? The poor brahmins, to whom you are giving them, will have to take the trouble of feeding them. This is not a good deed at all." The father told him to keep quiet.

But just like a little child Nachiketa went on asking him, "If you are giving away everything of yours, then to whom are you going to give me? To whom will you give me?"

When he asked this question several times, the father became very annoyed and said, "I will give you to death."

Man gives whatever is useless; you also distribute those things which are of no use to you. I see that a few things keep on rotating – they keep on going from one person to another. They are of no use to anyone, so people go on distributing them. You give it to someone, then he passes it on to another person. It is just giving for the sake of giving.

A friend of Mulla Nasruddin gave him a bottle of alcohol. Later on he asked him, "How was it?"

Mulla Nasruddin said, "Almost alright."

The friend asked, "What do you mean by *almost* alright? Either it is good or it is not good."

Mulla said, "No, it was *almost* alright. If it had been absolutely good then you would not have given it to me, and if it was less then alright then I would have given it away to someone else. It was almost alright, so I drank it."

Like this, such things are given which have no value. You give away in charity that which is useless. You don't have to make much effort to fast – it is only a little trouble to the body. You can do austerities also because it satisfies your ego. But the one and only revolution is the revolution of self-knowledge. Nobody can be free without that revolution.

Self-knowledge is the only liberation. Knowledge is salvation.

But knowledge doesn't mean knowledge of the scriptures, because that is very easy. It is easier even than fasting and charity. There is no difficulty in reading the scriptures and there is no difficulty in filling the mind with scriptures. You can memorize the Gita even when there is no song in your life. But when there is no inner harmony in you how can you sing the song of the divine? Yes, the Gita can be memorized without having any song within you.

When the inner music is so deep that you are absolutely lost in it, only then that music, that song, becomes the song of the divine. Then one doesn't remember or think of Krishna and Arjuna or the words of the Gita; you become what is said in the Gita. You yourself become that. Then there is no need to remember all that garbage. Scriptures are valuable for those who are interested in collecting garbage, but scriptures have no value for those who themselves have become scriptures. You cannot gain knowledge until you yourself become scriptures. You will have knowledge when every gesture of yours indicates truth. Even the winking of the eyes, this small gesture too will express the truth. Whether you speak or you don't speak, truth will be expressed through you.

You may undertake the journey to the Ganges.... Poor Ganges! Why do you bother it?

Someone asked Ramakrishna, "I am going to bathe in the Ganges. Do you think that by bathing in the Ganges all the sins are washed away?"

Ramakrishna was a very simple person. He said, "Certainly they get washed away when you bathe in the Ganges. When you dip yourself into it, the sins get separated from you and they go and sit on the top of the trees which are on the banks of the Ganges. But after the bath, when you come out of the Ganges, these sins jump back on you from those trees. They had to leave you because of the Ganges, not because of you. If you don't come out of the Ganges, if you remain in it for ever, only then can you be free of the sins."

That man said, "But I will have to come out at some time."

"Then there's no point in your going there," Ramakrishna said.

The Ganges will free you of your sins? But if *you* have done the sins, how will the Ganges free you from those sins? If the Ganges goes on freeing people of all their sins, then the Ganges itself will become very sinful because then it will be burdened with all the sins made by all the people.

Man goes on looking for excuses. Man sins, then tries to find some excuse so that his conscience may not prick him. By taking a dip in the Ganges he feels free of the sin and is again ready to sin. He will sin again and will again bathe in the Ganges. The Ganges did not free you from the sin; actually it made you an expert in sinning, because you found a cheap way of getting rid of it. You didn't have to pay much. The real journey is not very costly – and then most pilgrims travel without tickets, they are not bothered about paying money for the tickets. When so many sins are being washed away by the Ganges, then one more sin will not matter.

> He may undertake the journey to the Ganges or to
> the ocean, he may undertake many
> austerities and fasts, he may give away in charity,
> but if he does not have self-knowledge
> he will not be liberated
> even in hundreds of lifetimes.

Therefore,

> Oh fool! Always sing the song of the divine.
>
> One may be residing in the temple of God or under
> a tree, the earth may be his only bed,
> deerskin his only robe, he may have dropped
> all kinds of possessions and indulgences
> – who would not be made blissful
> by such a renunciation?

This is a very important statement. Shankara is raising a very serious problem. He is saying that if you have really renounced, then the proof of your renunciation will be your bliss. Bliss will prove whether your renunciation was true or not.

If the renouncer seems unhappy, then it means that his renunciation was false. If you say that you have lit a lamp in your house and still it is dark, then your lamp is false. If the lamp is lit, then there will be light in the whole house.

Shankara is saying that if you are living in a temple or under a tree and you are unhappy and sad, then you have not reached the temple yet, then you have not known the deity of the temple yet. *The earth may be his only bed....* One who is so free that the sky becomes his covering and the ground becomes his bed – that is why Mahavira was called Digambara. The sky became his cover and the earth became his bed.

When, *the earth may be his only bed and the deerskin his only robe, he may have dropped all kinds of possessions and indulgences – who would not be made blissful by such a renunciation?*

Blissfulness is the measuring rod. There is no other proof of your renunciation except bliss. Your bliss will prove whether your renunciation is true or false.

You may give up your home, your money, you may become naked, you may shave your head or keep long hair, you may wear ochre robes and go to the Himalayas or sit on the bank of the Ganges, but if you are not happy, if you are not blissful, then all these things are nothing but a deception. You may look like gold but you are not gold, you are just brass. Just as gold can be tested, your renunciation also can be tested by your bliss. True renunciation means bliss and the worldly enjoyment means misery. A blissful person proves that his renunciation is true and unhappiness, misery, is the result of the worldly enjoyment.

That is why Shankara says:

> He may be absorbed
> in the enjoyment of senses or in yoga,
> he may be engrossed with somebody's company
> or he may be alone,
> but if his heart dwells in the divine,

> then it is he who is blissful,
> it is he who is blissful, it is he alone who is blissful.

Then it doesn't make any difference whether he is living in the home or out of the home, whether he is sitting on a throne or on a stone on a mountain, whether he is absorbed in the enjoyment of the senses or in yoga, whether he is with someone or alone, whether he is in the company of the family or of the society or alone, whether he is in a palace or in a cottage.

> ...if his heart dwells in the divine,
> then it is he who is blissful,
> it is he who is blissful, it is he alone who is blissful.

Therefore,

> Oh fool! Always sing the song of the divine.

Dwelling in the divine, in *brahman*. The definition of brahman is *satchitananda* – to be engrossed in truth, in consciousness and in bliss.

One who is authentic, and who is the same from inside and outside; who tastes the same within and without; who is truth and consciousness; who is awakened and is not unconscious; who is blissful and who is full of the fragrance of the divine; whose very breathing is full of music; whose movements are like a dance; whose presence reminds you of the divine – if you go near him his coolness affects you, his bliss starts dancing in you. All your misery disappears by looking at him. His blessing means the attainment of everything. When you feel this, when you feel deep contentment, then that is the proof of his being engrossed in brahman, of being in a deep embrace with the divine.

There is a very interesting thing. You must have seen the image of Mahavira – he is very blissful. You must have seen his body also. But look at the Jaina muni. He looks so unhappy, so miserable. There is no bliss showering from him; he looks sad. It seems as if the bud has not blossomed into a flower, it has shrunk. But you say that this shrinking is renunciation. He doesn't bathe, he doesn't brush his teeth, so he smells of sweat and his mouth stinks and he thinks that this is renunciation. When you are with him you will never feel like dancing out of joy; when you are with him you will never hear the song of the divine music of the flute which you had never heard before. Rather, you will feel a little restless when you come back after seeing him. Perhaps his presence will create self-condemnation in you; perhaps in his presence you will feel that you are a sinner. But his presence will not make you aware of the divine within you.

And that is the difference – with the real sannyasin you will not feel self-condemnation, you will feel happy and joyful. With the real sannyasin you will feel gratitude. The real sannyasin will never show you your darkness, he will indicate the light which is within you. You may be a great sinner but the real sannyasin will never give you any hint about your sins because that is not worth talking about; that topic is worthless, meaningless. The glory within you is the real thing.

You are a sinner because you have not known your inner glory up till now. If you are made more aware of your sins then your inner glory will get even more suppressed. No, these sins are like the dream of the night. They are meaningless. You should be able to remember the godliness within you. But only that person can make you remember the divine, can remind you of the divine, who is in the deep embrace of brahman. In his presence someone within you will start waking up. In his presence – just as the peacocks start dancing when the sky is full of clouds – the same way in his presence....

Buddha has said that the inner peacocks of many people start dancing when someone's inner space is full of the clouds of the ultimate. Yes, you will dance in his presence. You must know that where you experience the bliss that is the abode of brahman, that is the temple.

> He may be absorbed in the enjoyment of the senses
> or in yoga, he may be engrossed in somebody's
> company or he may be alone,
> but if his heart dwells in the divine,
> then it is he who is blissful, it is he who is blissful,
> it is he alone who is blissful.

And that is the aim, that is the destination which has to be approached from all sides.

Therefore,

> Oh fool! Always sing the song of the divine.
> Sing the song of the divine,
> sing the song of the divine.
> Oh fool!

Enough for today.

6

THE GREAT TRANSCENDENCE

The first question:

> Beloved Osho,
> You have said many times that a dialogue is not possible through debate. But Shankara announced his universal victory and defeated innumerable intellectuals in a debate on the meaning of the scriptures. After the defeat, they had to become Shankara's disciples. Please explain what kind of debate on the scriptures this was.

Through argument and debate, through logic and debate, dialogue is never possible. Dialogue means the talk of two hearts; debate means the conflict of two intellects. Dialogue means the meeting of two individuals; debate means the conflict of two individuals. Nobody is defeated in a dialogue, both win; in a debate both are defeated, nobody wins.

But there was no other alternative for Shankara — he had to debate, because at that time only after the debate was dialogue possible. Shankara did not debate to explain truth. The fact was that people were so full of their own intellect, their ego, their scholarliness, that they were not ready to listen to any talk of the heart till their scholarliness and intellect were defeated. Shankara did not explain truth to them by debating, he destroyed their ego by the debate. And dialogue is only possible with that person who is ready to bow down.

Shankara's debating the scriptures was only negative; it was like taking out a thorn with another thorn. A mind which is full of logic can only understand the language of logic. A mind full of scholarliness can only understand the language of scholarliness. It cannot even hear the language of love, and even if it hears it, it cannot understand the meaning — and there is just no question of understanding the language of silence.

The scholarliness of this country was at its zenith when Shankara was born: that very scholarliness has ruined this country. It had just got stuck in the head and there was no way to reach the heart. To reach the heart, first it was necessary to cut off the heads. This disease was so acute that it could not be treated by medicines, so an operation was needed.

So Shankara had to debate, he was compelled to debate. Shankara is not at all the debating or argumentative type. It is just not possible for Shankara to be argumentative. He is not interested in logic at all; otherwise he couldn't have sung songs like Bhaj Govindam. He wanted to sing the songs of the divine from his very heart. If the time had been ripe, if the people could have understood the language of the heart, then Shankara would not have argued or debated at all. If he had got the opportunity, he would have danced.

But the country was sick; scholarliness was at its climax, people's heads were really heavy with learning and knowledge, so it was necessary to remove that useless weight from their heads. And scholarliness can only understand argument. Scholars may listen to the language of the heart after being defeated by logic. So Shankara defeated them in debate.

And remember, that a person who has known the truth can utilize logic in a right way, but logic can be dangerous if used by a person who doesn't know truth. Logic is the end, logic is everything for the one who doesn't know truth, but the one who knows truth can use logic in the service of truth; one who knows truth can make logic the servant. Truth can ride on logic also. Usually logic is like a sword in the hands of children, they will harm others and harm themselves with it. But a person with knowledge can use logic in a sensible way – like a grown-up person using the sword. He will not harm anyone with it, but will protect others from any mishap.

Shankara made the right use of logic. If used properly, even poison can become medicine. An intelligent person can always turn the poison into medicine, and Shankara did utilize logic in the service of truth. He toured the whole of the country – he went from one corner to the other. He debated and he used logic; he argued with people whose sick minds could not go beyond the intellect and who had forgotten the language of the heart. He debated whenever he saw that some genius was lost in words and could not find the door to truth. He argued with people who were overburdened with scriptures and who were struggling to come out of it. It was only the prologue.

Whenever someone was defeated in the debate of the meaning of the scriptures, at once Shankara made him a disciple. The real, important thing is this: as soon as someone was defeated in argument, Shankara utilized his defeat. In the moment of that defeat, when the individual was stunned, when his ego was shattered, when his intellect and his logic didn't work, when he became helpless and started sinking, Shankara at once put the other boat in front of him. "If the boat of your logic is sinking, let it sink. I have got another boat, the boat of the heart – the boat of love, the boat of devotion."

During such moments he must have sung: *Oh fool! Sing the*

THE GREAT TRANSCENDENCE

song of the divine, sing the song of the divine, sing the song of the divine. He has called these *pundits*, fools. You must understand that he debated so that your foolishness could be cut off. All illusions disappear as soon as your foolishness is destroyed. He utilized that moment of transition when your mind becomes thoughtless – when all the clouds disappear and for the first time you are looking at the open sky. Shankara didn't debate to explain truth, by debate he removed the clouds so that the sun of truth could be seen.

There is no need to prove truth, it is proof in itself. It is self-evident. And remember, that if anything has to be proved by logic, it can be disproved also by logic. Logic is only a play, it is not a strength. Anything which is proved by logic can be disproved by logic. Logic is just like a lawyer, logic is like a prostitute, it is not attached to anyone – it can take any side, it can be used on both sides, for and against anything. Just as a sword doesn't belong to anyone, logic also doesn't belong to anyone. Your own sword can be used by your enemy to cut your throat. You cannot say, "It is my sword, how can it cut my throat?" The sword belongs to no one. Similarly, logic too belongs to no one. That is why people who depend too much on logic will find one day that it is not dependable at all. One day, they will realize that they were riding a paper boat. One day they will discover that the logic which acted as a support for them to stand became the cause of their downfall.

If you believe in God, you say that there must be someone who created this world. Your logic is that this world must have been created by someone, so there should be a God. But then the other argument is: Who made God? ...Because how can God exist without being created? There is no difference between the two arguments. One believes in God, and the other is an atheist. But I see no difference between the two, because both of them depend on the logic that how can anything exist without being created?

You get annoyed with an atheist and you tell him, "Keep

quiet! Nobody has made God." But the atheist is only saying that if God can exist without being made, why can't the world exist without being made? The logic is the same, the argument is the same, so nobody wins.

Nothing is ever proved by logic. What is, is beyond logic; what is, is self-evident. But if you go to Shankara with logic, he will counter all your logic. There are very few people who are as logical as Shankara. You can meet people who have known the divine — like Ramakrishna — but such people are rare who have known the divine and can counter the arguments of the atheist. Ramakrishna could not counter the argument of an atheist. He didn't know logic; he was a simple and pure person. Vivekananda could counter the logic, but Vivekananda doesn't have any experience of truth. People like Shankara are unique. He has in him the qualities of Ramakrishna and Vivekananda both. He has known just as Ramakrishna has known, and he can use arguments in favor of what he has known, just as Vivekananda can do without knowing.

But Shankara has been misunderstood. The irony is that all his life Shankara tried to destroy the egos of the pundits, and those very pundits took him to be a pundit also! These pundits go on saying that Shankara conquered all. Shankara must be having a hearty laugh at this. The victory of logic is no victory at all. To defeat anyone with logic means nothing. If anyone is defeated in argument he just keeps quiet, he doesn't feel defeated at heart.

If you put a lot of arguments before someone, he may not be able to reply to you in the same way so he will keep quiet at that time, but in his mind he will go on waiting to take his revenge on you. To defeat someone with logic is like using the sword to make him surrender. He will surrender for the time being, but will wait for the right time to take his revenge. One who is defeated with a sword is not defeated at all. Only the one who is defeated with love is really defeated, because no other surrender is meaningful until you surrender from the heart.

So Shankara defeated with logic those people who existed on

logic. He cut down logic with logic. But in that moment of defeat Shankara told them, "Your logic is futile, my logic is also futile. I took out your thorn with my thorn, but my thorn is not more valuable than yours. And don't try to keep my thorn in your wound, otherwise this will also cause you as much pain as your thorn was giving you. It is better to throw away both these thorns."

This was the meaning of being his disciple: to move away from the intellect and come down to the heart. Truth has to be sought not with thinking, but with feeling. Truth has to be discovered not with logic, scriptures and principles, but with an open heart. When the flower of the heart blossoms, then the sun of truth shines on it. The rays of truth dance on the blossoming flower of the heart. This was the meaning of discipleship. But those who could not understand this, were made to understand in their own language by Shankara.

Shankara is a unique person. And it is very easy to misunderstand the unique person because he is beyond your common understanding. It seemed to people that he was also a logician, a great logician. But can a great logician say, "Sing! Dance! Sing the song of the divine"? It is just not possible for the logician to say so. Such words can be spoken only by a lover of the divine from the depths of his heart. So remember this.

"You have said many times that a dialogue is not possible through debate." It is never possible. Shankara cleaned the ground for dialogue, by logic and debate. You were full of debate, so he humbled you with debate. You were full of arguments, so he humbled you with arguments. He cleared the ground with these, then sowed the seeds of love and devotion.

Many people have been thinking that Shankara is contradictory. He is not contradictory. He seems contradictory, in the same way as when you see someone in your neighborhood demolishing his house. It takes him months to demolish it and then to clear the debris; then he lays the foundation and he builds a new house. Will you call this person contradictory? One day he demolishes his house, and the next day he builds it. It may seem contradictory, but you know that if a new house is to be constructed then the old one has to be demolished. There is no contradiction in this contradiction. The new house can be built only after demolishing the old one.

Shankara is not contradictory, he is fighting logic with logic. When the old house is demolished, then he gives the invitation to dance. You will say that this is contradictory – first he talks about thought and logic, then he talks about love and dance.

No, he used logic to destroy the old and then built the new with emotion. He cleared the ground with logic and then sowed the seeds of love. There is no contradiction.

You say, "But Shankara announced his universal victory." This announcement also was not made by Shankara; this announcement was made by the people who were following Shankara, but couldn't understand him. You cannot understand anyone just by following. It is very easy to follow anyone, but it is difficult to be a disciple. It is very easy to follow or to copy others, but it is difficult to understand someone and then to develop your life according to that understanding.

So those who followed Shankara announced his universal victory. They are still doing so. The Shankaracharya of Puri is still doing so, Karpatri is still doing so. They still go on saying that Shankara defeated the whole world. The Shankaracharya of Puri still says that he is *jagat* guru, master of the world. This is not Shankara's announcement, because Shankara knew that nobody wins and nobody is defeated with logic – it only means that the other person's logic was weaker than yours and you were more skilled, but tomorrow the other person can also become more skilled in logic.

Shankara knew that the victory of logic and argument was no victory, it was only a deception. And Shankara was not attempting to defeat anyone with logic. His attempt is unique, but this unique attempt cannot be seen by those who are following him, they will only see that he defeated another man.

Those who are following him can only understand the language of the ego. They cannot see that actually Shankara didn't defeat the person but made him victorious, he brought him on the path of the heart. The person was losing, sinking deep into logic – Shankara saved him, and showed him the path of victory. Now that person will be victorious.

That is why people like Kumaril Bhatt, who was defeated by Shankara, became his disciple – he didn't become his disciple in misery and anguish. If Kumaril Bhatt had become a disciple after being defeated, then it would have hurt his ego and he would have tried to take the revenge for his defeat. Kumaril was as great a logician as Shankara. By debating with Shankara, Kumaril realized that debating was futile. Shankara was not victorious, Kumaril was not defeated. Logic was defeated and emotion won.

It is necessary to understand this. By debating with Shankara, by playing with an expert player, Kumaril saw clearly that those things which he depended on fell down with just the blowing of a breeze. This doesn't mean that he accepted Shankara's logic. Shankara's skill is only that, through debate, he shows you that your arguments are futile, that my arguments are futile: logic becomes meaningless. Neither Kumaril was defeated nor Shankara won – *logic* was defeated. Because this defeat of logic came through the medium of Shankara, Kumaril bowed and fell down at his feet.

Those debates were full of sweetness, those debates were full of love, there was no bitterness in them. They were not fighting like enemies, it was like playing chess: an army of arguments was put at stake. Kumaril prepared the best of his logic and the best of his intellect, and Shankara went on destroying all his arguments one by one. He didn't try to put his own argument in Kumaril's mind, he just went on negating Kumaril's arguments until a space was left, and in that space discipleship was born. The opponent saw that the person standing in front of him had not brought any theory but truth: "He has destroyed all my arguments, but has not established any new argument in their place." Empty space was left. There was an interval, there was emptiness, there was void. In that state, meditation happened. In that moment of meditation, he bowed down. Don't think that he bowed down before Shankara; he bowed down before the truth which was expressed through Shankara. Shankara was only an image, a symbol. Kumaril was bowing down before truth. Kumaril was bowing down not because he was defeated, but because he was awakened.

But those people who were standing behind, all they saw was that he was defeated and was bowing down. The people who followed him announced that "Shankara has become victorious, he has defeated the world." Because of these stupid people, Shankara's image was polluted. The unique approach of Shankara was lost and instead of it a very ordinary tradition, a narrow path, came into existence. The vast path of the open sky was lost – that openness was lost. Therefore you will find that if a *sannyasin* of Shankara's is a logician, he will not accept Bhaj Govindam and such things.

There are people who say that songs like Bhaj Govindam were not written by Shankara, that they were written by others and are given the name of Shankara. They say, "How can Shankara write such songs?" Yes, Meera could write such songs, Chaitanya could write such songs, but how could Shankara write them? ...because he was a sharp logician, it was not possible for him to sing such devotional songs. These people say that those songs have been made by others who have taken advantage of Shankara's name. They think that these songs are not authentic, and they believe in arguments which really have no value.

Shankara used logic to destroy the old building, and gave these songs to construct the new building. This process of his is not contradictory; if you think so, then you will not be able to understand him.

Shankara never announced his universal victory. Those who know truth are not ambitious, those who know truth are not egoist. Such announcements of victory are very childish – little children indulge in such things. Who is there to win and who is there to lose? Shankara sees that there is only the divine: the multiplicity of things is an illusion, unity is the truth. Who will win and who will lose? If anyone wins, it is only the divine who will win, and if anyone loses, it is only the divine who will be defeated. When it is he who is winning and it is he who is losing, then who is going to announce the universal victory? No, Shankara could not make this mistake, and if he has made it, then he has no value. Shankara has awakened, and not defeated others.

No, Shankara made innumerable intellectuals really intelligent. Before this they had been involved with false intellect; they were taking care of bad coins. Now they were shown the real coins. You can only make out the bad coin after seeing the real one; there is no other way to prove that a bad coin is bad. Shankara showed the real coins and then the bad coins could be recognized. These debates were not like those which are popular now in the West. These debates were also not like the ones which go on in the East these days. These debates were very sweet. These were the debates of the seekers of truth.

There are two types of debates: one is that whatever you say is correct because you are saying it – because you cannot be wrong. Whatever you say it doesn't matter, but it has to be correct because you have said it. This type of debate is futile, useless. If you are seeking truth, then you don't insist that what you say is correct. Then you say that from whatever you have known up to now, this seems correct to you: "I am ready to know more if there is anything more to be known. I am open, I am not closed. I have not yet arrived at any conclusion. But up to now, wherever I have searched, this seems to be the most truthful. But if truth is revealed to me, I am ready to accept it and be transformed and to give up whatever I knew before this." Then debate becomes the process of approaching truth.

The East has utilized this type of debate. This tradition is thousands of years old. In seeking the truth, intellectuals used to think over and debate – not because they had found the truth, but because they were searching for it. This continued for thousands of years. Whenever a person showed the other's untruth, then he had the courage to bow down at that person's feet because in the search for truth whosoever showed it was the master. So those who were defeated by Shankara became his disciples.

Discipleship means: You have taken me one step farther than where I was, you have made me see farther than where my eyes could see, you have made me see the open sky by carrying me on your shoulders.

The search for truth is an absolutely different thing. If the aim is the search for truth, then debate can also be utilized. That is why I say that even poison can become medicine.

There have been debates in the West also, but they are not like the ones in the East. In the West they go on fighting, debating, and it can never be judged who has won and who has lost. They have never become anyone's disciples.

Shankara traveled to Mandala, Mandan Mishra's city; Mandala was named after Mandan. As he entered the city he asked the women at the well, "Where is Mandan Mishra's house?"

They laughed and said, "You don't have to ask this, because you will be able to recognize it yourself. The very atmosphere of that house will tell you. Even the parrots in the cage hanging in front of the house recite the words of the Upanishads. The aura of that house is ancient and sacred." The women laughed and said, "Stranger, you will be able to locate that house. Nobody needs to ask for it."

Shankara arrived at the house. It was true, the birds were singing at the door and they were reciting words from the Upanishads and the Vedas. Shankara went inside, and invited Mandan Mishra to debate with him.

Mandan Mishra was a very famous man. He was older than Shankara, and his prestige and fame were much more than those of Shankara. He also had more disciples than Shankara did. Shankara invited him to a debate on the search for truth. They welcomed him and made him stay in the house. He was not an enemy. Mandan was more than fifty years old at that time, and Shankara was about thirty years old. So Mandan said, "I am much more experienced than you. You are young. I am of your father's age, so we are not equal – this debate is not equal. So I give you the advantage of choosing the judge. You are young, so you choose the judge – he will decide who has won and who has lost."

This was not a fight at all, it was a very loving contest. The older person welcomed the younger one like his own son, and gave him an advantage also. Shankara looked around for a judge who could be of the same repute as Mandan, but couldn't find one. So he decided on Mandan's wife, whose name was Bharati. Shankara said, "Your wife will make the judgment."

Do you think that this is a fight? This is not the language of enemies. If the wife is to make the judgment, then there is the possibility of her taking the side of her husband. This is quite natural if the debate is based on enmity. But this debate was for the search for truth, and was full of love.

The wife became the judge, and after the debate she gave the judgement that Mandan had lost and Shankara had won. Bharati then said, "But wait, this defeat is incomplete. You have defeated only one half of Mandan – I am his other half. You now have to debate with me." This sounded like a joke, but it was a sweet fact – the wife being the other half of the husband, only half of Mandan had been defeated and now the other half, the wife, had to be defeated. This wife who gave the judgment of her husband's defeat must have been unique. She said to Shankara, "Your victory is incomplete. You have to defeat me too to make it complete."

Shankara agreed to debate with Bharati. But he found he couldn't reply to the questions asked by her, because she did not ask any question regarding *brahman*, or knowledge of brahman.

He had already defeated Mandan on that topic. She had understood from the debate with Mandan that it was useless to talk to this young man about brahman. She thought: "This young-looking person is actually a very ancient being."

And Mandan certainly knew more than Bharati. That is why Bharati had fallen in love with him, married him, and was looking after him. She had seen him defeated by Shankara on the subject of brahman, so she asked Shankara questions regarding sex. Shankara was young. He was thirty years old and was unmarried.

He found himself in a difficult situation. He said, "I want six months' time to reply to these questions because I am unmarried, a celibate – I don't know love, I don't know sex. So if I reply now it will not be from my own experience, and the answers which are not based on experience cannot be true or correct. Just as Mandan has lost by talking about brahman based on his knowledge of the scriptures, the same way, I can also talk about sex based on my knowledge of the scriptures and I am sure to be defeated, because I have no experience of sex. You will win because you are experienced. I have only heard about it, mine is only second-hand knowledge. So I need six months' time to have that experience. After that I shall be able to answer your questions."

These debates were really full of love and affection. Bharati said, "Alright, you go for six months, gain the experience and come back."

It is a strange story. Shankara was in a great dilemma. He had taken the vow of celibacy – he had given this promise to his master. Now if he gets married or he looks out for a woman then the whole pattern of his life will change. So, according to the story, Shankara left his own body and entered another dead body. A king was dying, so Shankara entered his body and stayed in that body for six months to understand the needs of the body and the meaning of sex. When he came back after six months Bharati looked at him and said, "There is no need of debate now. You have known it. I am ready to be your disciple." Mandan and Bharati became Shankara's disciples.

These incidents showed they were full of love and regard for each other; there was no enmity between them. Not that Shankara defeated intellectuals – he gave real intelligence to these intellectuals and he shook and awakened the defeated ones, he gave light to the people who were living in darkness. And the people who bowed down at his feet didn't do so out of any humiliation; they bowed down out of gratitude and thankfulness.

You say, "After the defeat they had to become Shankara's disciples." Don't say "had to." We are in the habit of using the language of the ego. Even if Shankara had refused they would have become his disciples. Not "had to" – they became disciples with gratitude and with great joy. That bowing down was not done on being defeated. That bowing down was out of a deep understanding. That was surrender and not defeat; they found happiness in bowing down at his feet. This bowing down gave them self-respect. In this bowing down they understood the meaning of life for the first time, in this bowing down they found the first glimpse of the divine.

Don't use the words "had to bow down." They bowed down out of gratitude, out of bliss, out of thankfulness.

The second question:

> Beloved Osho,
> The fall of an ordinary person can be understood, but how can the fall be possible of a seeker who is treading the path of renunciation, detachment and austerity?

An ordinary person cannot fall down. Where will he fall? Where can a person fall who is walking on even ground? Only a person who is trying to climb the summit of the mountain can fall down. You need mountain peaks to fall down – and there are hidden abysses and ditches near the mountain peaks.

But how can a person walking on the flat, even ground, on the main road, fall down? Where will he fall down to? He has already fallen down. An ordinary person cannot fall because there is nowhere for him to fall. So you have not understood what you have said: "The fall of an ordinary person can be understood." How can an ordinary person fall down? – because he is living at the point from where no more falling is possible. He is living at the zero degree. He is already living in the abyss.

Only extraordinary people fall down – only those who try to reach the mountain peaks, those who accept the challenges of the heights, those who are not ready to live in the abyss, who say that their life is meaningless until they have reached the golden mountain peaks; who don't accept to live in the darkness of the abyss, who say, "We will fly in the sky and we will go on a faraway journey." The longer the journey, the greater is the danger of falling down.

We have a word *yoga bhrashta*, one who has fallen from yoga. Have you ever heard the word *bhoga bhrashta*, one who has fallen from indulgence? There is no meaning to bhoga bhrashta. Yoga bhrashta is meaningful; it means that the attempt to climb the height was made, but one missed it.

With climbing there is always the danger of missing. Perhaps that is why many people don't try to climb the heights at all. They forget the heights. They take the abyss to be the height. In fact, they don't look at the peaks, because by looking at them they may have to accept the challenge.

I have heard that in countries where the mountain birds come from faraway places, the pet birds also start feeling like taking the challenge. Ducks from Siberia come to spend the winter in the southern parts of Europe. When the winter is over these ducks go back. The domestic ducks were also wild and free a few generations ago, so when the flocks of wild ducks begin to go back, and the ducks in the farms and fields see them flying in the sky, they also start fluttering their wings, they also try to fly for a few feet and then they fall down. Their wings are no longer strong, but when they see these mountain birds — birds like themselves flying, then something in them gives them the challenge and then they also remember the height of the sky and the unknown country. There is a very faint remembrance of Siberia in their minds. Though they fall down, yet they do try to fly.

Whenever a Buddha or a Shankara passes among you, you also flutter your wings a little in your fields and in your barns because his presence wakes up the sound of some sleeping music in you. Then you know that you can also fly to those heights, that that is your destination also — but you flutter a little and then forget everything after falling down.

Or, those among you who are very cunning will say that this is just not possible. They don't look at Buddha at all. They keep their back towards him. They don't look at Buddha directly, they just listen to the rumors about him. They don't look into the eyes of Buddha because it is dangerous to do so. They sit in their shops and go on saying that all this is nonsense — nobody has ever realized the divine, there is no brahman; these are all tall tales to impress people. This man must have become mad, or this type of talk is very poetic.

They just cannot accept that there are such mountains, such heights, such virgin snow-clad peaks where few have ever reached, because they are afraid that if they believe it then they will also try to fly. But they have no confidence in their own wings. They go on doubting: Will they be able to fly? Will they be able to reach? Or will they fall down? With flying, there is the possibility of falling, there is the possibility of slipping while moving forwards. But the creatures who crawl on the land cannot fall — where will they fall to?

So don't say that you can understand the fall of an ordinary man. Have you ever heard of the fall of an ordinary person? Only the seeker who is treading the path of renunciation, detachment and austerity can fall down, and that danger becomes more and more as he is nearing his destination. Then there is danger at every inch. You may miss a little – and you will fall down. The miss is small, the fall is big. If you make a mistake it doesn't matter, but if Mahavira makes the same mistake then he will have a big fall. Your mistakes are of no consequence because you live in mistakes, but if that mistake is made by Buddha....

Buddha was passing through a village. Ananda was with him. A fly sat on his shoulder while he was talking, and he removed it just like anyone else. Then he stopped suddenly as if he had made a big mistake, then he raised his hand and very consciously he brought it towards the shoulder and removed the fly which was not there now.

Ananda asked him, "What are you doing?"

Buddha said, "I had removed the fly unconsciously, mechanically. I should have done it consciously." Even a fly should be removed consciously, because if the act of removing it is done unconsciously, then other things are also done unconsciously. There was nothing to be worried about – the fly had not died – there was no violence. But Buddha was certainly worried. Even this little black spot is too much on his white sheet.

But nothing is visible on your black sheet. That is why many people buy such clothes that the dirt is not visible on them. Even a small spot is visible on a white cloth. Buddha's white sheet shows the spot immediately. That is why even the fly has to be removed consciously.

At night Buddha slept only on one side. Ananda asked him one day, "Whenever I get up at night you are always sleeping on the same side. Even your hands don't move, they also remain in the same position. Do you sleep consciously? Don't you relax in your sleep?"

Buddha replied, "One who is awake doesn't sleep. One has to sleep consciously. I sleep, but someone within me is always awake, because if there is no wakefulness within then dreaming starts. And if dreaming goes on inside, then thoughts will go on during the daytime. If one is not awake at night, then it is difficult to be awake even during the daytime. Waking should be natural all the time – day and night. The inner flow of wakefulness should continue."

So even at night Buddha slept consciously, he kept his hands in the same position. He didn't let unconsciousness come in even in his sleep. For Buddha, unconsciousness in sleep means falling down. The danger of falling down goes on increasing as you come nearer to your destination. As the height increases, the way to the summit goes on becoming narrower and narrower. Right on the top of Gourishankar, Everest, only one man can stand – there is only that much space there.

Just recently, when an expedition of Japanese women went to Gourishankar, the Chinese claimed that their expedition of seven people had also reached Gourishankar just two days before them. The Japanese women refused to believe this claim from China, because seven people cannot stand there at one time.

The way to the summit goes on narrowing. This is your ordinary Gourishankar – what can you say about Buddha's peaks? – they become so narrow that even one person cannot stand. If you stand there with your ego then you will fall down; there you can stand only if you are absolutely empty. On that summit of fulfillment, of wholeness, only emptiness can stand. A little bit of ego will cause the fall.

Always remember that the danger of falling increases as you grow. But this challenge has to be accepted. This will show your inner strength and inner depth. It doesn't matter if you have to fall down a thousand times, but you have to reach the summit; you cannot be contented until you have reached there. You may gain other things, but you will remain a beggar until you realize the divine within you.

Happiness is not possible until you become that which you are ultimately capable of becoming, until your future becomes the present; you cannot be in ecstasy until all your flowers blossom. That is why for 'ecstasy,' in Hindi we use the word *prafullata*, which means the blossoming of the flower. This full blossoming is ecstasy. So never accept anything which is even a little less than this blossoming, otherwise you will remain unhappy and will live in hell.

An ordinary person doesn't fall down, but he lives in darkness, in pain, in misery. It is better to take the risk of falling – instead of living in misery, it is better to get one glimpse of happiness. Instead of crawling on the ground it is better to fly in the sky just once. By flying even once, you will get confidence in your wings. You will certainly fall and rise many times, but every fall is a lesson and every rise is a new strength. Your falling down now, means that in future your possibility of falling has become less because you will become an expert in rising.

The journey is long and the destination is the divine. Don't accept anything less, don't be satisfied sooner, and don't sit on the roadside with closed eyes imagining that you have already come to the destination. This journey is uncomfortable, so many people have done this…it is easy and convenient to sit by the roadside. To continue the journey means to stake yourself, to work hard, to labor. Life is a gamble and only big gamblers can reach the divine.

The third question:

> Beloved Osho,
> The so-called sannyasins are doing business in
> the name of religion. And you have told your
> sannyasins to continue their shops, their businesses.
> This seems contradictory. Please clarify.

There is no contradiction at all. The so-called sannyasins do business in the name of religion because they have been forced to give up their shops. They were not yet mature, they were still interested in running the shop but they were forced to sit down in the temple. So they turned the temple into a shop.

That is why I don't ask my sannyasins to give up their businesses or their shops. I say that if the temple has to be changed into a shop, then it is better to change the shop into a temple. I don't force them to give up their shops, because I have seen that such sannyasins turn the temple into a shop. It is futile to take you away from the shop or from business till you yourself have lost interest in it, and the moment you lose interest in the shop there will be no need to take you away from it – you yourself will turn the shop into a temple.

Remember, if a temple can turn into a shop, then why can't a shop turn into a temple? The process is the same in both cases. I insist on the second one: if you have to change, then change the shop into a temple. And if you still have an interest in the shop, in business, it just doesn't matter, please continue it; then at least the temple will not get polluted.

I want you to become mature. Be mature wherever you are. The basic thing is maturity. The most important fact of life is this, that if you are forced to give up something while you are immature, you may give it up physically, but mentally you will not be able to do so. Your mind will continue to desire the thing which you had to give up. So you may live or go anywhere, but that interest will create its own world. The seed is in your desire, not in your circumstances; it is in your mental conditioning.

Sannyas is the inner revolution. It is the declaration, "I am going to change myself from within." And I believe that it is more convenient to change in the marketplace than in the Himalayas, because every moment in the market there is a challenge, every moment there is a chance of falling down and every moment there is struggle where you cannot deceive yourself for long. The market is the mirror – every person whom you meet lights some corner of your mind.

Try to understand this. You will not be able to know many

things about yourself if you don't meet people. If you don't meet anyone who abuses you, then how can you know whether there is anger in you or not? If nobody insults you, then you will think that you are without anger. You will know the anger within you only when someone abuses you. So in one way the person who has abused you has helped you to understand yourself, he has helped you to realize that there is some anger within you which was kept suppressed. That dark corner came into the light with his abuse.

But the sannyasin who runs away to the jungle doesn't get these opportunities of understanding his inner characteristics because there he is alone, because there there is no one to abuse him, no one to give him respect, no one to entice him with money. No one gives him any opportunity – he is alone there. Self-observation becomes difficult.

This world is the place where you can observe and understand yourself. Otherwise, God would have made innumerable jungles, and would have kept one person in each jungle. But you will have to admit that the divine is more intelligent than you. Listen to him, and be careful of these so-called saints who are pretending to be even more intelligent than God. They are trying to be very clever. They say that they will do their *sadhana*, their spiritual practice, in the jungle.

But sadhana cannot be done in the jungle, it has to be in this world. You will only vegetate in a jungle. But here in this world thorns will prick you the moment you walk on them. When you walk on these thorns and they are not able to prick you, that means that now you have become capable of going to the jungle – now if you want to, you can go, then I will not stop you. But then you yourself will say that there is no need to go there – for me there is a jungle in the midst of this very crowd. Wisdom will be born when you become mature.

How is wisdom born? It is born out of conflict, it is born by accepting the challenges of life, by getting defeated, by falling down and by rising again. When you are abused a thousand times and you get angry a thousand times, a moment comes when you will not become angry at being abused. This experience of a thousand times will make you understand that there is no point in burning with anger – somebody else is abusing you, so "Why should I punish myself for that?" Then surely one day you will not react when somebody abuses you, you will not get angry.

That very day, the thorn in you will become a flower and you will be a changed person. The peace which you will experience that day cannot be given to you by any jungle.

The peace of a jungle is a dead peace. If you become peaceful amidst these abuses, then your peace is real peace. The peace of a jungle is like the peace of a graveyard: the place is quiet and deserted, there is no one. It is negative. If you become peaceful in this world, then it is positive. The peace of the jungle is like death, and the peace of the world is very lively.

I am telling you that if you want to attain the divine then don't run away. There can be no relationship of the divine with cowards or with escapists. The only path is the path of courage, and there is a possibility of falling down in courage, but there is no other alternative.

Have you ever noticed that the children of rich families are not very sharp or very intelligent? They cannot be, because there is no challenge for them. The intelligent children always belong to the families where they have to struggle to attain even small things. The children of millionaires are usually mediocre.

Henry Ford used to send his sons to polish boots on the roadsides. He used to tell them to earn their own pocket-money this way. He was a billionaire, and yet he made his sons polish the shoes of other people. His friends said that this is a bit too much! He said, "I myself have earned money by polishing shoes. People who were rich when I was a child have now become beggars. I was like a beggar, but today I am the richest man in the world. I don't want my children to become beggars, so I send them to polish shoes on the road."

Certainly it was intelligent of him, very clever of him to make his sons work like this. Usually the children of rich people are lifeless, absolute fools – because there is no struggle and no challenge in their lives. If there is no struggle and there is too much security they become spineless. The spine becomes strong with struggle. The more the struggle, the stronger the spine becomes.

So I don't ask you to run away from the world. I ask you to wake up from this world. Sannyas is not an escape from the world, sannyas is a great struggle and an awakening. And never avoid challenge; always face the challenge till the work is completed. If you don't run away then you will wake up soon, because the energy which is spent in running away is turned towards awakening. I am not asking you for the peace of the graveyard. I am asking for the peace which one gets by one's labor, by one's effort. I am for the positive peace which is attained by living to the maximum.

The fourth question:

> Beloved Osho,
> It seems that Bhaj Govindam is written for the vanaprastha stage. But you are saying this for everyone.

What is the meaning of *vanaprastha*? Vanaprastha means, 'facing the jungle.' Everyone is facing the jungle. If not today then tomorrow, if not tomorrow then the day after tomorrow – one day that ultimate solitude which is called godliness has to be found. All are vanaprastha. Sometime or other, everyone has to enter that ultimate solitude; that inner jungle has to be found. Vanaprastha has nothing to do with your physical age; otherwise how can you explain Shankaracharya? He left his body at the age of thirty-three. Long before that he had become a *vanaprasthi* and a sannyasin.

You are clever, and this cleverness is your misery. You are clever, so you say that this is only for old people. When there is nothing left for you to do in this world, when people will forcibly retire you and when you will be at your last stage, do you think you will be able to sing the song of the divine? People don't want to give up anything till the last moment.

There is a medical college in London where they have kept a dead body. Two hundred years ago, that man had given some money to the college on the condition that he will preside over the board of trustees not only while he lives, but also after his death. So even today his skeleton is put in the chair of the chairman to preside over the meeting of the board of trustees. Even after death he is presiding! Even now, he is the president. Do you think such people would ever be vanaprastha? You are asking about living people, but he is presiding even though he is dead. Even now the trustees have to stand up and address him as "Mr. President." This is a trust deed which cannot be changed. This is his legal right. The corpse is full of straw, but still it is holding on to that position. There is nothing but straw inside his body now. He is stuffed with straw, yet he is holding the chairman's position.

You don't want to be vanaprastha; vanaprastha and sannyas seem unpleasant to you. You want to do these things at the end of life. But the person who wants to do them later will never be able to do so. Only that person can do them who wants to do them now. There is no other time except now. Even minor things create obstacles.

A friend had taken sannyas. He came yesterday and said that his wife would not let him wear orange clothes and a *mala*, and he agreed not to! Listening to his plight I said, "When you are defeated by your wife, you cannot win anywhere else." It is surprising that a man gives up the challenge so easily.

I am telling you that now is the time. There is no other way for the time to come — it is always now. If you can utilize this moment and your consciousness can turn towards the jungle —

the jungle is only a symbol – if you can turn towards solitude, towards the divine, then the result will be sannyas.

Vanaprastha is the preparation for sannyas. If your back is turned towards the world, if you gradually lose interest in the world – when happiness and unhappiness seem equal to you, when losing or winning makes no difference to you – then it means that you have become a vanaprasthi. It has nothing to do with the age of your body, it is related to your mental maturity. Some people are eighty years old, but their mental age is not more than eight or ten years old. But sometimes even a child of eight or ten years old has the maturity of an eighty-year-old. It all depends on the sharpness and intensity of consciousness.

The words spoken by Shankaracharya when he was ten cannot be spoken by people even at the age of one hundred years. The commentary on the Upanishads by Shankaracharya at the age of ten cannot be made by people who are one hundred years old. It all depends on sharpness, depth and maturity.

Awaken all your energy and allow it to flow and you will find that vanaprastha has happened at that very moment, sannyas has happened at that very moment. But if you go on postponing it till tomorrow…today you want to see a movie so you will go to the temple tomorrow. If you have to postpone something at all, then postpone the movie, see it in your old age, but you are postponing the divine till your old age! You give your youth to the world and old age to the divine. From this your values are quite clear: your youth is spent in useless things and your old age is meant for the divine. When you have energy you do wrong, and when you don't have any energy you want to do good. When you are incapable of doing anything, you intend to do good. You think of surrendering when you are about to die, but you didn't think of surrendering when you had all the vitality. Whom are you deceiving? That is why Shankara says, "Blind in the eye." Whom are you trying to deceive?

You should remember the divine when you have energy, because great energy is needed for this remembrance. There is no

THE GREAT TRANSCENDENCE

greater action than this – it needs your totality, your every breath, your every cell. When you become weak and old, when you walk with the help of a stick, when you are not able to see properly, will you then be able to remember the divine? Then your voice will become so weak that it will not be able to utter the song of the divine properly. What is needed is intensity, is a flooding of energy. For the remembrance of the divine you have to stake the whole energy of your life, and that can only be done today. The day you understand this, it will be vanaprastha for you.

The last question:

> Beloved Osho,
> Can a person who has cosmic consciousness really enjoy pleasures, or does he just act as though doing so?

Only a person who has cosmic consciousness can really enjoy. Only he can enjoy the ultimate bliss. Only he enjoys – the rest of the people are under the false notion of enjoying. They are carrying false coins; actually, they are suffering. Your happiness and pleasures are nothing but the misery and agony which you have experienced. You say and you think that you are experiencing happiness, but in reality you are experiencing misery.

Only the enlightened one enjoys. *Ten tyakten bhunjithan* – "those who renounced, only they enjoyed." He enjoys the divine. You are enjoying trivia, and the so-called enjoyment of the trivial is causing you great misery.

One day a man came and put a lot of money at Ramakrishna's feet. Ramakrishna said, "Please take it away."

That man said, "This is another proof of your being a great renouncer."

Ramakrishna said, "You are a great renouncer, not I, because

I am enjoying the divine and you are giving it up. You are collecting money and I am collecting the divine. So tell me, who is renouncing and who is enjoying? I am the lover of happiness and you are the renouncer."

A person who is not bothered about diamonds and is collecting stones must be a renouncer. One who is giving up the valuable and is taking care of the nonessential must be called a renouncer. Cosmic consciousness is the ultimate enjoyment. It is entering into the ultimate bliss of life. There is no greater bliss than this. Without it everything else is misery.

So don't ask, "Can a person who has cosmic consciousness really enjoy pleasures?" He cannot enjoy your pleasures, because your pleasures are not pleasures. He is enjoyment, he is bliss, but his enjoyment is different from yours.

To know it, you will have to give up your enjoyment and you will have to wake up your consciousness. You are in a dream at present; you have not experienced pleasure or happiness, you have only dreamed about it. But the enlightened one enjoys the truth. He enjoys bliss.

Enough for today.

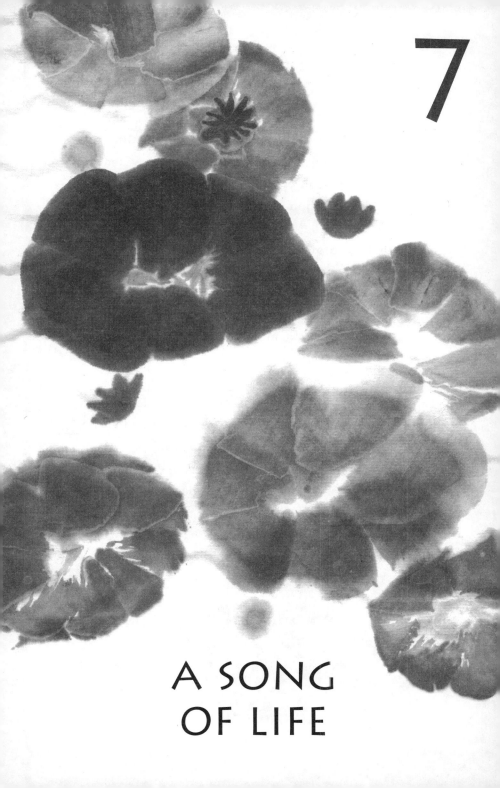

7
A SONG OF LIFE

One who has read even a little of the Gita,
has drunk even one drop of Ganges water
and has worshipped God even a little,
Yama, the god of death, cannot destroy him.

Oh God, protect me from this troublesome world
where one has to be born again and again,
die again and again, and
fall into the womb of a mother again and again,
and take me to the other shore.

He who has made his robe
out of the rags from the roadside,
whose path is free of the thought of sin and virtue,
who is engrossed in yoga,
such a yogi sometimes plays like a child
and sometimes like a madman.

Who are you? Who am I?
From where have I come?
Who is my mother? Who is my father?
Contemplate over these questions,
then you will find that the world
and its worry is meaningless and dreamlike,
and you will become free of this bad dream.

The same divine resides in you,
in me and everywhere else.
By becoming intolerant towards me
you are getting angry in vain.
So, dropping this ignorance
of discrimination in everything,
see only yourself in all.

Do not waste your energy over such matters
as enemy and friend, son and brother,
war and treaty. If you want to attain to the
feet of the divine soon, maintain equanimity
in everything everywhere.

THE SONG OF ECSTASY

I have heard a story. A wasp made its abode near a window outside a big building. In winter this wasp would sleep and rest, in summer it would fly, dance and collect the pollen of the flowers. It was very happy. But this wasp was a special one – it was a thinker – it used to think a lot and to look down upon other wasps because there was no thinking in their lives. Their lives were full of desire. They never did any thinking, they never contemplated, they never knew the scriptures.

Sometimes it used to fly into the building too. It loved that building. The people visiting the building seemed to be of its own type because they were thinkers. Actually, this building was a big library. Professors, teachers, writers, philosophers, poets used to come there. Usually people used to drive out the wasp, but it would always come back.

Gradually it started reading and writing. It started in the children's department, and soon it was studying the big books of philosophy. It began to read big volumes of science and poetry. It became very proud and just couldn't tolerate the other wasps

– they seemed very insignificant. It became very egoistic. It was thinking day and night. It forgot all about dancing in the sun, flying in the air and visiting the trees. Now, mostly it used to sit down engrossed in deep thoughts like, "Who made this world? Why was it made? From where has this existence come and where is it going?" It used to think about these serious questions all the time.

One day it was reading a book on the science of aviation. It was written in that book of aerodynamics that the body of a wasp is heavier than its wings, so theoretically a wasp cannot fly because its wings are small and weak and the body is big and heavy. On reading this, it became confused and puzzled. Up to now it didn't know that its body was big and its wings were small. It was the first time it had learned this and, of course, whatever is written in the scriptures cannot be denied. It is not possible to go against what is said by the scientists.

It became very sad. That day it didn't fly back to its hive, it crawled there. How was it possible for it to fly – to do something which was quite against science? It became very sad and stopped moving about altogether. It still saw the other wasps flying around, going to the flowers, but it thought that they were doing so out of ignorance – how can a wasp fly? – its wings are small and its body is big. It was full of pity for those who were flying because they didn't know the facts of science. If they knew, they would have stopped flying.

But one day a bird attacked the wasp intending to eat it for breakfast. In its nervousness and confusion the wasp forgot all about the scriptures and flew away. It sat on a bush, rested a little and became calm and realized that it had flown! "I was thinking that a wasp cannot fly, but I have flown, so there must have been a block in my mind stopping my natural capacity for flying which melted in the moment of danger" – it had read about mental blocks in the mind in a book on psychology. So it started flying again from that day. It gave up the knowledge of scriptures from that day, and from that moment it again became the wasp – the natural wasp! From that day it became free of knowledge and stopped looking down on other wasps. That day it experienced its true nature.

Religion is freedom from knowledge, and in that freedom is the ultimate knowledge. The scriptures are not meant to make you lame but to give you the capacity to fly. If the scriptures have made you lame, then it is certain that you have misunderstood them or interpreted them wrongly. If the scriptures have made you sad, then you must have missed something in them or must not have understood them properly. The scriptures which have snatched away your natural capacity to fly or flow are not your friends – you have turned them into your enemies.
A scripture is a scripture only if it gives you freedom: a scripture is a scripture if it makes you natural. And a scripture is a scripture if it doesn't fill you with condemnation for others and is able to make you realize that the divine is hidden within them also. These sentences of Shankara are very important.

> One who has read even a little of the Gita...

– take note of "a little" –

> ...one who has read even a little of the Gita,
> has drunk even one drop of Ganges water
> and has worshipped God a little,
> Yama, the god of death, cannot destroy him.

You have read the Gita many times. This country has been reading the Gita for thousands of years; people have memorized it. Every person is full of the Gita and yet there is no liberation for him. He can see only death. And Shankara is saying that death disappears for the one who has read even a little of the Gita, who has tasted the divine even a little, drunk even a drop of Ganges water! And you have taken a bath in the Ganges!

> ...who has drunk even one drop of Ganges water
> and has worshipped God even a little...

You have worshipped a lot, you have recited many times, you have performed many *yajnas*, you have bowed down at the doors of many temples. Even the stones of the gates of the temples are worn out by the rubbing of your head, but no revolution has happened in your life. Certainly there must be some basic illusion, some mistake somewhere – you have missed something.

"Even a little" can give you liberation provided you can understand it, otherwise all scriptures can become your imprisonment. Even one single word can give you freedom if you understand, otherwise the words will become a useless weight on your chest. It is not the scriptures which make you free, it is the understanding. And the understanding has to be created by you; scriptures don't give it. You must understand this. You have to create the understanding, only then can the scriptures be meaningful. If you don't have the understanding, then scriptures cannot give you the understanding. They can give you only theories, and theories have no value because you don't bother about theories – you behave quite differently in life.

One day I said to Mulla Nasruddin that I had not seen his children for a long time. He said, "I believe in family planning."

I was surprised to hear this because he had seventeen children, and he was saying "I believe in family planning." I said, "What do you mean? I don't understand."

He said, "I believe in the slogan of family planning: Two or three children are the ideal number for the home. So I send the rest of the children to play in the neighborhood. Now most of them have even started sleeping in the neighbor's houses. In my own house I don't keep more than two or three children."

By sending his children to the neighbors he is able to fulfill the theory of having two or three children at home!

Your understanding of the scriptures is also like this. You go on giving birth to children and then sending them to the neighbors. Man is able to fool himself. It is easy to avoid theory, but you cannot avoid understanding. You can avoid theory, because it is dead and you are alive. You can always save yourself from theory, but you cannot avoid your own understanding.

When the understanding is within you, you may run away anywhere, but it will remain within you. So you should not give any importance to theory; you should give importance to understanding. Theory can be borrowed, but the understanding has to be created by yourself. Theories can be stolen also from scriptures, from masters, but you cannot get understanding free. You have to pay for it, and you have to struggle inch by inch to gain it. Theories have no value, you get them free. Theories are garbage, and garbage cannot be valuable.

Who has read even a little of the Gita... – a little Gita, that is sufficient. Even if one word is understood, it is enough. Then there is no need to wait to hear the whole of the Gita. But the question is of understanding.

There is a story in the Mahabharata, that Dronacharya thought that the boy Yudhishthira was the most intelligent of all the Pandavas and Kauravas, but after a few days' experience it seemed that he was quite dull. The other children were learning new lessons every day and were making rapid progress, but Yudhishthira was stuck on the first lesson. In the end Drona's patience also became exhausted so he asked him, "How long are you going to take to learn the first lesson? Aren't you going forwards?"

Yudhishthira replied, "What is the sense in learning the second lesson while the first lesson is not understood?"

The first lesson was regarding truth. The other children had read it, memorized it and had proceeded to the second lesson. But Yudhishthira said, "Until I start speaking the truth, how can I go to the second lesson? Please don't hurry me."

A SONG OF LIFE

Then Drona understood! Looking at Yudhishthira's mental condition, Drona understood for the first time that there can be no other lesson after truth. Then he told Yudhishthira, "There is no need for you to hurry up. By learning, by understanding this first lesson, you will understand, you will know all the lessons. Just reading the lessons is one thing and living the lesson is an entirely different thing."

At the end of the story, when all the Pandava brothers were climbing up to heaven, then one by one they began falling down. Only Yudhishthira and his dog – who was truth – arrived at the gate of heaven. The truth reached heaven and the one who accompanied the truth reached heaven. It was his dog who had always lived with him and was of great integrity. Even his brothers didn't have that much integrity, they fell on the way.

But the dog had never doubted, his faith was unlimited. All his life he had obeyed Yudhishthira. Even Yudhishthira was surprised to see that all his brothers had fallen and only this dog could reach the gate of heaven with him. The door opened and Yudhishthira was welcomed, but the gatekeeper said, "Only you can come in, the dog cannot come in. No dog has ever entered heaven before this. Even human beings come here with great difficulty."

On hearing this Yudhishthira said, "Then I too cannot come in. This dog who was with me all my life, who has come all the way to the gates of heaven where even my brothers couldn't come, who has so much faith in me – I cannot forsake him at any cost, otherwise I would consider myself worse than a dog! I am not going to leave him. Please close the door."

Then the whole of heaven laughed happily. All the gods gathered there and requested him to come in. Then Yudhishthira noticed that the dog was not a dog, it was Lord Krishna himself. It was his test! If at that time Yudhishthira had forsaken the dog and had entered the gate without him, then he would have missed heaven. That was the test of his love, of his faith, of his integrity. Yudhishthira learned only one lesson – truth. That was enough to take him to heaven. Arjuna took a long time to learn it. Krishna spoke the whole of the Gita, but even then Arjuna went on doubting. Yudhishthira learnt only one small lesson in his life and that was the lesson of truth. Even the teacher had doubted his intelligence because he was stuck on the first lesson, but he soon realized that there is no other lesson after the first one.

Whosoever has learnt one lesson has learned all. Don't try to learn everything, otherwise you will miss – a little, ...*a little of the Gita*.... If there is a little awareness of the divine, if you have heard part of the song of the divine, if your ears have heard even a little of that song, if even one word has gone to your heart, then that will become the seed. It will sprout and become a tree, and you will be filled up with unlimited fragrance. All is hidden in that one seed.

The *pundits* remain empty. They are able to memorize the Gita, but they cannot hear its song. Their mind is full of the words, but their hearts remain unmoved, untouched. They can repeat the Gita, but there will not be a tear in their eyes, there will be no music in their hearts, there will be no dance in their feet – they will just go on repeating like a dead person, mechanically, without being touched inside. There is not even a scratch on their heart, not even a shadow.

So Shankara says, ...*who has read even a little of the Gita*.... Here 'Gita' doesn't mean only the Shrimad Bhagavadgita, because he who has read even a little of the Koran, he will also attain; he who has read even a little of the Bible will also attain. And he who has read neither the Bible nor the Koran nor the Gita, but has read life a little, he will also attain. The whole emphasis is on the awakening of understanding – he who has not passed his life sleeping, he who has been awakened, has opened his eyes and has recognized life a little.

If you can get a hold of even a little, then you can get a hold of the whole of heaven. If you get a hold of one ray, you can get a hold of the whole sun. You can get the sun with the help of that one ray. If you are sitting in a dark cottage and you can see one ray peeping through the thatched roof, you can find the whole sun in that ray. If you start with that one ray, you will certainly reach the sun. There is no need to have the whole of the sun in your house — what will you do with so much? You will get indigestion! Don't start accumulating scriptures, they will become your prison. Then your wings will not be able to fly, nor will your heart be able to dance, nor will you be natural.

It is the scriptures which make people more unnatural than anything else. If you can understand, I would like to tell you that it is the scriptures which have made people irreligious. More people have become irreligious because of scriptures and not because of anything else. As the number of scriptures goes on increasing, man is becoming blind because he thinks that the understanding is in the book, and that just by reading it he will be able to get this understanding. But if getting this understanding was really so easy, then the whole world would have been very understanding, very intelligent.

Every house has a Gita or a Koran or a Bible, but there is no understanding. Remember that you give up your effort when the scriptures are easily available. Don't get lost in the jungle of theories.

> One who has read even a little of the Gita,
> has drunk even one drop of Ganges water...

What will you do with the whole of the Ganges? There is no need; the whole of the Ganges is too much. One drop is sufficient for you. Which Ganges is Shankara talking about? He is not talking about the Ganges where you went for your pilgrimage.

Here 'Ganges' is a symbol: he who has drunk a drop of piety, who has drunk a drop of innocence, who has drunk a drop of simplicity, he has tasted the Ganges. There is no need to go to the Ganges — because there are many people living on the banks of the Ganges and nothing has happened to them. They have lived there, they have bathed there, but nothing has happened to them. The Ganges referred to here is not the one which can be seen outside, it is the inner Ganges. One drop of it is sufficient. Even one drop is more than necessary, because our limit is not more than one drop; our being is not bigger than one drop. We are like one drop in this vast existence. A small drop of Ganges water will bathe us and will make us whole.

But you must understand properly that the Ganges means innocence, the Ganges means simplicity, the Ganges means the virginity within; the Ganges means to become innocent like a child. By bringing back even one drop of your childhood, if you can look at the world again as you saw it in your childhood – with those fresh eyes, without thought, without any condemnation, without any judgment – if you can look at the world in the same way as you saw it when you first opened your eyes.... You only saw it, there was no thought within – you didn't say if it was good or bad, beautiful or ugly, a sin or a virtue – you only had a good look. The whole world was before you and there was no thought within. If you look at it again in the same way, if you can get even one drop of your childhood back again, then you have tasted a drop of the Ganges.

> ...has drunk even one drop of Ganges water
> and has worshipped God even a little...

Nothing happens by too much worship! "Too much worship" simply means that you don't know how to worship. "Too much worship" means that you are repeating dead rituals, otherwise it is sufficient to speak the name of the divine even once. And every day you are sitting with the rosary repeating, "Rama, Rama." When will your life be full of Rama? How many times are you going to repeat "Rama"? There are some people who keep an account of the number of their chants. They say, "I have chanted this mantra ten million times." But if nothing has happened by chanting once, then what is going to happen by chanting ten million times? Try to understand this. A *mantra* is not mathematics. A mantra is not quantitative, it is qualitative.

If anything is to happen, it will happen the very first time. If it is not to happen then, it will not happen even if you go on repeating it ten million times. If you have repeated it wrongly the first time, you will do it more so the second time, the third time even more so, and this will go on. You can repeat it a million times or ten million times, it makes no difference.

It is a question of calling properly; then one call of the heart is enough, then even one call becomes a revolution. The divine is not deaf. He doesn't want your flattery. Is he going to listen only when you say it repeatedly? He can hear without your saying it, but it should be from your heart. He will never hear if you go on repeating it in your mind, because the divine is not related with your thinking, the divine is related only with your prayer of the heart.

I have heard that it had not rained in a village for many years, so the whole of the village had gathered in the temple to pray. A small child was also going to the temple to pray. Everyone was laughing at him on the way. Even the priest said, "You're stupid! Why are you carrying that umbrella with you? It has not rained for many years, that is why we are going to pray."

That child had brought an umbrella. Thousands of people had gathered to pray, but none of them had brought an umbrella. The child said, "I have brought the umbrella because when we pray it will certainly rain and I will need it on my way back."

People just laughed, they said, "He is mad."

Can the prayer of such people be answered? Only this child's prayer could be answered. He had deep trust; he had no doubt in the prayer; his prayer was full of deep trust. But the older people put doubt in the mind of the child. They said, "Go home and put this umbrella away. It doesn't rain in this way." They are going to pray, but don't have the confidence that it will rain by praying. Then why pray at all?

It is better to be an atheist and be honest about it. What is the

THE SONG OF ECSTASY

use of being a theist if you are dishonest? You have prayed many times, but did you believe that it would be answered? When it is not answered, you say that you knew beforehand that the prayer would not be answered. You have knocked on the doors of the temple many times, but have you done so wholeheartedly? With full trust? Or did you go with doubt?

If you went with doubt then you should not have gone at all – that would have been honest. By going, whom did you deceive? By going you have harmed yourself. Your prayer was unanswered. If your prayer is unanswered again and again then you lose your self-confidence; then you pray from your lips and not from your heart.

And has worshipped God even a little... – yes, a little is enough. You must understand that Shankara's emphasis is not on quantity – how much you have worshipped – but on quality: how you have done it.

I have heard that there was a lawyer who used to pray daily. He prayed on the first day. Then on the second day he said, "Ditto." On the third day he again said, "Ditto." He thought that there was no sense in repeating the same words every day, so he used to say, "Ditto."

People are very calculating in life. Even their prayer is calculating and clever, they cannot be simple even while praying. If you get an opportunity you can pick God's pocket! Perhaps that is why he hides himself and is afraid to face you. Innocence in itself is a prayer.

> ...and has worshipped God even a little,
> Yama, the god of death, cannot destroy him.

He who has tasted prayer even a little, goes beyond death. Only those people die who are frightened. It is the fear which kills. Only those die who are egoists; death is always of the ego.

Only those die who have not known life. Those who have known life even a little, don't die. Then the god of death stops talking about you.

He who has understood the song of the divine even a little, doesn't die. Then you may not remain as you are, but your innermost being will always be. The mind, with which you have been thinking, may not remain; the body, through which you have enjoyed, may not remain; but your innermost self, where you have experienced trust, cannot be destroyed.

Trust is eternal, because trust is your ultimate, the last, the innermost. Death has never entered there, and can never enter. There you are eternal, ancient. There you yourself are the divine. Whoever has yearned for the divine, whoever has searched for the divine, has soon realized that it is hidden within himself. It is not found in a temple, but within oneself. It is not hidden in the mountains nor on the moon nor in the stars.

Russia is an atheist country, but when the first Russian spaceman, Yuri Gagarin, returned to earth the first thing people asked him was, "Did you see God on the moon?" He said, "I looked very carefully, but there was no God there." There is a very big museum in Leningrad where all the things regarding atheism in the history of human beings have been collected. On the wall of that museum the words of Yuri Gagarin have been carved: "I went to the moon, I went into space, but I did not see God anywhere."

If God had been in space then Yuri Gagarin would have met him. But Yuri Gagarin is wrong, and you are also wrong because you also think that the divine is somewhere outside. The atheist and the theist are both wrong, because the theist thinks that God is sitting somewhere in the sky and the atheist thinks that if he is in the sky, then we can look for him in the whole sky. But if he is not found there, then…?

Yuri Gagarin should have looked for God within himself. The divine is there. The one who was seeing the moon and the stars through Yuri Gagarin's eyes, that is God. The one who is looking for God cannot ever find him.

The divine cannot be seen, he is always the seer. He is not a thing to be seen, he is the seeing hidden within you. The one who is seeing is the divine, he is always the seer. You can never make him the object of your sight. But he who has heard even a little of the song of life – I call that the Bhagavadgita, the divine song. The song which Krishna has sung before Arjuna is the refrain of that ultimate song, is the refrain of the song of life; it is only a small part of that song.

That song is written on every tree, on every rock, on every wave of the sea. The emptiness of the sky is his silence, the rivers are singing the song of the divine. It is he who is seeing through your eyes, it is he who is listening through your ears, it is he who is throbbing through your heart – there is nothing else except the divine. One who has understood even a little of the song of the divine, who has recognized life even a little, who has drunk even a drop of simplicity, who has worshipped even a little....

Worship means, one who has made his ego bow down even a little, who has bowed down his head even a little. It doesn't matter before whom you bow down – your bowing down is enough. If you have bowed down in a mosque it is alright, if you have bowed down in a temple it is alright, if you have bowed down in a gurudwara it is alright – the question is of bowing down. It doesn't matter whether you bow down before a rock or a tree or the empty sky. It doesn't matter whether you believe in God or you don't believe in God. Mahavira bowed down without believing and attained. And Buddha never accepted God, but he became God. He knew the art of bowing down.

The question is not of attaining God, the question is of destroying one's ego. Worship means, one who has finished himself and who has said, "I am not." It is not necessary to say, "You are." Whoever has said "I am not," that very moment he has known "Only you are." The divine appears as soon as the I disappears. This I is the only obstacle.

Then

>...the god of death cannot destroy him.

Therefore,

>Oh fool! Always sing the song of the divine.

>Oh God, protect me from this troublesome world
>where one has to be born again and again,
>die again and again, and fall into the womb of a
>mother again and again...

Man is helpless, and nothing can be done by the resolution of man because whatsoever you will do will be less than you. The divine is vast, much bigger than you. He is in you, he peeps through you, but is much greater than you.

It is like the ocean being in a drop of water. If you taste the drop you get the salty taste of the ocean. If you analyze just that one drop you will get the substance of the whole ocean. A drop is very small, but the ocean has shown itself through the drop, just as the sky has shown itself through the window. The divine has shown himself through you also, but he is much vaster than you. The divine has shown himself through you just as the sky is seen through the window, the ocean is hidden in the drop, the tree is hidden in the seed.

You cannot attain him with your effort; your effort is very small. It is like trying to get the sky in your hand. You can attain him only with his grace.

That is why Shankara says, "Oh God, please save me! I am sure to get drowned. I can be saved only if you save me. My energy and my strength are very limited. Even if I think, what can I think? Even if I contemplate, what can I contemplate? – all the thinking will be mine. You are unknown, you are vast. To attain you, your help is needed."

That is why a devotee, a *bhakta*, is continuously wishing to get his support, his help. The day you start asking for his support you will find that you have it because you start growing – your shrinking stops and you start expanding. The day you ask for the support of this vast life you yourself start becoming vast; your smallness starts disappearing from that very moment. You have given the invitation, "Come!" Nothing else is needed.

Buddha has said, "I thought that I was searching for truth, but on attaining it I found that truth was also searching for me."

Truth is also searching for you. The divine is also searching for you, looking for you, but you are not giving the invitation. If by chance existence takes your hand in its hand, you then give up its hand.... Have you noticed small children? The father holds the hand of the child and takes him to the market. The father keeps on holding his hand, but the child attempts to free his hand because he wants to become independent, he wants to walk by himself. The father wants to hold on to the hand of the child, but the child wants to free his hand so that he can run by himself.

Man also behaves like this. The divine is holding his hand, otherwise man cannot even live. How are we going to breathe if existence doesn't breathe through us? How shall we live if existence doesn't throb in us? But we try to stand on our own feet. Ego always tries to stand on its own feet without the support of anyone else. It seems very insulting to ask for someone's help. It looks pitiable to ask for someone's support. That is why, as the ego of man goes on increasing, worship and prayer are disappearing.

Have you ever noticed that when you bow down in the temple you feel a little uncomfortable? You are afraid that someone may see you bowing down. You kneel down, you fold your hands, but at the same time you make sure that no one is looking at you, because people will say, "You are kneeling down, you are bowing down," and it will hurt your ego.

People have become afraid of bowing down. It is very unfortunate, because whatever is great in life can be attained only by bowing down. It is just like your being thirsty and you are standing in the river, but you are not bending down. You want the river to rise up to your mouth. But if you want to drink water then you have to bend down, you have to bend your head, take the water in your hands, and then drink it. But your ego doesn't let you bend down.

Most of the people deny the divine – not because they have come to know that there is none, but if there is a divine then they will have to bow down.

Friedrich Nietzsche has written, "If there is a God then we will have to bow down. That is why I say that there is no God. How can I bow down? If there is God then he is superior to me – that is why I say that there is no God, because no one can be superior to me." Ego is terrible.

Man is full of terrible ego. The ego in the soul is like a cancer in a body. Yes, ego is a cancer of the soul. Until you are free of this ego the song of the divine cannot be born in you, you cannot pray and you cannot worship. The divine cannot enter you while you are full of yourself. Come down from your throne, make some space and invite him.

> Oh God, protect me from this troublesome world
> where one has to be born again and again,
> die again and again, and
> fall into the womb of a mother again and again...

Whoever has understood the fact of life has come to know that life is just a repetition; everything is being repeated again and again. You have been born many times, you have died many times, you have earned wealth many times, you have earned fame many times, you were successful many times and you were unsuccessful many times. You go on revolving like the wheel of a vehicle, up and down, up and down.

It is a natural wish to be free of this repetition, because repetition is boring. That is why we have called this world the *chakra*, the wheel; we have named it the *dushta-chakra*, the bad, ominous wheel, because we go on revolving in the same way – nothing new happens. You are living today as you lived yesterday; tomorrow you will also live like this and the day after tomorrow you will also live in the same way. It is always the same evening, the same morning, the same anger, the same greed, the same attachment, the same birth, the same death – it is just repetition. There must definitely be a very deep-rooted idiocy in us – that is why we are not awakened from our sleep – otherwise we would have seen that why we go on repeating the same things again and again. If we didn't attain anything by doing them so many times, then it is certain that we will never attain anything by repeating them innumerable times.

We have to get out of this vicious circle. That is why in the East, and especially in India, this great desire was born of getting out of the circle of birth and death. This kind of desire was not born anywhere else in the world. In the West the religions like Islam, Christianity and Judaism are not inspired by this desire. They want to attain heaven. Heaven means that all the miseries of this life should not be there, but all the pleasures must be there. Heaven is only a greater expansion of such worldly types of comforts and pleasures. But in India a unique desire was born – and that is the speciality of India – the desire for *moksha*, liberation. It is the desire for liberation and not for heaven.

The meaning of the desire for liberation is that now neither misery nor happiness is wanted; we have had enough of both of them. There was nothing significant in them; now we want to be free of both. This desire to be free from both is unique. That is why it is not possible to translate the word moksha into any language of the world. It is possible to translate *swarga*, heaven, and *nareka*, hell, but moksha is a unique word. No other language of the world has this word. It cannot – because first the desire has to be born, and then the word is born to express it. First it is the experience, and then the words are born later on to express it.

The experience of moksha is the unique search of India. No other search has gone higher than this, and no other search can go higher than this. Only those people can have the desire to be free of happiness who have experienced happiness thoroughly, and have found that happiness is also a way of misery, a deception of misery.

> He who has made his robe
> out of the rags from the roadside,
> whose path is free of the thought of sin and virtue,
> who is engrossed in yoga...

— whose mind has become united —

> ...such a yogi sometimes plays like a child
> and sometimes behaves like a madman.

A person sitting by the roadside may look like a beggar, but if you look carefully there is an emperor hidden within him. ...Because if you look at the emperors carefully, you will find beggars within them. They go on asking for more.

There was a Muslim *fakir* named Farid. The people of his village asked him to request the Emperor Akbar to open a school in the village, as Akbar had great regard for him. Farid had never asked Akbar for anything. A fakir never asks, the fakir always gives. But since the people of the village had insisted on his seeing Akbar he couldn't refuse them, so he went. He had never visited the palace before this, but now he had to go. He arrived there quite early in the morning and was told that the emperor was praying in his personal mosque. So Farid went and stood at the back.

Akbar didn't know this. He completed his prayer, raised his hands towards the sky, and said, "Oh God. Whatever you have given me is not enough, I want much more than this. Please make my kingdom much bigger than this. Please increase my wealth and my fame."

Farid just couldn't believe his ears. The great Emperor Akbar, who had such a vast kingdom, was still asking for more. He was still begging!

So, Farid thought, how could he ask from a person who is still asking for more? – because opening a school means spending some money, what Akbar has now will be that much less. If Akbar is asking God, then I can also ask him directly. Why have an agent in between? He turned around. When Akbar got up he saw Farid going down the stairs. He ran after him and asked him the reason for his coming. Akbar had great regard for Farid and used to go for his *darshan* from time to time, but Farid had never before visited Akbar. Akbar asked him, "Why did you come? Why are you going back?"

Farid said, "I came to meet an emperor, to ask him for something, but instead I saw a beggar, so I am going back. How can I ask from a person who is begging, asking for more? I don't want to make you poorer. I had to come because the people of the village insisted on my asking if you would open a school. But now I won't ask you, I will ask God for it. When you go on asking him for so many things, I can also ask him directly."

Akbar told Farid many times that he will open the school, but Farid refused him saying, "One doesn't ask for help from beggars. Only real emperors can help."

But your emperors are actually poor beggars. They are asking for more. But this country has produced such emperors who are not beggars; if you look into them you will find they are more precious than all the precious stones.

> He who has made his robe
> out of the rags from the roadside...

Yes, he has made his clothes out of the rags on the roadside, but moksha has been born in him, freedom has opened its wings in him.

> ...whose path is free of the thought of sin and virtue...

Please note that religions say that if you sin you will go to hell and if you do a good deed you will go to heaven. But what will you do to attain moksha? Neither sin nor good deed.

> ...whose path is free of the thought of sin and virtue...

One who neither sees good nor bad, whose life has become free from choice, Krishnamurti calls this choiceless awareness. One whose life is only full of awareness – choiceless, without any alternative. One who doesn't choose, who neither says that this is right nor says that that is wrong; who doesn't choose, who says that everything is the same, there is nothing to choose – nothing is beautiful or ugly, nothing is sin or a virtue.

This is a very unique idea, which is connected with moksha. That is why, when the Upanishads were translated for the first time, the thinkers in the West couldn't understand what the Upanishads were saying, because in the West it was thought that the aim of scriptures was to preach to do good actions. Scriptures are to save you from sins and inspire you to do good. But the Upanishads say that scriptures save you from sin and good deeds both, because when you are full of the thought of sin and good deeds, then you are full of duality.

Scriptures are to take you beyond this duality and to make you one. Your mind is full of contempt while you say that "this is sin." Your mind is full of praise while you go on saying "that is good." When you say that something is good, it means that you have chosen. When you say something is sin, it means you have refused it. And the divine is in both sin and in good deeds, and by refusing something you have refused the divine.

In the life of the enlightened one there is neither refusal nor demand. He neither accepts nor denies; his consciousness doesn't waver, he has become stable.

> ...whose path is free of the thought of sin and virtue,
> who is engrossed in yoga...

A *yogi* is one who is united, who has become one; there is no duality for him. Heaven and hell, happiness and misery, sin and virtue, all will remain while there is duality. When only one remains, then heaven and hell, happiness and misery, darkness and light, they all disappear. In that one is the ultimate rest, in that one is the ultimate bliss. By achieving that one, everything is achieved.

> ...such a yogi sometimes plays like a child...

— so innocent, like a child —

> ...and sometimes like a madman.

— so full of bliss, so drunk with ecstasy.

In a yogi you will find both a child and a madman. A child means one who has not started thinking and a madman means one who has gone beyond thinking. The circle is complete in a yogi. He has become like a child, he doesn't think; and he has become like a madman, he has gone beyond thinking. That is why it is difficult to recognize a yogi. You cannot put him into any category and you cannot make any judgment about him. It is never known what he will do in the next moment because he doesn't do anything by himself, he does whatever the divine makes him do. He has entrusted himself in the hands of the divine. He just goes on flowing; wherever the river of godliness takes him, that is his destination. If he gets drowned in the middle then that is his destination! No longer does he have any aim of his own. 'Yogi' means the ultimate freedom. Therefore, *Oh fool! Always sing the song of the divine.*

> Who are you? Who am I?
> From where have I come?
> Who is my mother? Who is my father?
> Contemplate over these questions,
>   then you will find that the world and its worry
>   is meaningless and dreamlike,
>   and you will become free of this bad dream.

Therefore,

> Oh fool! Always sing the song of the divine.

The same divine resides in you, in me and everywhere else. By becoming intolerant towards me you are getting angry in vain. So, dropping this ignorance of discrimination in everything, see only yourself in all. Therefore, *Oh fool! Always sing the song of the divine.*

Don't waste your energy in the duality of enemy and friend, in son and in brother, in war and in peace. If you want to attain to the feet of the absolute then all should be equal to you. To see everything as equal is the journey to oneness, in happiness and in misery, in victory and in defeat, in success and in failure. Then gradually you will attain oneness.

You will remain two while you see the duality, because you become what you perceive. When you don't see conflict, when you don't see duality, and you start seeing the one in a friend and in a foe, in good and in bad, in sin and in virtue, in heaven and in hell, in blessing and in curse — when you start seeing one, then you will start becoming one. You become whatever you see. What you perceive becomes your nature. Therefore, to go beyond duality is *sadhana*, spiritual practice.

It will be difficult. How will you see it? How will you see

the one and the same in the person who abuses you and in the person who praises you? But if you look carefully, then you will find that abuse and praise are just on the surface; inside, there is only one. Try to see carefully that friend and foe, hate and love are just the two expressions of the same energy. That is why love can become hate and hate can become love; a friend becomes an enemy and an enemy becomes a friend. If both of them were absolutely different then this change could not have occurred. A friend of today can become an enemy tomorrow. A person who was an enemy yesterday becomes a friend today. Certainly the energy is the same. The feet that are taking a person away from you are the same feet which will bring him back to you one day. The feet are the same. To come near and to go away, these are just two ways of the one energy.

Try to understand it. Try to look for it. The old habits will create obstacles. The old ways of thinking will create obstacles, but the darkness disappears with continuous effort and the light appears. As you start seeing the one in the opposite also, you will experience deep peace, some wholeness starts coming within you. You are not the same as you were yesterday, a new consciousness starts being born in you. When the two disappears and only one remains, then you are ready for the divine. And the divine is always ready. When you are ready the cloud rains and you are full; the moment of bliss arrives.

But one has to awaken from the two, one has to avoid the duality, and has to see and hold onto the flow of the one.

You will attain oneness by disciplined equanimity.

Always try to see the one in the two; this should become your meditation, your sadhana. When you have success you should be able to see that this is also a failure – soon failure will be following it. And don't get upset when you fail, soon success will be following it. These are two sides of the same coin. When success seems like failure and failure seems like success, the difference disappears and sameness appears. Then your door for the divine will open.

The divine is always very near, but you remain away from him because of your differentiation. The divine is always before you – because whatever is before you is godliness. But your eyes are closed. Because of the differentiation your eyes are closed, but they open when differences disappear. Difference is like the eyelid on the eye, and indifference is like the opening of the eyelid.
Therefore,

> Oh fool! Sing the song of the divine.

Enough for today.

8

THIS WORLD IS A SCHOOL

The first question:

> Beloved Osho,
> When Shankara was very young, his mother would not give him permission to take sannyas. But one day, as he was bathing in a river, he was caught by a crocodile. At death's door, Shankara asked his mother to give him permission to take sannyas. The permission was given, and Shankara was saved.
> Please explain this event.

The event is not valuable – it is not even definite that the event really happened – but its meaning is to be understood. And always remember that the events in the lives of the enlightened ones are not just events but symbols; some secret is hidden in them. They may or may not be historical, but they are spiritual. It may or may not have happened in the flow of time, but it did happen in the flow of consciousness. Don't try to understand the buddhas through history; understand them through poetic experience, otherwise the whole thing is misunderstood. This is a parable.

"When Shankara was very young his mother would not give him permission to take *sannyas*." A lot of things are hidden in this. 'Mother' means, the love of the mother; 'mother' means attachment. It is difficult for attachment to give permission for sannyas, because sannyas means the death of attachment. Sannyas means that a person is becoming free of the family; the mother will now not be the mother, the father will not be the father, now the brother will not be the brother. That is why Jesus has said again and again, "Whosoever wants to come with me has to deny his mother and his father; whosoever wants to come with me has to give up his family." You cannot be a part of the family of Jesus until you give up your family.

Sannyas means that this life between birth and death is futile, meaningless. If this life is futile, then the mother who gave birth also becomes futile. Not only did she give birth, she created a dream.

Basically, sannyas is freedom from life. And freedom from life means freedom from the mother, freedom from the father, freedom from the family, freedom from the society. All this becomes futile, meaningless. So how can the mother give permission? Will a mother ever give permission for sannyas? It is impossible. It is very difficult. Attachment cannot give permission for sannyas; the love of a mother cannot give this permission. It is impossible to get permission to be free of life from the very source from where life comes.

"When Shankara was very young his mother would not give him permission to take sannyas." And remember, you may grow up to any age, but for your mother you will always be a child. You can never be older than your mother; you will always be younger than the mother who has given birth to you. You may be seventy years old, but for your mother you will always remain a child. "Shankara was very young," means that whenever a seeker asks his mother for the permission to take sannyas, his mother will always stop him from doing so, thinking that her child is very small and he wants to tread a difficult path.

"When Shankara was very young his mother would not give him permission to take sannyas. But one day, as he was bathing in a river, he was caught by a crocodile."

In the river of life misery gets hold of you sometime or other. You meet death in this river of life. You don't go into the river to meet death, you go there to bathe, to enjoy swimming, to enjoy the freshness of the morning. Nobody goes into the world to die, nobody goes into the river of life to meet crocodiles. One goes into life in search of happiness, in search of treasures – success, fame, prestige – but in this process gets caught by crocodiles.

Death takes hold of you sooner or later. And if a person is wise he understands soon that this river is the surface, death is hidden inside – 'crocodile' means the hidden death. On the surface the flow of the water seems so pure and peaceful, but deep down death is waiting. On the surface it looks very attractive, and the river also seems very innocent. Inside death is waiting quietly. Anyone who is clever, wise and conscious will be able to understand this quickly.

Shankara saw it at once. If you cannot see this for a long time, then it means that you have very little intelligence and understanding. Your mirror is covered with dust. Your intelligence is full of smoke, otherwise you could see it earlier.

In this story the only thing conveyed is that Shankara realized that in this life one gets nothing except death. And one cannot be free of the love of the mother, until the realization of death. Try to understand this a little. On one end is the mother – 'mother' means birth; on the other end is death – death means the end. Freedom from the mother is possible only if death can be seen; birth can be meaningless only if the end can be seen. So sannyas means, realization of death.

We go on postponing death in this world; we go on saying that it is always others who die, "I will never die." Every day you see dead bodies being taken to the graveyard or to the cremation ground; you help others carry these dead ones there, but it never occurs to you that you will also die. You always think that you are going to live forever and only others will die. But one day others will also carry your body to the graveyard when you are no longer alive. But man lives on false hopes.

Sannyas means, the awakening of the awareness that "death is mine; the news of the other person's death is actually the news of my death. The death of the other is pointing towards my death. And with the death of everyone, I also die a little."

If you have a little understanding, then everyone's death will become your death. But if you don't have this understanding, if you are foolish, then you will think that it is always others who die; "I will not die, I am immortal."

Shankara could see death. One gets free of the mother as soon as you see death, because 'mother' means life. 'Mother' means, the one who brought you into this world. 'Death' means, that which will take you away. The Hindus' imagination regarding this is unique. No other community on this earth is more imaginative, more poetic, than Hindus. Their poetry is very deep.

Have you ever seen the statue of Kali? She is the mother and death also; *kal*, means death – so her name is Kali. And she is the mother, so she is a woman. She is beautiful, beautiful like a mother. Nobody else can be as beautiful as the mother. Even if one's own mother is ugly, she seems beautiful. Nobody thinks in terms of the beauty of the mother, but the mother is beautiful ...because if you see your mother as ugly, then that means that you are ugly because you are her expansion. So Kali is beautiful, very beautiful! But around her neck she is wearing a garland of human heads. She is beautiful, but she is Kali – kal, death!

Western thinkers are puzzled over this symbol. They wonder why a woman should be depicted so horribly, so terrifying. And you call her mother also! How frightening! It is horrible, because death starts from the one who gives birth. It is terrible, because death has arrived along with the birth. The mother has given death as well as life. So on one side she is as beautiful as the mother, as the source, and on the other end she is like kal, death, as dark as death. Around her neck is a garland of human heads; in her hand she is holding a severed head, blood dripping, and she is standing, with her feet on her husband.

This is a very deep symbol: woman as life, and as death too! ... Because death comes from where life comes; these two are the two sides of the same coin. And nobody else on this earth realized this fact as the Hindus have done. When Shankara became aware of death...whether he was really caught by the crocodile or not should be asked of the silly historians; I am just not interested in it. What difference does it make whether he was caught by a crocodile or not? But one thing is definite – that he saw death, and when he saw death, sannyas happened.

One cannot escape from sannyas after seeing death. Then you remain stunned, wherever you are. Then life cannot be the same as it was just a moment before this realization. The ambition, the fame, the reputation – everything loses its charm. Death destroys everything. One has to die, so it doesn't matter whether one dies earlier or later – today, tomorrow or the day after – it is just a matter of time. If my death has to happen, then it has happened just now. And the arrow of death will pierce you in such a way that you will not be able to be what you were before now. This new change in you is sannyas.

If you ask me the definition of sannyas, I will say that sannyas is a state of being where death has not happened outside, but has happened inside. One is alive, but one knows death; while living, one is quite aware of death. This is sannyas. One lives, but doesn't forget death even for a moment: this is sannyas. You know that the dewdrop is just momentary. The world is like the morning star, it will soon disappear. You live, but you are not drunk with life. Then life cannot make you forget the fact of death. You remain awakened, you are aware all the time. Death awakens you. One who is awakened is a *sannyasin*.

One who is lost in life and is taking the dreams to be true is a worldly person, is a householder. One who is living in dreams, or who is creating dreams in the house, is a householder. But one who gets up from sleep, whose dream is over, who is awakened and is conscious, realizes that over here there is nothing except death.

Any colony, any place of living, is nothing but a graveyard, or a queue waiting to go to the graveyard. The queue is moving towards the graveyard. Someone may be a little ahead and someone may be behind, but all of them are going to the graveyard. The attachment to life is over as soon as one sees this. Losing this attachment is sannyas. Sannyas is not an effort for detachment. Sannyas is not a discipline of detachment. Sannyas is the loss of attachment – where attachment is over. If attachment is not over, then one has to make an effort to attain nonattachment, but that is not sannyas. If attachment is not over, only then one tries to attain nonattachment.

But when attachment is finished, then the empty space left by attachment is nonattachment. Then you become a sannyasin. That is why I tell you that there is no need to go anywhere for sannyas. Wherever you are, if you can open your eyes, if you become a little conscious, then you are able to see things as they are.

One night Mulla Nasruddin was coming home after getting drunk in the bar. He was merrily walking on the road humming a song when he collided with somebody. He lost his temper and shouted, "You fool! If you don't say sorry within five seconds, then…."

The other person retorted in a louder voice, in a threatening way, "Then?"

Hearing the threatening voice Mulla came to his senses, looked at the man carefully – he looked like the boxer, Mohammed Ali! All his drunkenness disappeared and he said, "Well, if five seconds are not enough, then how much time do you need?"

In this life you also go about as if drunk, humming the song of dreams, and you don't see things as they are. A hard hit is needed to upset your dreaming mind, only then you can see the empty sky. You will then see that you are surrounded by death. What you consider as life is actually death.

What you consider as happiness is really the mask of misery. What you consider as wealth is only a game of falsehood. In the illusion of money you remained poor. And in the illusion of life you remained unacquainted with real life...and time is passing away, life is passing every minute and your energy is diminishing.

This is only a symbol, that when death caught hold of Shankara, then before dying he asked his mother to give him the permission to take sannyas, and the permission was given.

Yes, this permission is granted only when death is standing at the door. One does not get permission before this – only when the mother realizes that her son will only be saved if he becomes a sannyasin; otherwise as he is, he will die. When the question is of choosing between a dead son and a sannyasin son, then the mother chooses the sannyasin son. This is the meaning, because a sannyasin son means a dead son. Sannyas means one has died while living.

Jesus has said, "You cannot come with me until you agree to carry your cross on your shoulders; you cannot come with me until you are ready to deny yourself; there is no way of resurrection until you are ready to die."

If this story is true, if things really happened in this way, then this symbol should be remembered. Shankara, a small child, is on the verge of death; a crocodile has caught hold of his leg. His mother is standing on the bank of the river and Shankara is asking her permission to take sannyas. He is saying, "I am dying, there is no hope of my being saved. Let me die as a sannyasin. Give me the permission for sannyas. The crocodile is taking me away – so give me the permission."

Even then the mother must have hesitated. Even then she might have hoped against hope that her son may be saved. But death was pulling Shankara away. A crowd of people must have collected and they must have said, "You had better give your permission now. He is dying, he is going. You cannot stop him from dying, so set him free before he dies."

Ultimately, she gave the permission, after hearing Shankara's words that he wants to die as a sannyasin so that he is not born again, so that there is no longer any attachment to life for him; he wants to die with no attachment to life. Even then, to me it seems that the mother must have hesitated; her eyes must have been full of tears. She must have prayed to God to save her son. But when there was no hope then very reluctantly, in a very helpless way, she must have said, "Since you are dying you had better die as a sannyasin."

But this incident may not have happened, because crocodiles don't worry about these things. When men don't worry, why should crocodiles worry? It is said that Shankara was saved. The crocodile thought, "Why kill this person now when he has become a sannyasin?" No, crocodiles are not so intelligent! When Hitler and Mussolini are not intelligent, then how can crocodiles be intelligent?

But this symbol is very valuable. Man is saved only when he becomes a sannyasin, then even death cannot harm him. Only he dies who tries to catch hold of life; death cannot kill the person who himself gives up life. How can you take from a person who is ready to give away? Things can only be snatched away from the person who wants to save them. That is why Jesus says, "That one who saves will lose; one who is ready to lose, is saved." You must understand this.

Shankara was saved. Did the crocodile leave him? No, it only means that death doesn't kill a sannyasin. There is no way of killing a sannyasin because, he says, "The I which could be killed by you was given up by me. I have given up the ego, and all the dreams of desire and ambition. I have killed myself with my own hands. Then only the nectar within, which was surrounded by death, remains in its purity."

You don't know anything about this nectar as long as you go

on holding on to life. That is why you hold life so tightly that it doesn't slip out of your hands. You are afraid you may die. You are afraid of death all the time. The more you try to hold on the more frightened you become, because you know that you cannot fool death. Yes, death is coming. Where can you hide yourself from death? It comes from all sides. If it was coming from any particular direction then that could be avoided, but it comes from all sides. You could save yourself if it was coming from outside; it comes from inside. You may run away anywhere, but death will come. You may hide yourself anywhere, death will find you, because death is hidden within you.

Nectar and death both are hidden within you. As long as you go on holding on to life outside you will see only death within. The moment you accept death within, you will start seeing the life within.

If you write on a blackboard with white chalk then the words are visible and clear. But if you write with white chalk on a white wall, then the words are not visible. If you accept that inner death, then in that blackness the little candle of immortality which is burning within you will become a thousand times more luminous. But you don't accept death, you don't accept the blackboard, so you cannot see the white words. Always remember this contradictory statement: Whoever can see death properly, has seen the nectar also.

"Shankara was saved" – because death cannot destroy you. It can destroy the so-called life. It can destroy what you call the body. It can destroy what you call name and form. But death cannot destroy you. You are immortal, you are *amrit putra*. You were never destroyed and can never be destroyed. You were never born, nor will you ever die.

One who is born will die. Your body was born, so it will die. Your name, your personality were born, and they will die. But you were always in time beyond name and form, and you will always remain in time. You are ancient, you are eternal.

The meaning of sannyas is that "I will give up whatever is

transient and I will go in search of what will not be destroyed. I will give up the transient and I will look for the eternal. Even if I am finished in this search it doesn't matter, because whatever is transient cannot be saved for long." But even after giving up the transient, if the intransient remains which cannot be cut by any weapons and which cannot be burned by fire, then that is worth saving. Sannyas is the search for this. Don't think that this event happened. It is just a very valuable symbol, a parable.

The second question:

> Beloved Osho,
> Sai Baba of Shirdi had gone to Narayanswamy's
> house in the forms of a dog and a leper, and
> Narayanswamy could not recognize him.
> My request is that you must come to my house,
> but in this very form, because I am very stupid.

If you have recognized me, then you will recognize me in any form. And if you have not recognized me, then how can you be certain of recognizing me even in this form? Recognition of form is no recognition. Bowing down before form is not bowing down. Worship of form is not worship at all. If Sai Baba had gone in the form which Narayanswamy thought that he recognized, then he would have definitely bowed down, he would have welcomed him, but that welcome would have been to the form and not to Sai Baba. In fact, a dog and a leper are more living, more animate as far as form is concerned. The form is only an outer covering. You must give up this hold on the covering. But I know why you go on holding on to the covering. It is because you know yourself also by this form.

I have heard, when Mulla Nasruddin went on a pilgrimage to Mecca he had two people with him; one was a barber and one was a bald fool. They halted at night in the desert. As it was an unknown new place and looked dangerous, they decided to keep a watch by turn at night. The first turn was the barber's. He stayed awake for some time, but soon he felt sleepy as he was quite tired. So, to keep himself occupied, he shaved all the hair off Mulla Nasruddin's head. He was getting bored, so he shaved off Mulla's hair!

After the barber it was Mulla's turn to keep watch, so the barber woke him up and Mulla, out of old habit, put his hand on his head and then he said, "My God! By mistake you seem to have woken up that stupid bald guy instead of me!" That shaven head gave him the idea that this was not him but that bald fool. His head had a lot of hair on it, so it must be the other person.

We identify ourselves with the form. Have you thought about it? If your face were to change at night during sleep would you be able to recognize yourself in the morning? No, you will not be able to. How can you? Because you recognize yourself through the mirror, there is no other deeper recognition.

If you go to sleep as a white man at night and on waking up in the morning you find yourself as a black man – if a scientist changes the shape of your nose and the color of your eyes, your hair, by doing plastic surgery at night – then you will also be in the same condition as Mulla Nasruddin was. What he has said is not absolutely wrong. He doesn't say wrong things: he says, "My God! By mistake you have woken up the bald fool instead of me!" You will also say and do the same thing. You will wake up screaming, "This can't be me, it must be somebody else!"

We recognize ourselves only through the form. Therefore, any recognition that we have of others is also of form. So long as you don't recognize your own consciousness you cannot recognize my consciousness either. Your recognition of me would be just as deep as your recognition of yourself. I may come to your house, but that will be of no use. Unless you come to your own house, my coming to your house would not mean anything really.

The third question:

> Beloved Osho,
> Yesterday, while narrating the story of the wasp, you told us about a mental block. Please tell us how to remove a complex by sadhana, spiritual practice.

You didn't even understand the story about the great intellectual wasp. In that story of the wasp it was made clear that there was no block, no complex, but it had read a book! There was not any block in the life of the wasp which had to be removed by *sadhana*. The only trouble with the wasp was that it had become an expert in reading, and it had read in a book that the wings of a wasp are small and its body is heavy so that a wasp cannot fly. Now the people who wrote this book certainly worked out the theory very nicely, but they didn't see the wasp fly! According to their logic it cannot fly, but the fact is that it flies. The wasp became confused after reading this. Its condition was like the centipede. It is a very old story.

A centipede with one hundred feet was passing by when a rabbit saw him and became very curious and puzzled. He stopped the centipede and asked, "Please tell me, how do you manage to move with these one hundred feet? And how do you synchronize them? Which one do you put forward first and which one follows? It is most baffling to me, how you manage all of them."

Until this moment the centipede had never even given a thought to his one hundred feet. He had just been moving. He had never thought of this matter, but when the rabbit asked him, he himself looked at his one hundred feet and became confused. He said, "My God! I have never given this a moment's thought before. But now, since you have asked me the question, I'll need to think it over, I will observe and experiment with it, then I will inform you."

But after this he became so conscious of his one hundred feet that he could not move and he fell down. Such a small body with one hundred feet – how was he to manage them all? He said, "You silly rabbit! You have created a problem for me. Now I will never be able to move. Now I have become conscious of the question: How to synchronize these hundred feet? This question had not bothered me before."

Have you noticed that all the minor things become a problem if you start thinking about them? You can try this: for seven days, whenever you eat food, start thinking how you digest it. Scientists say that it is quite a miracle. The food goes in, gets absorbed and becomes blood and bones, flesh and marrow, and all the fine nerves of the brain – thoughts and desires. And all this is transformed in the small factory of the stomach. How? Well, if you think it over for seven days you will get indigestion and you will never be healthy again. If you experiment like this the stomach will be out of order. Like the centipede, you will also start wondering.

Life is bigger than your mind. Whenever you bring in the mind it creates problems. Life is much greater than you, and your mind is small. You couldn't even understand the story of the wasp, and you want to know how to remove the complex by spiritual practices? What did the wasp do? It didn't do anything. There is no question of doing anything, because it was only an illusion of the mind. The wasp had been flying until it read the book.

The scripture was the cause of death. The wasp could not fly from that day; it just sat down and became fat by sitting, and it became more difficult to fly. And when it became difficult to fly the scriptures seemed quite correct. The other wasps were flying, but it thought that they were ignorant fools and they were flying in their ignorance. It thought that it was very learned, and that "these are ignorant fools so they don't know what is written in the scriptures; they are flying in their ignorance. They don't know that the scientists have said that the wings of a wasp are small and its body is so big it cannot fly." Man tries to cover up his idiocy and his diseases by knowledge. He is very skilled in this task.

That wasp was also under the impression that it was the only one who was sensible; the others were stupid. They were flying, and thus going against the theory and the scriptures. "They don't know what they are doing; they are doing what cannot be done." But the wasp didn't understand that what cannot be done, cannot be done even in ignorance. It was just a fortunate moment that one morning a bird attacked the wasp and in the confusion of the attack it forgot all about the so-called knowledge, the Vedas, and it just flew away! But later, when it sat down in the shade, then it realized that it had flown, which means it can fly.

So certainly these are the tricks of the mind. It didn't think that it was an illusion that it couldn't fly, and whoever had written this in the scriptures was not correct. Even man doesn't doubt the written word...and this was just a poor little wasp.

If anyone tells you something you may not believe it, but if he shows you that same thing written in a book then you will believe it.

I have a friend who writes poetry. His poems are just trash. If one listens to his poems one gets a headache. His poetry is just the opposite of an aspirin – it *creates* a headache. So no one listens to it. Sometimes he used to read them to me. One day he told me, "Nobody listens to my poems. People say that they are very busy. If I see my friends they just disappear. If I go to the coffee house then people don't sit at my table. What am I to do?"

I suggested to him, "Get the poems printed."

THE SONG OF ECSTASY

He said, "Who will read them? People are not ready to listen to them. Besides, getting them printed is quite expensive."

I said, "Printed words have a magical effect on people. But if that seems expensive to you then take this tape recorder and get them taped on this. Then go to the coffee house tomorrow with this tape recorder and tell your friends that you have recorded some poems."

When he came back after two days he said, "What a miracle! Those fools were not ready to listen to me, but were listening to the tape recorder very attentively." This is the effect of the machine. You can deny man, but you cannot deny the machine.

In New York, a thief with a gun entered a house, closed all the doors and broke open the safe. As people came to know about this, he stood with his gun at the window – it was very dangerous for anyone to enter, as he was standing at the window with the gun.

Then somebody went to a nearby house and telephoned that house. The telephone in the house rang, the robber put the gun aside and answered the phone and said, "Excuse me, I am very busy." But meanwhile he was caught.

When he was asked why he went to answer the phone, he said, "What could I do? The telephone was ringing so it had to be answered." So he left the gun to answer the telephone!

This is the magical effect of the machine. If anyone knocks at the door it doesn't matter, but if the telephone is ringing – even if it is not your house – you will answer it.

That friend of mine said, "Now I will certainly get my poems printed and they will read them. They will even buy the book and read it. When I ask them to listen to me for free they don't like it, but they listened to the tape recorder very attentively."

Certainly printed words are very effective. If someone is talking to you about something and you don't believe it, if he shows that very thing written in a book at once you will believe it — as if being written in a book is a proof of its being true. In reality, ninety-nine percent of things written in books are false, but they seem true because they are written in books. Yes, books are very effective.

The wasp came under the influence of books. It did not have any disease which was to be treated, it did not have any complex which was to be removed by yoga postures. Nothing was wrong with it except that it was under a false notion, a false idea. Nothing is to be done with a false notion except it has to be given up. A bird attacked it and it became nervous, that was all that was needed.

The master is also like this bird which attacks you. If you become nervous and confused, in that moment you have the realization. That is why one is scared of a master. He is not doing anything; he just laughs at you and at the same time feels pity for you, because you are not ill, but you imagine that you are. There is no doubt that you are miserable, but you are miserable without any reason. Misery is just mental — you *think* you are miserable, so that thinking has to be removed. By nature you are always healthy. The divine has not forsaken you, he is in your every cell. But somehow you think that something is wrong. Nothing was ever wrong, except this thought that something is wrong.

The wasp flew away. Even then it didn't think.... The ego of man never thinks itself to be wrong — not even in the past. The wasp thought that there must have been a block in the mind on account of which it couldn't fly. Now that block is removed. In the moment of crisis that block is broken, the energy has awakened, so now she can fly. She didn't realize there was no block. She was just sitting idly and she had read about this block in the psychology books.

Books are your death. Try to come into life a little. Please say good-bye to the Vedas, the Koran and the Bible. Yes, you should say good-bye to them in these words, "Please excuse me now, enough is enough. Now let me live a natural life as it is."

To be natural is to be religious. You have become unnatural. You don't suffer from any disease, but you have the illusion of suffering from disease. Actually the world is not, it is only an illusion. Only the divine is. That is why Shankara calls the world *maya*, illusion.

If you are suffering from an imaginary disease you want treatment – and there are people ready to treat you. Then all sorts of troubles start with the treatment – because the right medicine can prove to be harmful, dangerous for the patient who is suffering from an imaginary disease. Of course, if the medicine itself is wrong, then it is alright; then one trouble leads to another. But if you can diagnose the basic trouble then it will disappear. The wasp was a bit too wise and that was its foolishness.

Now you are asking, "Yesterday, while narrating the story of the wasp, you told us about the mental block." No, I did not say anything about it. You must have heard something else. And this is the trouble, that when I say something you hear something else and do something else, and later on you will make me responsible for this by saying, "You said so."

Sometimes some people come to me and they say "You said so" with so much confidence that I also keep quiet, because if they didn't understand before how will they understand now? I keep quiet – yes, I must have said so, otherwise how did you hear it? I *must* have said it. But just because you heard this, doesn't mean that I said it. Now you have heard that yesterday, in the story of the wasp, I had told you about the mental block. Not at all, I did not say anything about it. The wasp was absolutely healthy; it could fly, it could dance, it could enjoy the spring, it could happily hum a song in the light of the sun, but just by reading about the mental block in a book of psychology it got this illusion that it couldn't fly.

Now you ask, "How to remove the complex by spiritual practices?" You are also like the wasp – you just collapsed after reading the scriptures, because it is written in the scriptures that you cannot fly.

Have more faith in yourself than in the scriptures. You are the judge, not the scriptures. Listen to your very nature, obey your nature; your nature will free you. Whosoever listens to his own nature and acts according to it, is able to understand the scriptures also. Only then can the scriptures be understood in their right sense. It doesn't mean what you thought. But you always understand just what you want to understand. Even for your disease you take the support of the scriptures; then the disease becomes deeper.

What was wrong with this wasp? Why did it believe this so quickly? The disease was that it was already in the habit of running down the other wasps. It used to say, "These vagabonds are in the habit of wandering here and there – they don't think, they don't study the scriptures, they have no idea about how to lead a high, pure and peaceful life. They are wasting their life dancing on the flowers." The wasp already had the ego of being extraordinary. It considered the other wasps to be very inferior.

It was this illusion which was the cause of the trouble it faced with the scripture. When it read that a wasp cannot fly, it said, "This is absolutely correct and I am the only one who has attained this knowledge. All these other wasps are ignorant fools." The ego of this knowledge made it sit down. It was enjoying running down and condemning other wasps. But by doing this his ego was getting inflated.

Go and see your so-called *sadhus* and sannyasins – they are also sitting like this wasp. They don't fly, they keep away from life, and they greatly condemn the people of this world. They say, "You will go to hell because of your attachments, because of your worldly involvements." They also think that it is because of ignorance that people are attached to this world. According to them, the whole world is ignorant; only the one or two persons who are sitting like corpses in the temple are full of knowledge.

I say to you, God wants you to go through this attachment. There is a secret behind going through attachments: one gains maturity only after experiencing this attachment. These escapists who are hiding themselves in the temples are going to be proved wrong. They only think in terms of ego. You enjoy food, they enjoy fasting, because then they can show off that they are not interested in eating while you are fond of food like animals. You like comfort, and they deliberately stand in the sun or lie down on a bed of thorns to torture the body. What madness! But their only enjoyment is your condemnation, and that can be done very easily by lying on a bed of thorns. You cannot lie down on thorns, you have not read the scriptures, but these people have read all the scriptures.

Your so-called sadhus and sannyasins do all sorts of austerities and renunciations just to satisfy their egos. They have not attained any heaven; it is nothing else but ego gratification. To enjoy their ego trip it is necessary for them to indulge in things which are just the opposite to whatever you do; they will do the opposite. And you are very impressed by these things – you think that they have done miracles. You are foolish, but they are more foolish than you. You are standing on your feet and they are standing on their heads, and they say that they are doing *shirshasan*, the headstand.

Man is meant to walk on his feet, otherwise God would have made arrangements for him to walk on his head. There is no need to stand on your head, but the one who is doing it can certainly look down upon you, thinking that he is doing something wonderful, something great, and that you are standing on your feet like ignorant fools. And the fact is that those persons who have egos are highly impressed by the exhibition of such a type of ego and they also start doing the yoga postures.

Now you are asking, "How to remove the complex by spiritual practices?" I don't see any complex in you which has to be removed. You are just as you should be – just forget the illusion of a complex. The day you give up this illusion of a complex you will be surprised to realize that you were always without it and you wasted time under this illusion.

When Buddha became enlightened, the first sentence he said

was, "Oh Lord, the maker of the houses of desire. Now you will not have to make any more houses for me, because I have caught the source of desire and the source of desire is my imagination. I have understood that this was all the web of imagination. But now I have found the original source – it is the imagination! Now that journey of desires has stopped."

Your complex is in your imagination. Your desire is also in your imagination. Your world is also in your imagination. Truth is always as it was. Even now it is the same, even tomorrow it will be the same. The day you drop this web of imagination you will realize that you missed a lot of joy in vain.

But there are hypochondriacs – you must also know some of them – who go on creating disease after disease. They are always running to doctors. Sometimes they are running to the allopathic doctor, sometimes to the homeopath, sometimes to the naturopath and sometimes to the ayurved. They are never at rest, they are always running to different places for treatment, and everywhere they are told that they don't have any disease. But they get very upset to hear this and they say, "We are suffering so much from these diseases, and you say we have no disease!" They can be satisfied only if they are told that they are suffering from a very serious and dangerous disease – "You are the first one to get it, and such a rare disease!"

I have heard about an old woman who was always complaining about being ill, but nobody believed her because actually she was not ill. And if the doctor treated her for one particular disease she would start complaining about others – either she had a headache, or her hands and feet ached, or her whole body ached.

Certainly, there is no end to imaginary diseases. At last she died, but before dying she told the people that the inscription on her grave should be: "Now you will have to believe that I was ill." Now she has died, so people must believe that she died because of her disease.

Once a mentally unbalanced man was brought to me. He was a healthy young man, but he was suffering from the idea that two flies had entered his body through his nose while he was sleeping, and now they go on buzzing inside him and because of them he cannot eat, he cannot sleep, he feels uncomfortable all the time. All sorts of treatments had been given to him, but they had no effect on him. The doctors had told him that there were no flies inside; the X-ray doesn't show them. He said, "Your X-ray must be wrong, because I hear the noise of their droning all the time, I can feel them moving in my bones! Your X-ray doesn't show them, but I go on suffering." He was right in saying that he was suffering.

I said, "Okay – let me try. Now lie down and close your eyes. Don't open them until I ask you to do so. Meanwhile, we will try to take out the flies."

He liked my telling him that I will try to take out the flies. He at once touched my feet and said, "You are the only sensible person I have met up to now. The other people just start laughing when I complain to them about the flies, and one feels very bad if the doctor laughs at him. But you will certainly cure me."

I said, "Yes, I can see the flies. It is surprising that the X-ray doesn't show them."

I blindfolded him and made him lie down. I ran into the house and with great difficulty caught hold of two flies and put them into a bottle. He opened his eyes and saw the flies in the bottle. I told him, "See! I have taken them out."

But he said, "These are not the flies. The ones inside me are big flies, these are the small ones found in houses. They are big flies, and they are still moving inside me."

I said, "Well, I could only take out these two."

He said, "These two also might have been there, but the real ones are still inside."

Now what can you do with such a man? He who can imagine two flies, can also imagine four. You may catch two, now he says they are not the same as the ones which are moving inside him. Then I understood that if I get two more flies, he is not going to accept these either. What to do with such a man?

You pity him because he is suffering without any reason. The suffering is imaginary. If it had been real, then it could have been treated. But the suffering is so false that it cannot even be treated.

One feels like laughing at him because it is entirely up to him to give up the disease. If he had believed that these flies were the same which had been troubling him, then he could have been cured. But he found out another way of not getting cured, by saying that these are not the same flies: "You have worked hard to get these flies, but they are not the same ones."

Your diseases and your complexes are just like that – they are imaginary. Nothing is wrong with you, it cannot be. When the divine is everything, then how can anything be wrong? It is just a web of your imagination.

If you can wake up, you can wake up this very moment; then there is nothing to be done. This not doing anything is *bhaj Govindam* – bhaj Govindam means that nothing else is to be done: just by singing the song of the divine the disease will be cured.

If the disease was real, then it could not have been cured by bhaj Govindam. By singing the song of the divine, how can the real disease be cured? How can cancer be cured by singing the song of the divine?

But the enlightened ones have said that if you even remember the song of the divine then all the diseases will disappear, because there is no disease. In the moment of remembrance, in the moment of dedication to the divine, you will suddenly realize that there never was any disease – you are a pure buddha, you are without any name, without any form, without any blemish. There is not even a black line on you. It is all a web of imagination. Try again to understand the story of the wasp. It is your story.

The fourth question:

> Beloved Osho,
> Is it possible for a man's mind to become like the mind of the newborn baby?

Definitely. A lake is absolutely calm, peaceful, but with the incoming breeze the waves start rising. But if the breeze stops, the waves will also stop and the lake will become calm. It will again become like a mirror. The lake is clean; with the falling of the leaves it becomes dirty, but when the leaves settle down the lake will again become clean and fresh.

A child is born – the lake is still clean, there are no ripples, there are no leaves of thought, no waves of desire. Then with the advent of youth storms arise, strong winds blow and the lake is full of waves. The mirror is lost. There is a terrific onset of passion. Then old age comes and the storm is over – the lake is calm again. A little understanding – let the leaves settle down. A little understanding – let the winds of passion stop. The lake will become calm again; there is no difference in the nature of the lake.

When the mind again becomes innocent like the mind of a child then we call that man a saint. A saint becomes like a child. That is why Shankara has said that the ultimate yogi ...*sometimes plays like a child and sometimes like a madman.* Sometimes he looks as innocent as a child – he is absolutely empty, there is nothing inside him. And sometimes terrible unknown storms arise in him – then he looks absolutely insane, mad.

There is a childlike innocence even in a madman, and there is insanity like the madman even in children. Small children get mad at small things. When they want a toy they will dance, they will jump, they will even break things because they want the toy, right now! They may be very angry now, but they will start laughing after a moment and will forget all about the anger. There is some similarity between mad people and children – that is why mad people have the innocent look of children in their eyes and there is something of madness in the eyes of children.

The enlightened one becomes both at the same time. Sometimes he looks like a child and sometimes he looks like a madman. Because he no longer observes any rules, he doesn't bother about dignity, prestige, sin or virtue, so to people he seems mad. That is why he looks like a child also – because the child also doesn't know anything about dignity, sin or virtue. A child is before dignity starts, and a saint is beyond dignity. In between the two is the world where there are limitations: dignity, prestige, morality, rules, sin, virtue, lucky, unlucky, worth doing and not worth doing – both the ends are there.

Certainly a moment which was once in your life can come again. You were a child – that child became lost, but he still exists in the crowd of your thoughts. When these thoughts calm down, suddenly the child will be rediscovered. That is saintliness.

The fifth question:

> Beloved Osho,
> Sometimes Shri Shankaracharya says that nothing will happen by the pilgrimage to the Ganges and sometimes he says that even by drinking a drop of the Ganges water, a man conquers death.
> Please clarify this contradiction.

The outer Ganges and the inner Ganges.... Nothing will happen if you undertake the journey to the outer Ganges, because the journey of the outer Ganges is an outer journey, it cannot send you inside. But if you drink even a drop of the inner Ganges then you will attain, because to drink even a drop of the inner Ganges you will have to go absolutely inside – only then you can drink a drop of that water. The pilgrimage is not outside – outside is only the world. The pilgrimage is within, inside. The more you go in – the more you enjoy within yourself – the nearer you get to the pilgrimage. All the pilgrimages like Girnar, Shikharji, Kaaba, Kailash, Kashi, are within you. Save yourself from the illusion of the outside.

But we are in the habit of looking out, so when we try to look for the divine, we look for him outside. When we are looking for the temple, it means outside. Godliness is within you. It is hiding within the one who is seeking it. It is the one who is searching. Try to recognize your consciousness; one drop of it is sufficient.

The story is that when the Ganges came down onto the earth, only half of it came, the other half remained in heaven. That means that when the Ganges came, only half of it came, half of it remained within. Heaven means within, heaven means sinking deep within oneself. And hell means getting lost in the other.

The great thinker of the West named Jean-Paul Sartre has said, "The other is hell."

Heaven is within oneself. You live in hell while you are dependent on others. When you gain your freedom, your individuality, your autonomy, your being yourself, and you don't depend on others, you don't remain a beggar and you become your own master – then it is heaven.

Begging for anything from others means humiliation; that is hell. From the other you will only get misery in your begging-bowl. You will never get happiness from the other.

Come inside. The inner Ganges is the other half of the heavenly Ganges. Even one drop of it is enough, it is nectar. Nothing will happen by bathing in the outer Ganges. The fish and the crocodiles live in the Ganges, other animals also bathe in the Ganges: does that mean that all these creatures go to heaven? They don't, and you cannot bathe more than them – you will take just one dip and come home. Whom are you trying to deceive? You are like a blind man who has eyes – you have eyes and yet you are blind.

Don't deceive yourself. The Ganges is inside.

Whatever is valuable is inside. Whatever is garbage is outside, but the real wealth is inside.

The sixth question:

> Beloved Osho,
> You say that one attains truth through the grace of the master. Then why do you also encourage the effort of ego?

Truth is attained through the grace of the master, but you cannot receive the grace of the master without your effort. The divine is attained through grace, but one has to seek the master, one has to have the ability to be near the master.

Effort has to be made, but always remember that the ultimate is attained without effort. This will seem contradictory to you, but these are the two wings, the two oars – effort and grace. The journey is completed with these two.

In this world there are two types of illusion. Some people think that they will attain the divine by their effort. They never attain because their ego never disappears; the effort makes it even stronger – the doors remain closed instead of opening. There is also the other type of person who believes that the divine cannot be attained through effort, but only through grace. They just sit idly and do nothing – they don't attain because of their laziness. Some fail because of their ego and some fail because of their laziness. The divine is found through untiring effort and yet without effort.

From your side you have to do it wholeheartedly; nothing should remain undone by you. You should put the whole of yourself at stake, only then will you deserve his grace. Then you can say, "I have nothing more to stake, now please bless me with your grace." You will have the right to ask for his grace only when you have done all that was possible for you to do and now there is nothing remaining.

You cannot get grace for free. Grace is a very valuable diamond which you cannot get for free. When you have put everything at stake then prayer can rise from your heart – then you can say, "Nothing happens by my doing. Now it is all up to you." In that very moment when you realize that nothing can be done by you and you say, "I have staked everything, I have poured myself completely, even then nothing is happening. Now your grace is needed." Then you will certainly attain his grace.

The divine is always attained through grace, because your effort is very small and the divine is so vast. You will not attain with effort, but with your effort you come near the point where the drop is ready to bear the ocean.

The last question:

> Beloved Osho,
> You said, while in misery live it thoroughly, find out its cause and wake up.
> What happens when one wakes up?

Waking up or awakening means that the dream is over – whatever was known up to now remains no longer. So it is difficult to say what awakening means, because your language is of sleep. At present, whatever can be told to you or whatever can be understood by you will be in the language of the dream. If I say that you will get happiness, then you will think of the happiness which you have known in the dream. If I say that you will not get misery, then you will think of the same misery which you have known in the dream.

If you think, you will not attain. That is why all the buddhas have kept quiet. Whenever someone asked what will happen after the awakening they just kept quiet. They said, "Wake up and see," because this is beyond the language which you know, or this is beyond your understanding which you have through language. Neither your happiness nor your misery is there. Neither your peace nor your restlessness is there. Neither your satisfaction nor your dissatisfaction – whatever you have known up to now is not there. The scriptures you have known up to now are also not there. The images of the divine which were made by you are also not there. Your notions about heaven and hell are also not there. When you are not there, your notions also will not be there.

There is something which cannot be described, which cannot be defined – you can call it *brahman, Vishnupad, jinpad* or buddha-hood, but even by these words nothing can be known. If you wake up, only then can you know. A dumb man cannot describe the taste of sugar, but he can enjoy it.

What will happen after awakening? You will taste the divine, the taste which you have been trying to get all these past lives but could not get – you missed it always. It just cannot be described. If you are bored of the way you have been living, then wake up. But if you have not even a little bit of interest in it yet, then just turn over and go to sleep again.

But you will have to wake up one day. Sleep cannot be eternal, and sleep cannot be the ultimate rest, and darkness cannot be the experience of the ultimate truth. Sooner or later you will have to get up – it all depends on you. But whenever you awaken you will repent for not having woken up earlier – it just meant spreading out your hand – it was so near.

Jesus says again and again, "Repent – the kingdom of God is at hand."

Enough for today.

9

THE ESSENCE IN LIFE

Dropping sex, anger, greed and attachment,
meditate upon yourself: Who am I?
Because fools without self-realization
suffer the anguish of deep hell here.

Only the Gita and the Sahastranam
— the one thousand names of God —
are worth singing; only the form of Vishnu
is worth meditating upon incessantly.
One should always seek
the company of good people,
one should give money to the poor only.

One indulges with woman for pleasure,
but what a pity that in the end
one only has a worn-out body.
Although death is the only certainty in this world,
people do not stop sinning.

Money is disaster — always contemplate over it.
The truth is that there is
no happiness in money at all.
It has been seen everywhere that the rich man
is afraid even of his own sons.

Pranayam and pratyahar,
intelligent discrimination between
transient and intransient,
disciplining of samadhi with japa —
discipline all these with caution,
with great caution.

Totally surrendered
to the lotus feet of the master,
free from the bondages of the world,
having disciplined the mind along with the senses,
you will be able to see the divine within your heart.

THE SONG OF ECSTASY

There is a Greek mythological story: There was a very handsome young man named Narcissus, who fell in love with a young woman named Echo. This name is worth pondering over. People fall in love with echoes. You always fall in love where you hear your own voice, where your own ego is satisfied, where you find yourself in the hidden form. Your love is nothing but the extension of your ego. Echo also fell in love with him. Echo has to fall in love, because she is the echo of your voice. There is no possibility or way of her being separate from you.

But one day a mishap occurred. It had to be so, because mishaps are certain in the life of one who is deceived by echoes – one who falls in love with his own voice. Narcissus had gone to the forest. There in the lake, which was absolutely calm, there was not even a ripple, he saw his own reflection. He was enchanted. He saw his own face in the lake, which was like a mirror. He saw it for the first time. It was so lovely! Who doesn't like his own face? People love only their own faces. Narcissus became hypnotized, he couldn't move, he became still. Attachment creates this type of stillness. He was afraid to move lest the reflection breaks. He didn't move from there. Echo kept on waiting for him, and when Narcissus did not return, love died.

Echo – your voice can echo only if you go on humming. If your humming stops, then for a little while the echo will be heard in the mountains and then it will be lost. Narcissus didn't come back. They say that standing at that lake Narcissus became a plant: there is a plant named Narcissus which is often found on lakes, streams and rivers. If you ever come across it you must watch it carefully: it is always looking into the water, it is always looking at its own reflection.

This is a wonderful, mythological story. If you become enchanted by yourself then you lose consciousness; then you don't remain a human being, you become a plant. Then the humanity in you disappears, your inner soul is negated, you fall back. A plant has no freedom. Man is free, he can walk – a plant cannot do so, it doesn't have feet, it has roots. Narcissus became a plant – it means that any person who gets caught in the reflections of the ego, his feet become roots, he stops; his pace stops and he loses his freedom of movement.

This happens to almost all people. The Upanishads say that when a man loves his wife, actually it is not the wife whom he loves but through the wife he loves himself. A man doesn't actually love his children, but in the children, through the children, he loves himself. Children are a mirror, the wife is also a mirror. And every man is Narcissus.

The doors of the ultimate freedom cannot open with this kind of mental condition of man, in fact it finishes whatever little freedom he has. You should have had wings so that you could fly towards the divine – but you lost even your feet!

Do you understand the bondage of the tree? It cannot move, it has to stand wherever it is, it cannot move even an inch from where it is standing. It is helpless, it has no freedom to move.

Man can move, he can walk. A bird can fly. But there is a limit to the movement of the body; at a certain point it gets tired, and that tiredness will become the bondage. And even if a bird is able to fly for miles, you cannot measure the sky in miles. It will get tired – there is a limit to the body. And freedom can be freedom only when it is unlimited. The freedom of soul is needed. When the soul has wings and it can fly without any limit, without any obstacle, without any chains, then that is *moksha*, liberation.

The search is for moksha. Your search for happiness is actually the search for this moksha. That is why every happiness of yours becomes a misery, because when you find that instead of salvation you have got bondage, then the happiness doesn't appear like happiness. When you are in search of money, even that is for moksha. You think that with money you will get a little freedom, you will be able to move about a little. The poor man's sky is small; a rich man's sky is a little bigger, more convenient. But when you have money you find that your space, your sky, has become even smaller than the poor man's sky. The money did not give you any freedom, it has become a bondage. Now you cannot even give it up.

There are stories about wealthy people, that after their death they become serpents and they guard their treasures. It is not necessary to know what happens after their death, because the fact is that even when they are alive they guard their wealth like serpents. Those who have money are always afraid of losing it, they are always guarding it. They don't enjoy it. They are not even the masters of their money; they are just guarding it. Very seldom does one come across a wealthy man who is really the master of his wealth. A poor man may be the master of his poverty, but the rich man is not the master of his money.

If you watch carefully you will find that man wants money for freedom, he wants position for freedom. If you have position, power, the capacity, then you think you will be able to break away from a few bondages and you will be able to enter a little

THE ESSENCE IN LIFE

into the unknown and the unknowable.

Man wants freedom from every side. Deep down in the consciousness of man the yearning is only for moksha. That is why every type of bondage makes him restless. Even when you fall in love you do so in the hope that this love will become a sky, that you will be able to fly. You hope to get somebody's support in attaining freedom. But when you fall in love you find that, never mind flying, you cannot even move. You expected to get support from the other, but the other, the lover, finished all your freedom, and thus love became a bondage. Freedom is only in dreams, and in reality it is only bondage.

The Prophet is a unique book by Kahlil Gibran. In it a person asks, "Speak to us of love." And the hero of this book, Almustafa, says, "Love each other, but don't possess each other. Be near each other, but not too near. You should be like the pillars of a temple which hold the same roof and yet remain far from each other. If the pillars of the temple come nearer, then the roof will fall down. Keep a little distance from the lover so that there can be some free space between the two. If this empty space is absolutely lost then you will be trespassing on each other, attacking each other."

But all these things are written in books. In real life we take away all the freedom from the person we love because we are afraid that his love may turn somewhere else: "Somebody else may become the possessor of the love which I have." We are always afraid of losing whatever we have. If we have money, then we are afraid of losing money. If we have love, then we are afraid of losing love. Because of this fear, freedom becomes impossible.

The flower of freedom blossoms only in a state of fearlessness. The only yearning one has is for freedom. Everyone's inner search is for liberation.

Wherever you get this freedom, you will be overjoyed. You will become sad whenever you feel the bondage. If you are sad, then the reason is very clear: you wanted freedom but got chains; you wanted the sky but got a prison; you wanted wings for flying but even your feet were cut off; you wanted ultimate freedom and you staked and lost everything you had for it. There is no chance of getting what you hoped for. That is why you are sad.

The meaning of the word 'god' can only be moksha. That is why the great enlightened people have not used the word 'god.' Mahavira talks about moksha and not about God, because there are many illusions with the word 'god' and even the word has created prisons. Buddha also talks about *nirvana* and not about God, because even the word 'god' has created new bondages – of being a Hindu, a Muslim or a Christian. A Hindu is tied down to being a Hindu, a Mohammedan is tied down to being a Mohammedan. Somebody is tied to a temple and somebody is tied to a mosque.

Religion is the ultimate freedom. That is why there cannot be any temple or mosque of religion. The day you become really religious, you will see the divine in the temple as well as in the mosque. Then sometimes you will pray in the temple and sometimes in the mosque. Actually, there will be no need for you to go to the temple or the mosque; you will be able to see the divine in your own house, you will see him everywhere.

You can understand this last sutra of Shankara only if you keep in mind that religion is the ultimate freedom.

> Dropping sex, anger, greed and attachment,
> meditate upon yourself.

Sex, anger, greed and attachment, these are the four bondages which keep your moksha, your freedom, suppressed. The base of all these four is sex. Because sex creates attachment, attachment creates greed, and anger is born towards the person who creates an obstacle to our greed. The basic disease is sex.

You must understand the meaning of 'sex.' The meaning of 'sex,' is the hope of getting happiness from the other. 'Sex' means, that my happiness is outside myself. And 'meditation' means, that my happiness is within me.

The journey will become very easy if you understand these two definitions properly. The meaning of sex is that my happiness is outside of me, in someone else; if the other gives then I can get it. I cannot find the happiness alone. It is miserable to be alone and it is a pleasure to be in the company of the other. That is why you don't want to be alone. You are afraid to be alone. You feel uncomfortable when you are alone even for a short time. As soon as you are alone you start throwing all types of garbage into yourself. You will start reading the newspaper all over again – you will not mind if you have read the same paper three or four times! Or you will switch on the radio so that there can be some noise to save you from being alone. Or you will play cards, or you run to a hotel or a club – anywhere, anyhow.

A young man came to me three days ago and said that because he is meditating, his fear of being alone is increasing – sometimes he just runs out of the house and goes to the bazaar, and by being in the crowd of the bazaar he gets the feeling of relief that he is not alone. He comes home feeling reassured.

You say that you are very busy, but most of the busyness of your life is not necessary; that time can be utilized for your rest. It is not that work is very important, but you feel lost without work.

In the West, the psychologists have a new worry, and this is troubling people for the first time in the history of mankind. In the Western countries like America and Sweden, the worry is that by the end of this century when all the work will be done by robots, man will have a lot of free time. So the psychologists are worried about what man will do in his free time, because as yet man doesn't have the ability to be empty or to sit quietly. Just think of the situation: all the work is being done by the machines and there is no work for you!

Now you say that there is too much work and you want to have some free time to rest – although even when you do have free time now you don't rest; you just cannot spend the Sunday holiday sitting at home so you go on a picnic. On Sunday you get bored and you start thinking of Monday, you wait eagerly for Monday so that you can start your work again.

But if your whole life becomes a Sunday holiday, will you be able to tolerate that much rest and peace? No, you will find ways and means to keep yourself involved and occupied.

Psychologists say that we will have to find some types of work which may not be of any utility, but which can be given to the people who cannot sit idle. And a unique idea has come to their minds. The government will give money to those people who are ready to sit idle; it will pay you for sitting idle! But those who work will not get paid, because two things cannot be given at the same time − work and pay.

It seems very strange to us now, but the Western countries are getting nearer to this point. The Eastern countries just cannot imagine this, because there is so much poverty, so much conflict in these countries. But at the close of this century the people who are ready to sit idle will be called gentlemen and those who are not ready to do so will be called non-gentlemen.

But only that person can sit idle who has tasted meditation. That is why people are now keenly interested in meditation in the West. They are very eager to know about it. Nothing happens without reason; whenever anything is going to happen the consciousness becomes eager about it.

It is not by chance that people from faraway Western countries are coming to me. They have an acute desire to know the happiness of being with oneself − because one doesn't find, one *cannot* find happiness, by being with the other. It is always miserable to be with the other. But the problem is that we don't know the art of being alone. That is why we go on tolerating the hell which the other is making us suffer. And there is no way out, because to be alone is absolutely intolerable, *more* hellish. So we prefer to be with the hell of the other rather than suffer the hell of being alone. At least we can talk a little with the other − never mind if it turns out to be a quarrel.

Have you ever thought about it? If you are left alone, you think that it is better to be in the company of the enemy than to be left with oneself. You can fight with the enemy, you can abuse him and feel a little lively. But you can do nothing when you are alone; you just sit like a dead person. One must do something. Then people start pottering around in the room.

I used to travel a lot by train. Very often I would be left alone with another passenger in the compartment, so I used to watch what the other person was doing. I would not talk to him, because if I talked his reality would not be revealed.

He would make attempts to converse with me by asking, "Where are you going?" I would reply in monosyllables and close my eyes. When he could understand that it was impossible to make conversation with this man, then his real self would be revealed. I would watch him quietly. He would open his suitcase, then close it, again arrange it properly; he would open the window, then close it, and feel very restless. He would start the fan and then put it off. He would go out and bring tea. He would get down at every station to buy some snacks, or would call the servant and talk to him.

But I understand his restlessness. He is unable to tolerate the aloneness of twenty-four hours in a train. He just cannot relax in these twenty-four hours, although he would also claim that he cannot even get a minute's time for meditation because he is very busy. If a man becomes absolutely peaceful, absolutely empty for just twenty-four hours, he will surely become a Mahavira.

In fact, twenty-four hours are too much time because Mahavira has said that if a person becomes absolutely empty for forty-eight minutes he will become enlightened. Just forty-eight minutes, not even one full hour! I am saying twenty-four hours, so that the Jainas are not angry with me. Mahavira has said that if a man becomes empty just for forty-eight minutes, that is sufficient. Just forty-eight minutes, not even an hour. The fact is that you cannot be peaceful even for forty-eight seconds. You yourself will create many disturbances.

Sex means happiness in the other. One never gets it, and that is the idiocy of man. There is certainly some reason for Shankara to call you a fool; he says it after a lot of contemplation. You go on hoping against hope, and you know it. You go on trying to extract oil from sand. If you didn't know this it means you are ignorant, and an ignorant person can be excused. But a fool cannot be excused. A person who goes on hoping against hope is certainly a fool. He knows that oil cannot be extracted out of sand, yet he goes on trying because he cannot sit idle.

Just look at your life carefully. Really, you are foolish! Just think: how many times have you had the urge for sex? How many times have you indulged in sex? Have you ever been satisfied? Have you ever been happy? But you are afraid of even thinking about these facts. You are just keeping yourself involved in this way to pass your life away. You will feel lost without it.

So you carry on this game, and the name of the game is sex. In fact, this is the only game, this is the whole world. You are too much entangled, too involved in it. You know that this path won't take you anywhere – it has never taken anyone anywhere – yet the mind goes on deceiving you by saying, "It might not have taken me anywhere until now, but tomorrow it may take me somewhere – I may prove to be the exception." Everyone thinks like this.

It is said that there is a very famous proverb in Arabia, that whenever God creates anyone he whispers in his ear, out of fun, "I have made you very special, you are an exception. The rest of the people are very ordinary, but you are extraordinary." That is why each person thinks that he is unique. "The others are just ordinary people, but I am special!"

Because of this joke of God's, each one of you has this idea of being unique. You don't tell it to the other person, but the other person also thinks in the same way. And without saying anything, you try to tell the other about this: the other one also tries to tell you without saying anything. And those who say it loudly are put into mental asylums. But each one has the illusion that he is an exception.

Buddhas have said that after searching in all the deserts of sex, no oasis of happiness could be found. Mahavira has said the same thing. Shankara says, that in spite of the long journey no oasis, not even the shadow of a date palm could be found. A date palm hardly has any shadow, but even that could not be found. But you go on thinking that others may have just missed it. They might not have been able to find it – they may not know its location, or they may not have been sensible enough to get a map – and since they did not get it they go on saying that it is impossible to find. Or, they may be thinking, "It doesn't exist and I didn't want it anyway."

You are always under such illusions, and hence you will never be able to get rid of sex. And if you don't wake up from sex, you cannot be aware of the divine. Only he who is able to wake up from sex can become aware of the divine. It is no use chanting the name of the divine, because if the mind is full of sex then your chanting itself will be polluted.

When the mind is empty of sex then there is no need to chant; then the call will arise on its own, your every fiber will be calling out to the divine – this is not something which you can do yourself. This is not something which needs the support of your throat or of your lips or of your tongue. This will be possible only when sex disappears from your being. Suddenly you will find a perfume arising from your being. When the energy being used in sex is freed, it turns towards the divine.

'Sex, means the false hope of happiness in the other.

The divine, means to find the happiness within oneself

And that is the only place of happiness. Everyone who has lost happiness has lost it in the same manner as you have lost it. That is why Shankara says, "Oh fool! Wake up!" But it is very difficult to see the fool in oneself.

A play was being staged in Mulla Nasruddin's village. They needed a fool in the play, so they chose a political leader for this role. This leader was a big fool: if he had not been a fool he could not have been a leader! Anyone with a little bit of sense doesn't like to be a leader, because people throw shoes and rotten tomatoes at them, curse them, abuse them. But a leader doesn't mind all these things; he is only worried about remaining in the chair. This leader was also the same type of person, so the people requested him to play this role. The leader asked Mulla Nasruddin for his advice on how to act this role correctly.

Nasruddin looked at him from top to toe and said, "Please go on the stage as you are. There is no need to make any change."

The leader was very annoyed. He said, "I know that you go on spreading the rumor in the village that I am the number one fool. Now you have said it to me."

Nasruddin protested vehemently, saying, "I might have called you a fool, but I didn't say that you are a number one fool. I know that you will never miss being first, even if it means being the number one fool!"

Really the leaders are always trying to be number one.

You are quite blind. You cannot see what the whole world is seeing. What sort of idiocy is this, that you go on desiring again and again the same experiences which you have had a thousand times and still haven't found happiness? When will you wake up? One who is asleep in sex is really asleep, and one who has awakened from sex is really awake.

And the journey of meditation starts only when you wake up from sex, because meditation means that happiness is within oneself. Admit defeat in the other. You have searched enough in the other; now repent it and return home.

> Dropping sex, anger, greed and attachment,
> meditate upon yourself.

Shankara is deliberately saying that you can meditate on yourself only when you give up these four. If sex is given up, if the hope of getting happiness from the other is over, if it can be realized that happiness is not in the other, then the revolution has happened, because as soon as you realize that happiness is not in the other, you will not have attachment for the other.

We are attached to those things from which we hope to get happiness. We look after them, we save them, we protect and guard them so that we may not lose them, so that others may not take them away from us. We have attachments for things which give us the hope of happiness. We go on thinking that "tomorrow we are sure to attain happiness," so we save these things for tomorrow. We don't learn anything from the experiences which we had in the past, and we go on hoping for tomorrow.

The question of greed doesn't arise if there is no attachment. Greed means the desire to get more pleasure out of the things which have given you some pleasure. If you have ten *rupees*, then you want one thousand: this is greed. If you have one house, then you want ten houses: this is greed. Actually, greed means the desire for multiplication of the thing which has given you pleasure. Attachment means to get hold of the thing which has given you pleasure, and greed means the desire for multiplication of that thing.

But why should you try to multiply the things which have given you no happiness? There is no reason for it. What does anger mean? When someone puts obstacles in the path of your desires which you think will bring you pleasure, you get angry. When you are trying to earn money and somebody is creating obstacles for you, then anger will be born. You are wanting to marry a particular woman and someone is putting obstacles in the way, then anger will be born. You were about to win an election when someone decided to stand against you with much noise and sloganeering; then anger will be born. Anger means when someone puts obstacles in the way of your desire.

So anger, greed and attachment are the shadows of desire.

People come to me and say that they want to give up anger. I tell them that this is a wrong thing to ask. Someone wants to know how to give up greed and someone asks how to give up attachment, but hardly anyone asks how to be free of desire. This means that you don't even know the basic problem of life. How can you find the solution? How can you be cured when you have not even diagnosed the illness?

Many people want to get rid of anger because it is troublesome – because of it people fight, and enmity is born unnecessarily. It is quite clear that anger creates a lot of trouble and unpleasantness, but this is like trying to get rid of your shadow while you are walking in the sun. For that I will have to say, "Don't go in the sun." But your answer is "It is impossible. I will walk in the sun, but there should not be any shadow. I will live in this world of desire, but there should be no anger."

Many times a desire is not fulfilled because of this anger. When one speaks one wrong word in anger the whole plan may be upset. So you want to get rid of anger, but you want this so that your sexual desires can be fulfilled more conveniently. But anger is nothing but the shadow of sex.

That is why Shankara has mentioned sex first, the second is anger...because whoever has lust has anger as well. When you have desire, competition will be born, enmity will be born.

You want to have money. The whole world wants to have money. The day this desire arose to gain money, you became the enemy of all those people who were also having the desire of gaining money. The seed of enmity is sown from that moment. Anger follows desire immediately. It may take years for its expression, but the journey has started. When you ask for something, when you desire something, anger is born – and this anger is so unpredictable!

You are sitting happily when a car passes by and you wish you had that car. You didn't even speak about this to anyone of course; you may say, "What is wrong? There is no quarrel, no conflict." But I say unto you that this is the beginning of anger in you against all those who will be obstacles in your way. The shadow of anger is forming in your subconscious. Soon it will enter the conscious, because you will have to struggle to get this car, you will have to compete with others to get this car and this will create enmity. If you have desired to have something which belongs to someone else, then surely anger will be born.

But this anger will not be born if, by your desiring and having something, the other person doesn't have to lose what he possesses. But there is only one such thing, and that is the divine – however much you attain, it is never snatched from others. If I attain the divine, then it will not make any difference to your attainment of the divine. In fact, if I attain, then you will get some help in attaining; then you will be able to attain sooner because by my attaining the door has opened.

If one has attained, the other can also attain. The stair is there, ready; only a little effort is needed. Now the confidence and the assurance are there. If one person has attained then he can show you the path, and he is called a *guru*, a master. One who has attained you call a master. He will be able to guide you.

The divine is the only thing which doesn't become less if one attains it. The divine is not a subject of economics. If anyone attains the divine, he doesn't become less; in fact he becomes available in greater quantity. If one person attains the divine all become rich. The attainment of one seems like the attainment of all. When Buddha attained, when Shankara attained, when Christ attained, that day the divine showered on the whole earth.

Nothing could be done for those whose pitchers were upside down, they couldn't get anything. But other pitchers were filled up. When Krishna attained, then thousands of pitchers were filled. When Buddha attained, thousands of pitchers were filled. When Shankara attained, then thousands of souls danced. This festival of ecstasy was not Shankara's alone.

Try to understand this. Only happiness is something which can be shared. Happiness is that which shares itself, which spreads. Happiness is something which doesn't have to be snatched from the other to get it. In fact, by your attaining it, others will also.

That is what we call bliss; that is what we call great happiness.

What you call pleasure is something very shallow. It is like the story in the Purana.

One kite caught hold of a dead rat and flew away. As soon as it had caught hold of the rat, the other kites started hovering around and attacking it. They went on pecking at it and the kite started bleeding badly. It was quite surprised at this attack, but it didn't give up the dead rat. But when the other kites attacked, it accidentally dropped the rat. As soon as the rat fell, all the kites which were hovering around left it alone and started chasing the rat. The kite sat on a tree and started thinking.

That kite must have been more intelligent than you. Shankara could not call it 'fool.' It thought in this way: "First I thought that all these kites were my enemies, but they went away as soon as I dropped the rat, which means that there was no personal enmity with me. The cause of their attack was this rat. The mistake was mine, I was holding the rat. I should have thrown it away earlier, but I was stupid enough to think that they are angry with me."

Ramakrishna used to tell this story often, and he used to say that holding a desire is like holding this dead rat in your mouth.

Yes, all around anger will be born, enmity will be born. You may go on saying that you have never harmed anyone: "I live quietly in my home, I am only concerned about my family. I don't have anything to do with others, then why do people become my enemies?" But indirectly you are concerned with others and others are concerned with you. You married the beautiful woman in whom the whole village was interested. Now you say, "I live with my family." But the whole village has become your enemy because you married that beautiful woman.

There was a custom in ancient India, which continued until Buddha's time, that the most beautiful girl of the village or town was not allowed to get married, because her marriage to one man would create a lot of trouble. Instead she was made the bride of the whole town – *nagar vadhu*. She was made the prostitute. That was the only way of keeping peace in the village.

You must have heard the name of Amrapali. She was a nagar vadhu – wife of all. The most beautiful woman of the village was not allowed to be the wife of one man because then people would start fighting, so it was better for her to be everyone's wife. But fighting is inevitable as far as sex is concerned. There used to be fights at Amrapali's gates also, because Amrapali could only be available to one man for one night, and all the men from far and near were keen to be with her. There must have been queues of people standing outside her door, there must have been competitions between the rich and the poor and the kings; there must have been a lot of suffering because of her. But this was the only solution.

If you have a dead rat in your mouth, then it is natural that all the other kites will attack. Just give up the rat, and suddenly you will find that the whole world has become friendly. With the disappearance of sex and desire the whole world seems friendly, there is no enemy. There was no enemy; the fight was because of the dead rat. You thought that it was because of personal enmity: it was because of the dead rat in your mouth.

That day the kite must have been in meditation, sitting alone on the tree. It could understand that there was no happiness in having that rat; it was the source of unhappiness. It was the cause of the enmity.

Anger cannot disappear if desire doesn't disappear. People ask me, "How to get rid of anger?" I tell them, "It is difficult. You are asking me the wrong thing. You want to cut the branches and save the root. This will create more branches. The root should be cut off."

That is why, first of all, Shankara says lust – that is the root; then anger, its shadow; then greed, its growth, its by-product; then attachment, its last conclusion. After giving them up, meditate on yourself. One can meditate on oneself only after giving them up, because then the mind is not on others.

When the desire is no more, then the mind is not attracted towards the subjects of desire. When anger is not there, then all the subjects of anger disappear. When there is no greed, then the anxiety involved in greed is also over. When you are free from all these, then the inner journey starts. And this inner journey is the only pilgrimage, the other pilgrimages are just deceptions. One who goes within has really reached the pilgrimage. The others who are wandering outside are fooling themselves.

> Meditate upon yourself: Who am I?
> Because fools without self-realization
> suffer the anguish of deep hell here.

Don't think that people without self-realization will suffer only after going to hell. People try to deceive themselves by saying that they will be miserable when they will go to hell – as if they are happy here. Will they suffer only when they go to hell? What are they getting here?

I have heard that recently, when people reach hell, Satan asks them, "Where have you come from?"

"From the earth," they reply.

He says, "Then you can go to heaven. You have already suffered hell on the earth."

Now the latest news is that those people who sin in hell are being sent to the earth for punishment. In hell, people are told that if they sin they will be sent to earth!

Shankara is saying that you are suffering hell here – what makes you think that you will go to hell in the future? These are just ways of fooling yourself. You think that you will suffer in hell – but aren't you suffering now? You have never gained anything but misery and unhappiness. You are full of suffering.

Ask yourself "Who am I?" But this can be asked only after the disappearance of the four. If you then ask, "Who am I?" you will get the reply. Actually, then there is no need to ask the question.

THE ESSENCE IN LIFE

You just close your eyes. Don't ask, "Who am I?" – you don't have to utter these words because now there is no one else to speak to, only you are. Whom are you going to ask, "Who am I?" You are facing yourself. Better see and recognize – What is there to ask? But Shankara is saying this for the sake of saying.

Shankara was very fond of a story:

A disciple used to ask the master, "What should I do to get self-realization?" The master just used to become deaf when he heard this. He used to reply to other questions, he used to hear everything, but whenever the disciple asked, "What am I to do to get self-realization?" suddenly the master used to become deaf. He became busy with some other work and never replied.

At last one day the disciple caught hold of him and shook him, and asked, "You reply to all my questions, but only when I ask you this...."

The master said, "I reply, but you don't listen. This is the only way of attaining self-realization, to keep quiet. I keep quiet so that you may listen, that you may understand."

This is the only secret: if one becomes quiet within. When the dead rat falls then the inner silence is natural. In that moment one becomes aware who one is.

> Only the Gita and the Sahastranam
> – the one thousand names of God –
> are worth singing; only the form of Vishnu
> is worth meditating upon incessantly.
> One should always seek
> the company of good people,
> one should give money to the poor only.
>
> Oh fool! Always sing the song of the divine.

Until all sex, anger, greed and attachment disappear, you can ask in your inner space without words, "Who am I?" — until then go on singing the Gita and the thousand names of the divine. Go on meditating on the form of Vishnu, be in the company of good people, give money to the poor — distribute as much as you can, and hear as much about truth as possible. Sing the songs of the divine. Go on making all these preparations until the arrival of that moment.

> One indulges with woman for pleasure,
> but what a pity that in the end
> one only has a worn out body.

You go in search of happiness, but you get only sickness. You go in search of life and you meet death.

> Although death is the only certainty in this world,
> people do not stop sinning.

Death is absolutely certain. Everything else can be uncertain, but death is not uncertain. To die is the only certainty. Even then people don't give up sinning. Everyone has to die, yet they are always ready to sin for a very small amount — as if they are going to live here forever, as if it will be very inconvenient for them to live here forever without this paltry sum of money.

People think that this waiting room of the railway station is their home. They arrange their luggage in such a way as if they are going to live here forever. But the bell is about to ring and the train is coming and they will soon have to pack up and board the train.

You must have seen in the waiting rooms of the railway stations that people don't even open their bed or suitcases, they just sit waiting, because why take the trouble of opening them when you have to be going in a short while? This life is also like a waiting room. It is just a night's halt, and everyone has to go on his journey in the morning.

If this could be seen, then it would become difficult to sin. For whom are you sinning? Why should it be done? Everything remains here in the end. Then why sin at all? You are able to sin because you live as if you are going to be here forever. You can sin only when you believe that you are not going to die. But your sinning will become less and less as you go on remembering death. That is why I consider the remembrance of death as a good deed. Sin becomes impossible in the life of a person who remembers death.

> Money is disaster – always contemplate over it.
> The truth is that there is
> no happiness in money at all.
> It has been seen everywhere
> that the rich man is afraid even of his own sons.

Therefore,

> Oh fool! Always sing the song of the divine.
> Pranayam and pratyahar,
> intelligent discrimination
> between transient and intransient,
> disciplining of samadhi with japa –
> discipline all these with caution, with great caution.

Pranayam and pratyahar...pranayam means that you should not think yourself to be small. Expand your energy, enlarge its dimension. You are big, you are vast. But you believe that you are small – it is only your belief that you are small.

Just see carefully: from where do you begin and where do you end? You are not limited to the body only, because if this sun which is millions of miles away finishes, then you will also be finished here. You are connected with it. You are also connected with the moon and the stars which are billions of miles away.

You cannot live without the atmosphere of the earth, you are breathing in it. Those who know say that it is not right to say that we are breathing in it; actually it is more proper to say that it is breathing in us. The breath which was mine just now will become yours after a moment, and before I finish saying this it will become somebody else's. The body which is yours today was sometimes in the trees, sometimes in the animals, sometimes in the birds. When you are dead, water will flow into the river, dust will go into dust; again plants will grow, again trees will grow. Maybe your sons will eat the fruits grown out of your dust.

Everything is connected, everything is united, there is nothing separate here. We are not small islands. There is a big continent, and we are its different parts.

Pranayam means, expand yourself. The process which is known as pranayam in yoga, is actually the method of expanding. Take such a deep breath in that it fills all the pores of your lungs; then let out the whole of the breath. As you go on deepening this process you will suddenly find that it is not you who is breathing, but it is the divine breathing in you. This is only a method. This is how pranayam happens. The bio-energy expands with this method, and it seems that we are small particles of a vast consciousness, we are drops of a vast ocean. Then even a drop becomes full of the grace of the divine. The ocean in your small cup also begins to stir.

Pranayam and pratyahar.... Pranayam is expanding your life energy, and *pratyahar* is the return to your home – to return, to come in. Pratyahar is to return within yourself from where you have come. Pratyahar is like the shrinking of a tree – as if it were to become a sapling, and then a seed, by shrinking. If you start shrinking inside, going in and in, then you will find the original source from where you have come. If the Ganges goes back to Gangotri, into Gomukh, the source, then that is pratyahar. Pratyahar means to regain your source. Zen monks say, "Come to know your original face, the face which was yours before you were born." To know your face when you were not yet born is pratyahar.

THE ESSENCE IN LIFE

Pranayam and pratyahar, intelligent
discrimination between transient and intransient.

...And to go on knowing, thinking and seeing every moment what is meaningful and what is meaningless. This is not to be forgotten even for a moment, because as soon as you forget you catch hold of the futile and forget the meaningful. It doesn't take long to catch hold of the dead rat. But you leave it as soon as you become conscious.

Disciplining of samadhi with japa.

Here Shankara is saying something very sweet. He is saying, *Disciplining of samadhi with japa*, disciplining of enlightenment with chanting. Patanjali says that eventually the *samadhi* should be without *japa*. Nanak says, *ajapa jap*, chantingless chanting. Buddha and Mahavira also say that everything should disappear, only void should remain.

But Shankara is saying *japa-samadhi*, disciplining of samadhi with japa. He is saying that void, emptiness should be there, but the dance of the whole should not be lost. The whole should be present in the emptiness. Thoughts should disappear, but emotions should not disappear, because with the disappearance of emotions you will become dry. You will become peaceful, but no song will be born out of that peace.

Then Meera will not dance and Chaitanya will not sing songs of the divine. You will become silent, you will attain, but you will not be able to express it. Your song will remain buried in you; nobody will be able to hear it. Your bliss will not overflow; its waves will not be able to drown others in it. That is why Shankara says one has to become thoughtless, but not without feelings. Knowledge should be attained, but one should not lose devotion. It is a unique coincidence, but it happens. It is an impossible happening, but it happens. Thoughts disappear, but emotions do not. Thinking and worry disappear, but the heart dances with joy.

> Disciplining of samadhi with japa
> — discipline all these with caution.

He repeats again: ...*discipline all these with caution.* And,

> Oh fool! Always sing the song of the divine.
> Totally surrendered to the lotus feet of the master, free from the bondages of the world,
> having disciplined the mind along with the senses, you will be able to see the divine within your heart.

The divine is not very far away. It is in your heart. You don't have to go anywhere in search of him, you just have to return to your own home. You have never lost him, you have only forgotten him. He is ever-present even in that forgetfulness. You have forgotten him, you have your back towards him, and even then he is present.

Actually, who are you? Only the divine is. You have forgotten him so you think that "I am." When you remember him you will disappear, only godliness will remain.

> You will be able to see the divine within your heart.

Therefore,

> Oh fool! Always sing the song of the divine.

Actually, Shankara is emphasizing an integration between meditation and devotion. He wants a harmony between meditation and bhajan. He wants an impossible bridge to be created between meditation and *bhajan*.

There have been many *bhaktas*, devotees, but they have not experienced the *shunya samadhi*. They are always full of the image of god; the duality always remains. There have been many *gyanis*, self-realized people; duality disappears in them and only *advait*, nonduality, remains. But with the disappearance of duality, the sensitivity of the heart also dries up.

Shankara says, try to bring such a moment – which can come, which has come sometimes – when you can become empty like the gyani and whole like the bhakta.

The synthesis of knowledge and devotion is the ultimate happening. It is the event. There is nothing higher than this – where bhakti and gyan are united; where devotion becomes knowledge and knowledge becomes devotion; where samadhi sings, where samadhi flowers, where samadhi is not a desert, it becomes greenery; where mind is totally finished and the heart fills it. There is the temple of the divine.

> You will be able to see the divine within your heart.

The devotee is not separate from the divine. The day the bhakta comes to know this, then only godliness is.

Many realized the divine; then their inner bhakta was finished, only the divine remained. And many have tried to save their bhakta; then bhakta remains and the divine remains – a duality remains, a distance remains. Is it not possible that you become a bhakta and the divine at the same time, that your *kirtan*, your divine song, goes on automatically – that you dance and you watch also?

It is possible. And that is Shankara's hypothesis. Such a unique personality flowered in Shankara where the culmination of knowledge and devotion could be found together. If the saying, "Fragrance in gold" has ever been actualized, it is in Shankara.

> Bhaj Govindam, Bhaj Govindam,
> Bhaj Govindam Moodhamate.
> Oh fool! Sing the song of the divine.

Enough for today.

10

JUST ONE MOMENT...

The first question:

> Beloved Osho,
> Yesterday you explained that pranayam is the method which expands the bio-energy and pratyahar is to return to the original source.
> First it is expansion, then it is return to the source.
> Why is it so?

Because life is made of contradictions, and there is no other way for life to exist. Breath goes out, then goes in – have you ever asked why it is so? When the breath has to go in, then why does it go out? But if the breath remains in and doesn't come out, then the result will be death and not life. If the breath remains out and doesn't go in, even then it will be death and not life.

Life is movement, a movement between two opposites. It is like the flowing of a river between two banks. Breath goes out, goes in; comes in then goes out. Every moment it is *pranayam*, and every moment it is *pratyahar*. When breath goes out it is pranayam, when the breath goes in it is pratyahar.

If your consciousness gets used to this type of rhythm, if this type of movement goes on in your consciousness, if like this you expand outwards, unlimited, if like this you reach the emptiness inside you — if there is emptiness within and unlimited expanse outside, if you flow constantly between these two banks, only then you will become godly because the divine is like this: empty within, whole outside.

This whole existence is the divine's pranayam. Creation is pranayam and destruction of the world is pratyahar. When the breath goes out, creation takes place; the breath goes in, the destruction of the world takes place.

If you can understand it properly, then you will see this everywhere in life. Birth is pranayam, death is pratyahar. In birth you expand, in death you shrink, you return, and life is in between the two banks of birth and death. Birth is not life, death is also not life; that which is flowing between birth and death, the unknown which is dancing in the beat, which is engrossed in the rhythm, that is life.

Mind tends to be logical, and life is contradictory. Life is illogical. Those who wanted to know it through logic lost their way and never attained. Logic will say: pranayam and pratyahar are contradictory, so only talk to us about one. Knowledge and devotion are contradictory, so only talk to us about one. Emptiness and wholeness are contradictory, so only talk to us about one. But remember that life is always contradictory, because life is greater than the contradictions; life is able to absorb all the contradictions. Logic is very small, it is the method of the small mind, so it can absorb only one and not the contrary. The opposite therefore is left outside.

That is why when Buddha said *shunya*, emptiness, it doesn't mean that the whole was not included in it. Buddha's emptiness included the whole. But followers of Buddha said that if it is emptiness then it cannot be whole. When Shankara said 'whole', the emptiness was included in it. But Shankara's followers asked, "If it is the whole, how can it be empty?"

This is how the follower misses the point, because the follower lives by logic and by mind, and those who know have known the contradictions together. But they also feel difficulty in expressing the contradiction because they have to explain it to you. If the contradictions are said at the same time, then you think that these are inconsistent things. Your mind goes on trying to make life logical and to add up. But life is not a calculation. Life is a flood which flows with such a force that it breaks all boundaries and limits of arithmetic. Life is a flood.

The second question:

> Beloved Osho,
> Yesterday you discussed how to be
> without passion, how to go beyond passion.
> Please tell us the alchemy of being without
> passion, sex, even in dreams.

Don't worry about dreams. You should first attain it in your waking state. Whatever is attained in your wakefulness, automatically starts appearing in your dreams, because your dreams are the echoes of your wakefulness. Whatsoever you do when you are awake, you go on hearing its echoes again and again in your dreams. Nothing new appears in your dreams, they go on echoing whatsoever you do in your wakefulness.

If you go on collecting money during the daytime, then at night you are counting it. If you are full of passion during the daytime, then at night you dream of sex. Those who are devotional, are devotional even in their sleep; and people who are empty and peaceful during the daytime, they remain empty and peaceful even at night – night is the shadow of the day, it just follows the day. Don't worry about changing the night. If lust disturbs you in your dreams at night, then it means that some deception is going on during wakefulness.

Just understand: Dreams can give you an indication; they indicate clearly whatever your understanding has missed during the daytime. Maybe during the day you behave like a saint, but this saintliness is like the crane standing on one leg and pretending to be very saintly. He looks so white, so austere; he stands like a *yogi* and looks so pure. But don't be deceived by his appearance. He is thinking only of the fish, he is waiting quietly to devour fish. He has done all these manipulations, these postures, just for the fish. Like this, the crane can fool others, but he doesn't fool himself. He knows why he is standing quietly holding his breath. But man is more dishonest than the crane; he not only deceives others, he deceives himself also. When other people start believing him, he also starts believing in whatever deception he is using.

There is a contradiction between your wakefulness and sleep. You don't feel any lust during the daytime because you have suppressed it very strongly. You just don't let it arise. Not that it is finished – you just don't let it be expressed. You go on suppressing it within your chest. At night, when the suppressor goes to sleep, then the suppressed wave arises and starts roaring and that becomes the lust in your dreams. Those who have suppressed it in the daytime will see it in their dreams.

The dream is the indication. It is your friend. It is telling you that it is no use suppressing anything, it will appear at night. "You may suppress us during the day, in the night we will reappear. You may deceive others and you may deceive yourself, but you cannot get rid of us."

Now you want to know how to get rid of lust even in your dreaming. You think that you are free of lust during wakefulness, that you only have it in your dreams. This is illusion, a wrong notion. The dream itself is the proof of your not being free of it during wakefulness. The moment you are free from this during wakefulness you will not even see it in your dreams. The dream is just your subtle story.

You are asking how to suppress in dreaming what you have been able to suppress in your wakefulness. But then there will remain no way for you to become liberated from it. You must understand that whatever is suppressed will be ever-present and will be expressed sometime or other. It is like a sleeping volcano. The flames are not coming out, but so what? – you will smolder and burn inside. This disease will spread like a cancer in your existence. No, try to understand your dreams.

Your dreams are saying that during the daytime you have deceived yourself and you have suppressed something. So now try to uncover what you have suppressed. Try to understand this deep rule about the mind.

The mind is like the root of the tree. If the roots are deep down in the earth then the tree goes on flourishing; new leaves, flowers and fruits go on sprouting. But if the roots are pulled out of that dark depth and put in the light, then the tree dies. This is exactly what happens with the mind. Whatever may be the disease of the mind, bring it out in the light. Light is death for disease.

But you do just the opposite. Your so-called religious *gurus* have been telling you just the opposite. They have been telling that you should suppress it so much that even the root cannot be seen. But the deeper the root, the more dangerous it is. Then your life will become poisonous. You should uncover yourself and bring it before your eyes. Don't run away or hide. Dig up your roots during the daytime and look at them in the light.

I call this meditation. Meditation is not any method which can be done once and then forgotten. Meditation is a continuous process of awareness. You have to be aware all twenty-four hours; while standing, while sitting, be aware. When a beautiful woman passes by on the road a licentious person will gaze at her. But if you are a gentleman you cannot gaze at her openly. You try to see her indirectly, you make an excuse of looking at a shop which is in her direction. But if you have suppressed yourself very deeply then you don't look anywhere – neither at the shop nor at the woman, you just go on with your head down without looking left or right. Then at night you will see that beautiful woman in your dream because you really did want to see her.

And this is also possible – that you have got into the habit of walking with your head down and with your eyes looking down. Out of habit your eyes must have looked down automatically as soon as you became aware of the presence of the beautiful woman.

You might have made your character in such a way. You have decided the rules of behavior for yourself which you go on following mechanically. Outwardly you may not realize that a woman has passed by, but your looking down proves that some breeze blew within you, something fluttered within you, a ripple arose in you which made your eyes look down. This looking downwards was your way of saving yourself from that woman. You passed by.

For this behavior the world will call you a gentleman or a saint. You will get a lot of respect. So your ego will be satisfied, will be nurtured. You will try to be more religious. For that you can even go to the extent of blinding your eyes. But who are you trying to fool? Can you deceive your innermost self? In the darkness of night, in your deep slumber when your gentleman, your saint is sleeping soundly, then all your suppressed feelings and desires will come to the surface and they will create your dreams. Don't think that anything is wrong with dreams. A dream is your friend, it is trying to tell you that you have deceived yourself and you will gain nothing by this deception. The dream proves that you have suppressed your lust. So awaken yourself, and recognize this instinct of yours.

The real question is not of looking or not looking at the woman passing by, the question is, are you aware of the ripple that arose in you caused by the desire to look at her? It doesn't matter whether you look at a woman or you don't look at a woman, but what matters is the rising of the ripple of passion in you. If you suppress it, then you will dream of her, but if you become aware of the passion rising in you by looking at her then you will not dream of her. If you go on watching every moment the passion, the desire arising in you, then you will become dreamless.

Yesterday I was reading a song written by a friend of mine, Kumar Barabankvi, who is an Urdu poet. A line of the poem is:

*The destination seems to be near,
as the path is deserted and lonely.*

Yes, as one starts approaching the destination the paths of the mind become deserted and lonely. Even the dreams are not there. The markets and even the shadows of the market disappear; there will be no more friends and enemies, and even their wavering shadows will disappear.

*The destination seems to be near,
as the path is deserted and lonely.*

When all your inner paths seem to be lonely, then you must know that the destination is not very far away, it is quite near. As long as your inner paths are full of dreams it means that you are in the marketplace. The world may be calling you a saint – and you may be thinking yourself to be a saint – but the worldly man in you is not dead, he is only hidden, and the hidden worldly person is more dangerous because he is like a hidden disease. If it is manifest it can be treated, but if it remains hidden it cannot be treated. And what can a doctor do if the sick person goes on denying that he is sick?

This is not the problem of ordinary people, this is the problem of the so-called great *mahatmas*. During the last days of his life even Mahatma Gandhi used to have dreams of sex. He was a very honest man although he was on the wrong path, because if, in spite of a lifelong effort, lust arises in your dreams, then it means that the effort was being made in the wrong direction.

JUST ONE MOMENT...

He had worked very hard, he was not lacking in effort, and he was very honest about it. But by honesty and integrity alone you cannot reach the destination. You cannot reach the destination by integrity alone and you cannot reach the destination only by going through right paths. You reach the destination only when the integrity, effort and the right paths unite.

If you try to extract oil from sand very honestly, you will not succeed. Your honesty is not enough for this purpose because there is no oil in the sand. You can go on trying with full faith, with all your integrity, but it will be of no consequence. On the other hand, another person with less integrity may succeed if he is trying to extract oil from oil-seeds. But a person with no faith and no integrity may have the oil-seeds, but he will not get the oil because he is not making any effort to extract it. That is why a revolution in life takes place only when the integrity and the right path unite.

To the end of his life Gandhi used to be disturbed by dreams. But I must say that he was an honest person, he was not like your other so-called *sadhus* and saints who are disturbed by dreams but never talk about them to anyone. Gandhi talked about it openly. His followers didn't want him to because it hurt their egos to know that their guru had such dreams. His followers thought of him as 'Mahatma.' So they were very worried about what people would say if they come to know about his dreams. That is why they used to ask him not to talk about it openly.

During his last days Gandhi began sleeping naked with a young woman. At this, some followers just ran away. Out of those who ran away at that time, some of them now claim to be the inheritors of Gandhism! Yes, it is those very people who had run away, who had opposed Gandhi, saying "I never heard this, I've never seen any such thing."

But none of them could understand Gandhi's agony. His agony was that he had wasted all his life in the vain effort of being a celibate. During his last days he came to know about the Tantra scriptures, which say that if you want to be free of passion then you have to wake up, you have to be aware. If you have to wake up then you have to be in that situation – it is no use running away from it. That is why, to create this situation, he slept with a young naked woman for one year so that if passion then arose in him he would see it, he would recognize it. All his life he had suppressed it, so now he had to make a great effort to uncover it. Sleeping with a young naked woman was an effort to awaken the passion which he had earlier suppressed.

Escapism is not the solution of life, life is solved by facing it, by confronting it. You have to face all the problems of life. Don't ask what you should do to be free of this lust in your dreams. You should know that the passion coming in your dreams is due to your suppression when you are awake. Don't suppress it when you are awake! You should uncover it and see it during your wakefulness. It will not be easy for you to do so because it will hurt your ego. You will say, "I am a celibate. I am a *sannyasin*. How can there be any passion within me?" But it is there, whether you see it or you don't see it makes no difference. Your false pride has no meaning, you will have to give up your false attachment. You must understand that you can be free of the passion only by watching it.

Try to experiment with this for a few months. Don't suppress anything. Whatever is coming in through the eyes, let it come – the whole of it. Don't condemn it even a little, because condemnation causes suppression. Supposing you have a thought of sex and you say that it is bad, it is a sin; immediately the suppression will start. Even if you don't say it is bad, that it is a sin, but you watch it very unwillingly, if you feel that it was better that you had not seen it, even then suppression will start. So you say to existence, "My God, what are you showing me?" Immediately, the suppression has started. Whenever you make a judgment of something being good or bad, or you complain or repent, or you feel a sense of guilt or you try to evaluate, the suppression starts.

So you should see every thought as if you have nothing to do with it. You should see it just as you see the flowers on the tree, as you see the clouds floating in the sky, or as you look at the people passing by on the road. You have nothing to do with them. Just watch without any prejudice or any bias, then all the instincts appear in their real form. You have suppressed them in many lives, so when they appear in their full form for a moment you may feel that you have gone mad. "What is happening to my morality, to my religion, to my character? Everything is going to pieces – my reputation which I have built with such arduous effort will be shattered!" But don't be frightened at this. Keep calm...and this takes courage, and this sort of courage is the real *tapasya*, the real spiritual discipline. You don't need courage to stand in the sun or to stand naked in the snow, these things can be attained just by a little practice. The greatest courage is to be able to see yourself as you are within yourself. And this creates the transformation, this creates the inner revolution.

Just watch, and as you start watching the dreams will start to disappear, because whatever you have seen during your wakefulness will not then be shown in your dreams. There is no need to show you what you have already seen. Then your nights will become dreamless – and if your nights become dreamless, then you will attain *samadhi*.

Patanjali has said that there is very little difference between *sushupti*, dreamless sleep, and samadhi – very little difference. The difference is that sushupti is unconscious and samadhi is wakeful – when all the dreams have disappeared.

Have you ever noticed that in the morning when you wake up you can remember that you have dreamed, that you had dreamed the whole night? That means there is some awareness in you which sees the dreams, which recognizes the dreams and which remembers the dreams. If all the dreams disappear, then this awareness which was so engrossed in seeing the dreams will now see samadhi, because now there are no more dreams – the path is without travelers, the path is lonely and deserted. Now the lonely path itself can be seen. In the morning when you get up, you will say that you saw sushupti and not dreams – and seeing sushupti is samadhi. The path was lonely, there was no crowd. There were no people, so the path could be seen. The sky could be seen as there were no clouds. The sky becomes covered with clouds because of dreams – sushupti is covered, and sushupti is samadhi.

Every night you attain to where Buddha attained. Every night you attain to where Shankara lives. But there is a big crowd between you and samadhi. There is a big fair between you and samadhi – and it is you who have collected this crowd, this circus. You go on collecting this garbage by treating life in the wrong way. Deal with it every minute. Watch with care whatever comes in front of you. Don't hesitate even a bit in seeing it properly, then it will have no reason to appear in your dreams. You see it in your dreams only because you didn't see it properly during the daytime, so it insists on coming back again and again.

Have you ever noticed that if you experience anything totally, then it doesn't recur in your memory. If you look at someone or something deeply, thoroughly, then you will be free of it, your mind no longer thinks about it. If you live intensely, deeply, then no love or affection can bind you – but incomplete experiences will always haunt you because the mind wants to fulfill them. The incomplete experiences of life always collect in you. Now please don't repeat this behavior and don't ask me how to stop it in your dreams. You should know from these dreams that you have suppressed it when you were awake; now don't stop it even when you are awake.

I am not saying that go and satisfy any passion that arises in you. I am not saying that, because many times you have tried to satisfy it but it has not been fulfilled. You have been doing that birth after birth. Anger has not disappeared by getting angry. Lust has not disappeared by indulging in sex. Greed has not disappeared by being greedy.

This is the conflict. If you indulge in it, it becomes stronger because it becomes a habit. You were angry today, you were angry yesterday, you were angry the day before yesterday – and thus the chain of anger becomes stronger. Then you become an habituated angry person. Then any small excuse will flare up your anger.

If you do it, if you indulge in it, it becomes a habit, it becomes a practice. If you suppress it, then it makes wounds inside. But there is a way in between these two: don't indulge in it, don't suppress it; just watch, just see. This is the thread of witnessing. Don't be a doer, just be a witness, just be a watcher.

Either way you are doing something – if you are angry, then either you are throwing your anger onto the other person or you are suppressing it within you. Both are wrong. If the desire for sex arises, then either you are forcing it onto the other person or you are suppressing it within you. Both are wrong. Don't force it on the other – by forcing it on the other you are dragging them also into the mud and dirt of passion. The other person has enough problems of his own and now you have added more to them.

No, don't force it on anyone, because if you force it on the other, he can also force it on you. If you make anyone the object of your passion, then he will also use you in the same way. That is why passion is a bondage. You bind the other and the other binds you. You enjoy the other and the other starts enjoying you. You hold on to someone and he holds on to you. So don't force your passion, anger or anything on anyone, and don't suppress it either. If you have been kind to the other person, then be kind to yourself and don't suppress it.

And in between these two there is a very subtle journey. Just see it properly, just watch it properly, that it doesn't harm anyone. And as you go on seeing you will feel awakened; you will become aware and conscious.

People that bow down towards a temple or a mosque should know that life itself is a prayer if you remain conscious, aware. There is no other prayer, there is no other meditation, no other worship. Life itself becomes worship if one is full of awareness.

The third question:

> Beloved Osho,
> You said that desire always creates misery.
> Then do the desires for good deeds, for religion,
> for God, also create misery?

Desire itself leads you to misery; it doesn't make any difference what you desire. The object of desire can be anything – you may want money or you may want religion – desire is desire.

Desire means that you are not satisfied, you are not contented with where you are and as you are. You think that if you get more money you will be satisfied, if you get more religion you will be satisfied. Desire means that you are dissatisfied and discontented. Desire is anguish born out of dissatisfaction. It doesn't matter what type of dissatisfaction it is, there is no satisfaction. What you desire makes no difference. Some people are desiring a good house on this earth and some people are desiring a good house in heaven....

One day, as I was going along a road, a woman came and gave me a pamphlet in which was shown a picture of a beautiful building with a garden full of flowers and a stream. On it was written, "Are you in search of a nice bungalow?"

Out of curiosity I turned it over and found that the bungalow was not of this earth, it was some propaganda from the Christian missionaries. That beautiful bungalow with the garden and the stream is in heaven! It was written in that pamphlet that if you want such a house in heaven, then nobody can take you there except Jesus.

Even if you desire heaven, it is you who will desire. It is the expansion of your mind – it will be in your language and it will color all that you do. One day you should sit down and make a list of all the things which you want in heaven. You will be surprised to read the list: it will contain all the earthly things. You will want to have a Rolls Royce, you will want to have the most beautiful of the actresses, you will want the Taj Mahal. Yes, make this list and read it to yourself. Don't be afraid. You may tear it up afterwards. Don't show it to anyone. It will certainly reveal the things you want to possess!

If God is ready to give you heaven and if he tells you to ask for anything, what will you ask for? Your desires will reveal to you that your heaven is nothing but the expansion of your world here. It may be a little refined.... Even in heaven you will ask for these same worldly things, but there they will be permanent, here they are temporary. The differences will be merely of details.

Here an actress becomes old, but in heaven she will always remain young, because in heaven women never become older than sixteen years. Urvasi was sixteen years old millions of years ago and even now she is still sixteen years old; she will always remain sixteen years old. This doesn't give any information about Urvasi, this reveals the desire of man. He desires that a woman should not become older than sixteen. In heaven streams of wine are flowing – it is not sold in bottles, it is flowing in streams. You may have prohibition here, but so what – there you can swim in wine like a fish, you can drink as much as you like, because there there is no prohibition. If there are rules and regulations in heaven and if you have to take a license for alcohol, then it is no freedom. No – there is not even a policeman at the crossroads. Heaven is nothing but a network of your dreams.

When you desire the divine, what is behind it? This desire is created out of your sheer misery, pain, your restlessness of mind. For this same reason people desire money, for this same reason people desire fame and status. So in the same way your desire for the divine is only a desire for the ultimate position. And your so-called sadhus and sannyasins even say the divine is parampad, the ultimate position.

You will be surprised to understand the language of the sadhus and sannyasins. They say, "What is the use of money? It is definitely going to be snatched away from you sooner or later – it is better to be in search of that money which will never be snatched away from you." But if you analyze this language of theirs, then you will be amazed. One who is looking for the money which will be snatched away is a sinner, is materialistic, is a debauchee – he will go to hell because he is in search of temporal money. And those who are looking for the money that is not of this world are saints, virtuous.

What is the difference between these two? The only difference which seems to exist is that the one who is looking for the transient is not very clever, and the one looking for the intransient is more clever, more dishonest and cunning. When little children collect pebbles you tell them not to be so silly – they should be collecting precious stones and diamonds. Your advice shows that the child is as yet very innocent and you have become worldly wise and very calculating

I see that compared to your so-called sadhus and sannyasins, the people you consider to be worldly are more simple and innocent. Your sadhus and sannyasins are more cunning and more dishonest because they are in search of unlimited, eternal wealth. But the desire is the same, there is no difference.

What I am saying is quite a different thing, what Shankara is saying is quite different. What Buddha is saying is quite different. They are not saying that you should desire the truth, that you should desire the divine. They are saying that when all desires disappear, then the divine is attained. This is a different thing altogether: only when all desires disappear, then the divine is attained. Therefore you cannot desire the attainment of the divine, because that very desire will become the obstacle.

When all the desires disappear without any condition – when there is no desire in the mind, when there is no passion – then only the divine remains. One cannot desire the divine. When desire is given up then godliness will be attained, but you cannot desire the divine. The very desiring is wrong. If you hope to get something in return for this then you will get nothing, then you have not understood at all.

Godliness is the result of the disappearance of desire. But if you deliberately give up all desires in order to attain it, you will not be able to attain. You cannot make any claims, you cannot become the claimant. This is not a business, it is a prayer of the divine. Try to understand this.

When there is no desire left in you, you say, "I am satisfied as I am, I don't want anything else, I don't want to be anywhere else. It is sufficient for me to be here, I am fortunate." You sing and you dance because you are in great happiness as you are. There is no desire; you have become an emperor, you are no longer a beggar. Then this emperor meets the ultimate emperor. To meet the emperor you have to become the emperor. Only an equal can meet the equal. If you desire even God, that will lead you to misery.

That is why you will find many *fakirs* in your temples and mosques who are unhappy and miserable. You are unhappy because you didn't get money, you didn't get fame, you didn't get position. They are unhappy because they have not yet attained the divine. But the unhappiness continues.

Desire means misery, because desire does not get fulfilled. The nature of desire is nonfulfillment. Buddha has said that desire cannot be fulfilled; it is not that you are not capable of fulfilling it, it is because its nature is nonfulfillment. You may do anything, but it is never fulfilled. It cannot be fulfilled. To get fulfilled is not its destiny. The moment a person understands that desire cannot be fulfilled, he doesn't desire the divine also. He gives up all desiring, drops it, and in that moment of dropping he finds that the one he was looking for is within him. He couldn't see this because the desire had made him blind.

That is why Shankara says that the divine is within you. The day you come home after giving up all the running around and the desire, when you sit down in your own home in a relaxed way with gratitude in your heart, you will hear a new music within you. The music is always there, but you cannot hear it because of the noise of desire. That music is very subtle, it is going on day and night, but you are never at home – and the divine is in your house! You never come home – you never find the time. You have a chain of desires to follow, one after another. You just don't have the time to come back to your home and see the one who is living there.

You don't have to go anywhere in search of the divine, you have to return to your own home, and that is pratyahar.

The fourth question:

> Beloved Osho,
> This pratyahar looks like an impossible experiment. Is it possible for the Ganges to return to Gangotri and is it possible for the tree to again become a seedling and a seed? Shankara and you are both asking us to do this.

The return of the Ganges to its source, Gangotri, and the tree becoming a seed look impossible to you, but this is what is happening every day. The tree is becoming a seed again daily. Just look at the seeds hanging on that *gulmohar* tree: the whole tree has become seeds. And every day the Ganges returns to Gangotri through the dark clouds; then it rains on the Himalayas and returns to Gangotri. This is happening every day.

You ask what has to be done? Well, the only thing to be done is to carefully observe this phenomenon that takes place every day. Many times you return home, but you are not conscious. You have become so used to staying in guesthouses that even when you return to your own home you think it is a guesthouse.

A friend of mine has to travel day and night in connection with his work. He is at home for only four or five days at a time, and he just cannot sleep when he is at home because he has become used to sleeping with the noise of the train. For the last twenty years he has been traveling. He told me that he is in great trouble because he cannot sleep when he is at home. So

I suggested to him that it will be better for him to rent a house near a railway line.

This appealed to him. He said that he had been to many doctors, but nobody could give him the right advice. So he took a house near a railway line and he is very happy because now he can sleep at home. A train passes by every ten to fifteen minutes. Certainly he is happy! It is difficult for you to understand his situation because when you travel in the train for the first time you cannot sleep. Habit...all of us are slaves of habit.

You have lived out of your home so much that when you do come home, it is not home, you just don't recognize it. The home also looks like a guesthouse to you – a place where you stay in the night and start the journey again in the morning. Every day the Ganges returns to Gangotri – and you say that it is difficult. You are already in your original source, and you say that it is difficult!

How can you go away from your original source? Where will you go? You must have gone away in your thoughts; you cannot go in reality. It is just as if you go to sleep in Pune and you see Calcutta in a dream; when you wake up in the morning do you have to catch the train to come back to Pune? You were in Calcutta in your dream, but that doesn't mean that you have to catch the train in the morning. When you wake up in the morning you will find yourself in Pune.

To be away from oneself is only a thought, an idea. If you ask me, and if you can understand, then I would like to say that the Ganges has never gone away from Gangotri. The seed never became the tree; it only saw the dream of becoming a tree. It was a dream that the Ganges came out of Gangotri and went towards the sea, because one cannot go away from one's nature.

You are saying that it is very difficult to return to one's nature. I am telling you that it is not only difficult but impossible to go away from your nature. Nobody has ever gone. At this very moment you are the buddha, at this very moment you are the *jina*, at this very moment you are the divine. But your thoughts...you think otherwise. You say that this thing doesn't appeal to me – I, who run a pan shop, how can I be a buddha? How can the pan shop become an obstacle in your being a buddha? Does one become a buddha just by sitting under a *bodhi* tree? I say that sitting in your pan shop you *are* a buddha. Be-cause you run a pan shop or something else – you may do anything, but you cannot go out of buddhahood.

A fish may come out of the sea, but how can you come out of the divine? Because the sea has a limit – it has a shore, a beach – but the divine has no limit, it has no shore; it is unlimited. So it is only your idea that you are running a pan shop. Yes, do it by all means, but this should not make you think that you are no longer a buddha. If you become that much aware, then the Ganges returns to Gangotri. This awareness, this consciousness....

A lot of obstacles will come in the way. First of all the world will stop you – the shop will stop you, money will stop you, position will stop you. If somehow you get free of these, then after that the temple and the mosque will stop you, the Vedas and the Puranas will stop you, the Gita and the Koran will stop you. You can come home only after being free of them. A lot of obstacles will come in the way, but you have to free yourself a little from them. I call this awareness. Shankara has called this carefulness, great carefulness. If you are awake, then nobody can stop you. A shop is very weak. The temple and the mosque also will not be able to stop you; books and account books, nothing will stop you; the Vedas and the Koran will not be able to stop you.

> *A lot of obstacles came in the path of the beloved.*
> *Even the temple and mosque became the obstacles,*
> *But thank God we could proceed with a little care.*

The fifth question:

> Beloved Osho,
> Your meditation techniques include yoga and bhakti. Are both of these necessary for pratyahar?

Life is of two kinds. One is based on the necessary and the other is based on abundance, on affluence. Just see the peacock dancing: is the rainbow coloring on its feathers necessary? If you cut off the feathers, will there be any difficulty in the life of the peacock? In spite of it the peacock will be able to live, because the life force is not connected with the feathers, nor is the getting of food connected with it. There will be no difficulty in breeding too; these colorful feathers are not a necessity. They are the symbol of excess, of abundance, of affluence.

The birds here are singing. If you stitch up their beaks it will not make any difference. These birds will still be able to live, but they will not be able to sing; the songs are not necessary, they are born out of abundance.

You dance – why? Why don't you just go to your business and come back home? You sing, you love: if you don't sing and don't love what difference will it make? To do your business is sufficient to survive. Will you die if you don't love? Those who don't love are also living, those who don't sing are also living – maybe they are living in a better way because that much energy saved is spent by them in earning money. But the splendor of their life will be lost. To live by necessity is the way of the miser. Here I am not teaching you to live by necessity, I am teaching you to go beyond the necessity, to live life in abundance.

I also know that the divine can be attained by knowledge, *gyana*, alone and there is no need of *bhakti*, devotion. The divine can also be attained by only bhakti – there is no need of knowledge. But then the attainment of the divine will be just like a business deal. You only do what is necessary. If you can do something by spending two *paisa*, then you hesitate to spend even three paisa. You remain miserly even on the path of the divine. But I want to teach you to be a little more carefree, more happy-go-lucky!

I also know that people have attained by knowledge and there is no need of bhakti, there is no need for everyone to dance like Meera. But even then I will say that if you can dance then a new form of the divine will appear before you that is not of mathematics, that is of poetry. Yes, the divine can be attained by knowledge, by dryness, by mathematics, but if you reach the divine by necessity, then even this relation is calculated. If even in this relation you did not jump, you did not melt and you did not flow, you did not enjoy the ultimate bliss, then it means that this was also a business.

People *have* attained by bhakti alone; knowledge isn't necessary. But I am saying: why only try for the necessary when you can have in abundance, you can have in excess? When life can become the ultimate luxuriance, why be miserly and calculative? If you want to dance, then you cannot be calculative. A calculative person cannot be a good dancer.

When will you get rid of your miserliness? When will you be able to flow without any hesitation? According to me, the ultimate fortune is in abundance. Look at the peacock: existence has put so many colors on its feathers, it has worked so hard on them!

If a scientist were to create the peacock, then one thing is certain, that he will not make feathers, because they are absolutely unnecessary according to him. A food-pipe will be there, a stomach will be there, the genitals will be there for breeding, but feathers will not be there at all. There will be no poetry, no song, no dance. The colors in life are lost because of these stupid people, because everywhere they are advising us to do only what is absolutely necessary.

Look at existence. Existence doesn't agree with having only what is absolutely necessary. It doesn't stop at the necessary, it goes on flowing into the unnecessary. Birds are singing, it is not necessary; trees are flowering, it is not necessary; fragrance is flowing from the flowers, it is not necessary. Rivers are flowing rapidly towards the sea, and the sea goes on roaring and its waves go on dashing against the shore. It is not necessary. Just think over what is necessary.

If God had been an economist then he would have made only the necessary things in this world. Then this world would not have been fit for living; it would have been good only for committing suicide. There would have been no pleasure in living in a world which had only necessary things.

You will attain by the path of knowing, you will attain by bhakti, but it is entirely a different thing to attain by the paths of knowing and bhakti both. That is a different enjoyment. But it all depends on you – the choice is yours. If you like to live in small courtyards and you are afraid of the open sky, then you may live in small, dingy rooms.

But I say unto you that the open sky, the vast sky is also available with this same effort. Do you think you are so small? Why do you talk about the necessary? Let your knowledge increase to the extent where it will become bhakti, and let your bhakti be so deep that it reaches the point where it becomes knowledge. Rather, touch both ends so that nothing remains untouched. Try to get the maximum out of what you have in this world.

The sixth question:

> Beloved Osho,
> I am listening to you daily and I understanding you. Tears flow out of my eyes, my heart palpitates like an earthquake, and it seems as if the day of self-realization has come. But it doesn't come.
> The next day, again this experience gets repeated. I don't know what is the meaning of this play of the sun and the shadow.

THE SONG OF ECSTASY

There is no sun and no shadow. It is only an illusion of your mind. We are never happy with what we get because the mind goes on asking for more. Has there ever been a moment in your life when you did not want more than what you had?

I am distributing self-realization, and you are getting it every day. It showers on you. Your eyes say the right thing, because tears are coming out of them. They recognize because they are more sensible than your mind. And your heart is also giving the right indication, because it starts throbbing. But your head is very strong, it goes on thinking, yes, something is happening but it is not complete yet, self-realization has not happened yet. But what is self-realization? When will it happen? When you agree that yes, now it has happened, how will you know it? What criterion do you have for it?

The mind is deceiving you. Thoughts will always deceive you. So listen to your tears and listen to your heart. Mind will say, "Yes, it has happened, but not yet completely." But what is complete? What is full? Even if you are standing before the divine you will say, "Yes, I have attained him, but not fully." You can make some additions even to God: the nose should have been a little longer, the ears should have been touching the shoulders just like Buddha's and Mahavira's…the ears are small, they should have been longer. Do you think that if you meet the divine you will be able to accept that you have him in his totality?

Mind never says that it has got it, the mind is in the habit of saying, "Yes, I got it, but much more is yet to be received." Don't listen to the mind, trust your tears; they are more innocent, more simple and more natural, more internal, more hearty, more primary. Trust the throbbing of your heart because it is here that the dance starts for the first time. Mind is of man, of civilization, of society. It is borrowed, it is of scriptures. Mind has been given to you by others. But nobody has given you tears, you brought them with you. The heart is yours, the sensations in it are yours, the sensitivity is yours; nobody has given it to you, although others have snatched it from you and created many obstacles in its path.

If you can listen to your heart and to your eyes, if you can listen to your inner life, you are not worried about tomorrow, then you are not worried about self-realization. This moment of bliss will make you most fortunate. You will be full of gratitude and a deep prayer will rise in your heart – then you will be thankful to the divine for giving you more than you deserve. He gave it when you were not expecting it at all. Then you will not think that it is a play of the sun and shadow. Today is enough for today. Tomorrow, when he will give again, you will thank him again.

And don't compare today with tomorrow, because all this comparison is of the mind. Every moment of life is unique. Tomorrow again it will be morning; again he will shower. But don't compare, because no two moments can be the same at the same time. All these comparisons are of the mind. There is always one moment at a time. In existence there is no possibility of measurement or comparison, and if you go on advancing like this – thankful, grateful, full of deep gratitude.... Self-realization is not something which you get all of a sudden, it just goes on advancing, increasing, deepening. Self-realization is not an object but a process. Self-realization is not something which you can attain just by grabbing. Self-realization is your transformation. It is your development.

And there is no end to self-realization. That is why the soul is called unlimited: it goes on increasing, it goes on growing. You never reach the point where you can say that now it is enough. It is unlimited. The more you see the divine the vaster he becomes. New doors open, new flowers blossom; there are thousands of lotuses of consciousness, and there are thousands of petals in each lotus, and each petal has thousands of colors. You will go on seeing, you will go on going deep into it and you will go on increasing.

Don't keep an account of the past, because if your mind is full of this account then you will miss what you are getting now.

Don't worry about tomorrow, because he has given you today and he will give you tomorrow also. If he has given today, why should he not give tomorrow? Don't worry about tomorrow. Let the past be past. Don't think of tomorrow, today is enough.

If this trust goes deeply into you — that today is enough, that this moment is enough — then this very moment will become one of *bhajan*.

> Oh fool! Sing the song of the divine,
> sing the song of the divine.

Enough for today.

ABOUT OSHO

Osho is a modern-day buddha whose wisdom, clarity and humor have touched the lives of millions of people around the world. He is creating the conditions for the emergence of what he calls the "New Man" a qualitatively new kind of human being who is aware, life-affirmative and free.

According to Osho, the spiritual traditions of the past have made a deep split within the individual, and this is reflected in all the institutions of society. His way is to heal this split, to restore the unity of body and spirit, earth and sky.

After his enlightenment in 1953, the evolution of this New Man became his dream. In 1966, Osho left the academic world and his post as a philosophy professor at the University of Jabalpur and began touring India intensively and speaking to many hundreds of thousands of people. At the same time, Osho was developing practical tools for man's self-transformation.

By the late 1960s, Osho had begun to create his unique Dynamic Meditation techniques. He says that modern man is so burdened with the traditions from the past and the anxieties of modern-day living, that he must go through a deep cleansing process before he can begin to discover the thought-free, relaxed state of meditation.

By 1974, a commune had been established around Osho in Pune, India, and the trickle of visitors from the West had become a flood. Today, his Commune is the largest spiritual growth center in the world. Each year it attracts thousands of international visitors to its meditation, therapy, bodywork and creative programs.

Osho speaks on virtually every aspect of the development of human consciousness. His talks cover a staggering range — from the meaning of life and death to the struggles of power and politics, from the challenges of love and creativity to the significance of science and education. These talks, given over thirty years, have been recorded on audio cassette and videotape, and published in hundreds of books in every major language of the world. He belongs to no tradition and says, "My message is not a doctrine, not a philosophy. My message is a certain alchemy, a science of transformation."

Osho left his body in 1990 as a result of poisoning by U.S. government agents, while being held in custody for technical immigration violations in 1985. He asks always to be referred to in the present tense. The words on his Samadhi, which Osho himself dictated, read:

OSHO
Never Born – Never Died
Only Visited this Planet Earth
December 11, 1931 – January 19, 1990

OSHO COMMUNE

Osho Commune International in Pune, India, is a place to relax from the outward stresses of life and nourish the soul. Osho describes the Commune as a laboratory, an experiment in creating a "New Man" – a human being who lives in harmony with the inner and the outer, with himself and his environment, and who is free from all ideologies and conditionings that now divide humanity.

Set in thirty-one acres in the tree-lined suburb of Koregaon Park, this meditation resort receives thousands of visitors every year from all countries and from all walks of life. Visitors generally spend from three weeks to three months and stay in nearby hotels and apartments.

The Commune houses the unique Osho Multiversity, which offers hundreds of personal growth and self-discovery programs and professional trainings throughout the year, all of which are designed to help people find the knack of meditation: the passive witnessing of thoughts, emotions and actions, without judgment or identification.

Unlike many traditional Eastern disciplines, meditation at Osho Commune is an inseparable part of daily life, whether working, relating or just being. The result is that people do not renounce the world but bring to it a spirit of awareness, celebration, and a deep reverence for life.

At the center of the Commune is the Gautama the Buddha Auditorium, where seven different one-hour-long meditations are offered every day. These include:

*Osho Dynamic Meditation:** Osho's technique designed to release tensions and repressed emotions, opening the way to a new vitality and an experience of profound silence.

*Osho Kundalini Meditation:** Shaking free dormant energies, and through spontaneous dance and silent sitting, allowing these energies to be redirected inward.

*Osho Nataraj Meditation:** The inner alchemy of dancing so totally, that the dancer disappears and only the dance remains.

*Osho Nadabrahma Meditation:** Based on an ancient Tibetan humming technique to harmonize the energy flow.

Osho No-Dimensions: A powerful method for centering the energy, based on a Gurdjieff technique.

Osho Vipassana Meditation: Gautam Buddha's technique of dissolving mental chatter through the awareness of breath.

Osho White Robe Brotherhood: The highlight of the day at the Commune is the evening meeting of the Osho White Robe Brotherhood. This two-hour celebration of music, dance and silence, followed by a videotaped talk by Osho, is unique – a deep and complete meditation where thousands of seekers, in Osho's words, "...dissolve into a sea of consciousness."

*Service mark Osho International Foundation

FURTHER READING

THE SECRET OF SECRETS
Talks on The Secret of the Golden Flower
In this book, among many valuable techniques, Osho gives specific instructions on the Taoist Golden Light meditation – to harmonize the male and female elements and transmute sexual energy.

SHOWERING WITHOUT CLOUDS
Reflections on the Poetry of an Enlightened Woman, Sahajo
This book contains the powerful insights of two enlightened beings, Osho and Sahajo, on the woman's path to enlightenment, and what it means to be a woman and a seeker of self-realization.

THE LAST MORNING STAR
Talks on the enlightened woman mystic, Daya
Using the playful and provocative poetry of Daya and other poets, Osho takes us on a journey of the heart – a way that is spontaneous joyous, and at times uncompromising.

RETURNING TO THE SOURCE
A delightful book of Zen teaching stories. Here Osho takes each anecdote and reveals the teaching within each one in his own way. This is no-nonsense Zen carrying the essence, the essence of Osho.

THE VOICE OF SILENCE
Discourses on Mabel Collins': "Light on the Path"
"It is out of you that the path will be born, and in the end the destination will also arise from you." Osho gives us step-by-step guidance on how to find our inner voice, the voice of silence, so that we can begin, travel on and complete the journey from unconsciousness to enlightenment. "Once you have heard the inner voice there is no more going astray in life."   OSHO

FURTHER READING

My Way: The Way of the White Clouds
Osho responds to questions from seekers and sannyasins
Osho has chosen the symbol of the white clouds to represent the way a seeker moves on the path, and this book addresses all the states — storms, winds, sun, rain and rainbows — that are a part of the adventure called life. The questions and answers that comprise this book have been selected by Osho to introduce his work to those looking for a new way of life.

The Path of Meditation
A step-by-step guide to meditation
Osho takes us step by step through preparations for our own meditation. He then explains the different stages on the path. This is not a book just to read, but an invitation to experiment with the extremely powerful techniques that are given.

Notes of a Madman
This small volume is one of three unique books of Osho's talks given in the unlikely setting of his dental chair: Osho speaks in a poetic way on anything that comes to him. It is a rare and intimate glimpse into an enlightened one's world.

Flight of the Alone to the Alone
"*The Kaivalya Upanishad* is a longing for the ultimate freedom. Kaivalya means the moment in your consciousness when you are utterly alone, but you do not feel lonely.... Your very being becomes the whole. This is the longing of man that is hidden in his deepest, innermost core."   OSHO

FURTHER INFORMATION

www.osho.com
A comprehensive website in many languages, featuring Osho's meditations, books and tapes, an online tour of the meditation resort at Osho Commune International, a list of the Osho Information Centers worldwide, and a selection of Osho's talks.

For information about visiting the Commune, your nearest Osho Meditation Center and general information, contact:
Osho Commune International
17 Koregaon Park,
Pune 411 001 (MS), India
Tel: +91 (0) 20 613 6655
or   +91 (0) 20 612 8562
Fax:+91 (0) 20 613 9955
e-mail: osho-commune@osho.com

For publishing and copyright information regarding Osho's books, contact:
Osho International
570 Lexington Ave,
New York, NY 10022, USA
Tel: +1 212 588 9888
Fax: +1 212 588 1977
e-mail: osho-int@osho.com